The Daily Telegraph

200 MILES AROUND THE [illegible]NT

A Yachtsman's Guide t[illegible]

Claim your berthright

for as little as a year, or as long as you like.

With marinas and Marina Villages strategically positioned close to Britain's premier cruising and racing waters, we can make everything in your life plain sailing, both afloat and ashore.

We have coastal and inland marinas with safe, secure berths for annual rental or for long-term lease. All in prime sailing locations, from Plymouth to Woolverstone, with services and facilities to keep you and your boat on an even keel.

For the truly fortunate, a luxury home and adjacent berth at one of our magnificent Marina Villages will make returning home every bit as exciting as setting sail. Find out more about our marinas and Marina Villages by sending for an Information Pack and free Video. Sailsmanship, pure and simple.

Please send me further information on:

- ☐ marina berths for annual rental
- ☐ marina berths for long-term lease/sale
- ☐ Hythe Marina Village, New Forest
- ☐ Ocean Village Marina, Southampton
- ☐ Millbay Marina Village, Plymouth
- ☐ Brunel Quay, Milford Haven Waterway
- ☐ Brixham Marina, Brixham

Please send me a copy of your video:

- ☐ The Village by the Sea

DT10.90.

Boat Type and Length ______________________

Name ______________________

Address ______________________

____

______________ Tel. No. ______________

MARINA DEVELOPMENTS Plc

Marina Developments, Shamrock Quay, William Street, Southampton SO1 1QL. Tel: (0703) 229461/638090 (24-hr). Fax: (0703) 333384. Telex: 47669 SHAMQY G.

The Daily Telegraph

200 MILES AROUND THE SOLENT

A Yachtsman's Guide to Channel Harbours

Philip Bristow

BOWLINE
BOOKS

First published in Great Britain by Bowline Books Ltd

British Library Cataloguing in Publication Data
Bristow, Philip
The Daily Telegraph 200 miles around the Solent
1. England. Solent. Navigation
I. Title II. Daily Telegraph
623.8929422

ISBN 1-872912-02-8

Designed and typeset by Spiral Design, Poole, Dorset

Printed and bound in Great Britain by Stephens and George Ltd

Contents

CHANNEL WEST

Harbours included in full:

Lesser harbours:

CHANNEL ISLANDS

FOREWORD

BY TIMOTHY JEFFERY, YACHTING CORRESPONDENT, THE DAILY TELEGRAPH

It's too easy to dismiss the Solent as boating's M25 even if that is how it seems at times. On a summer bank holiday, there are sufficient boats afloat to carry the population of a town comparable in size to Winchester.

It is to those people that Philip Bristow's book is aimed. For all its density of yachts, the Solent contains real treasures for the waterborne visitor. To have the Beaulieu River or Newtown Creek just around the corner from the refineries and power stations of Southampton Water is a gift too many yachtsmen take for granted.

Bristow offers his readers the chance to appreciate what is on their doorstep as well as what awaits beyond the horizon. Modern sailing yachts are efficient to a degree that destinations in his 100 range are not limited to lengthy cruises or fast motor boats. There is a wealth of ports, bays and marinas to be sampled and for the most part savoured.

Not all destinations are appealing, as Bristow makes plain. It is the insight of his narrative together with really practical information on entry, shops, water, fuel etc. that bridges the gap between the traditional navigational pilot book and wide ranging cruising guide.

We hope you will find *200 Miles Around the Solent* has more genuinely useful information between its covers than most other cruising books for the area put together.

TIMOTHY JEFFERY
December 1990

INTRODUCTION

by Philip Bristow

Sitting around in the cockpit at sunset, how often have you heard the question,

"Where shall we go tomorrow?".

And how often has the decision been in favour of some harbour you know – because there has been no guide to what it's like in Channel harbours you don't know?

Thus this book; intended NOT as a guide to navigation, not a guide to "How to Get There" but a guide to "What it's Like WHEN you Get There". All of the major Channel harbours have been included, and some of the lesser harbours, from Ramsgate to Penzance and from Dunkerque to L'Aber-Wrac'h, and also the Channel Islands.

There are quite a number of "How to Get There" guide books and I have listed them in the bibliography at the back of this book. You will see that there are twenty six such guides to Channel Harbours. Admirable though these navigational guides may be, it is obvious that no author/publisher can equal the coverage of Admiralty and SHOM Charts with their detail and accuracy. No amateur author, particularly if he has several guides in print, can hope to compete with the full time professional resources of the Hydrographer of the Navy and the Service Hydrographique et Oceanographic de la Marine. Having said that, yachting guides *do* give some detail of specific interest to yachtsmen.

I hope that this guide will encourage you to venture further afield, to harbours new. With a boat you are always learning, and by extending your repertoire of familiar harbours you are sharpening your navigational skills, apart from the delights of new experiences.

Obviously, as a thoughtful skipper, your overriding consideration will be crew satisfaction (particularly where the crew is the family) and you will be surprised at the general enthusiasm for trying new harbours. This intelligence I have gathered from visiting numerous craft over the years.

"Can you recommend somewhere new for us to go?"

"Can you tell him not to go to the same old place every time?"

It really is worth trying. It really is a thrill to tie up in a new harbour, to go ashore in a new town. Do try it more often and you will gain confidence, and you will soon feel like Joshua Slocum and Sir Francis Chichester rolled into one.

Obviously you will not venture forth without the necessary skills, one of the most important (though not sufficiently grasped) being an understanding of the weather; by which I mean making sense of weather patterns as far as possible *all the time* and not only when you are getting ready to leave. Understanding weather changes as they occur will give you the necessary confidence for extended voyaging.

From a navigation point of view, when preparing to set out it is tempting to rely upon push-button electronic marvels without even drawing the proposed track on an up-to-date chart. At the present time we are told that the electronic position finder of the future is GPS (Global Positioning System) and this is probably true, but not necessarily of the immediate future. For the area covered by this book you could use a radio navigation system, like Decca (Loran-C for the Mediterranean) for the next four or five years until the price of GPS comes down.

You will be familiar with the various arguments concerning Decca and Loran-C, and also of Transit which gives fixes from low orbit satellites but perhaps not as often as one would like. The new GPS is based on a constellation of twenty one satellites orbiting the earth at very high altitudes and claims to give pinpoint positions anywhere in the world twenty four hours a day. In no time at all, it seems, you'll have one on the dashboard of your car to show you where you are and where you are supposed to be going.

You have probably heard about the new rules regarding Customs regulations but, if not, as from 1st July 1990:-

Before proceeding foreign (every time) you must complete Part 1 of Customs form C1328 which you can get from your local Customs office; and deposit it in the Customs' box before you sail. You keep Parts 2 and 3 as arrival documents for when you return;

- on returning from foreign you fly the yellow flag on entering the 12-mile limit and complete Form 1328

- if you have nothing to declare you place this form 1328 in a Customs box, take down the yellow flag and go home

- if you have something to declare, you telephone Customs who will

a) either assess Duty over the phone so that you can deposit your cheque and form 1328 in a Customs box and go home or

b) board you to assess Duty

Whilst on this subject I should mention that visiting the harbours named in this book does not entitle you to ship Duty Free stores for your outward passage (for which privilege you have to be going south of Brest or north of the Eider to qualify).

In 1993, of course, all Customs restrictions of this sort should disappear between EC countries – a pity in a way. Nothing would ever feel so good, nor look so good, nor taste so good as "Duty Frees".

The "Welcome Scale" rating indicates my impression of the effort made to provide facilities for yachtsmen, particularly visiting yachtsmen.

I hope that you will find this guide to be helpful and interesting. Having compiled a number of such guides over the years I am aware of the difficulty of getting every fact and figure correctly up-to-date; please tell me if you have any information to add or comments to make.

Note that bearings when given are in TRUE; Most UK yacht harbours and marinas have installed VHF Ch 80 as their main working channel for 1991. Times relative to high water are given thus: 2h-HW-1½h which translates as 2 hours before highwater to one and a half hours after highwater.

Happy sailing to NEW harbours.

Acknowledgement

I would like to thank George Taylor (Editor of *Practical Boat Owner*) for all his help and assistance in the production and proof reading of this book.

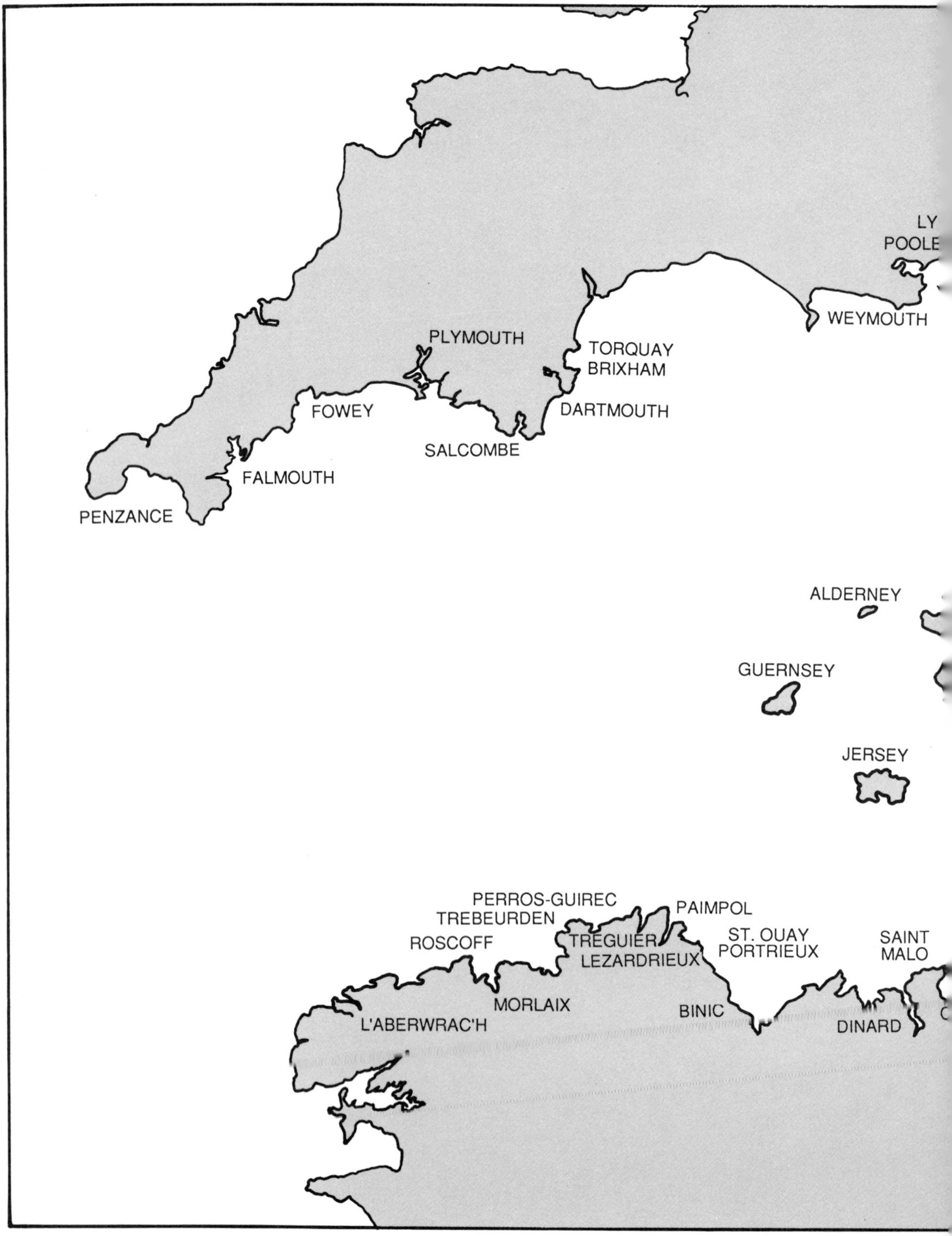
LY
POOLE
WEYMOUTH
PLYMOUTH
TORQUAY
BRIXHAM
FOWEY
DARTMOUTH
SALCOMBE
FALMOUTH
PENZANCE
ALDERNEY
GUERNSEY
JERSEY
PERROS-GUIREC
TREBEURDEN
PAIMPOL
ROSCOFF
TREGUIER
LEZARDRIEUX
ST. QUAY
PORTRIEUX
SAINT
MALO
MORLAIX
L'ABERWRAC'H
BINIC
DINARD

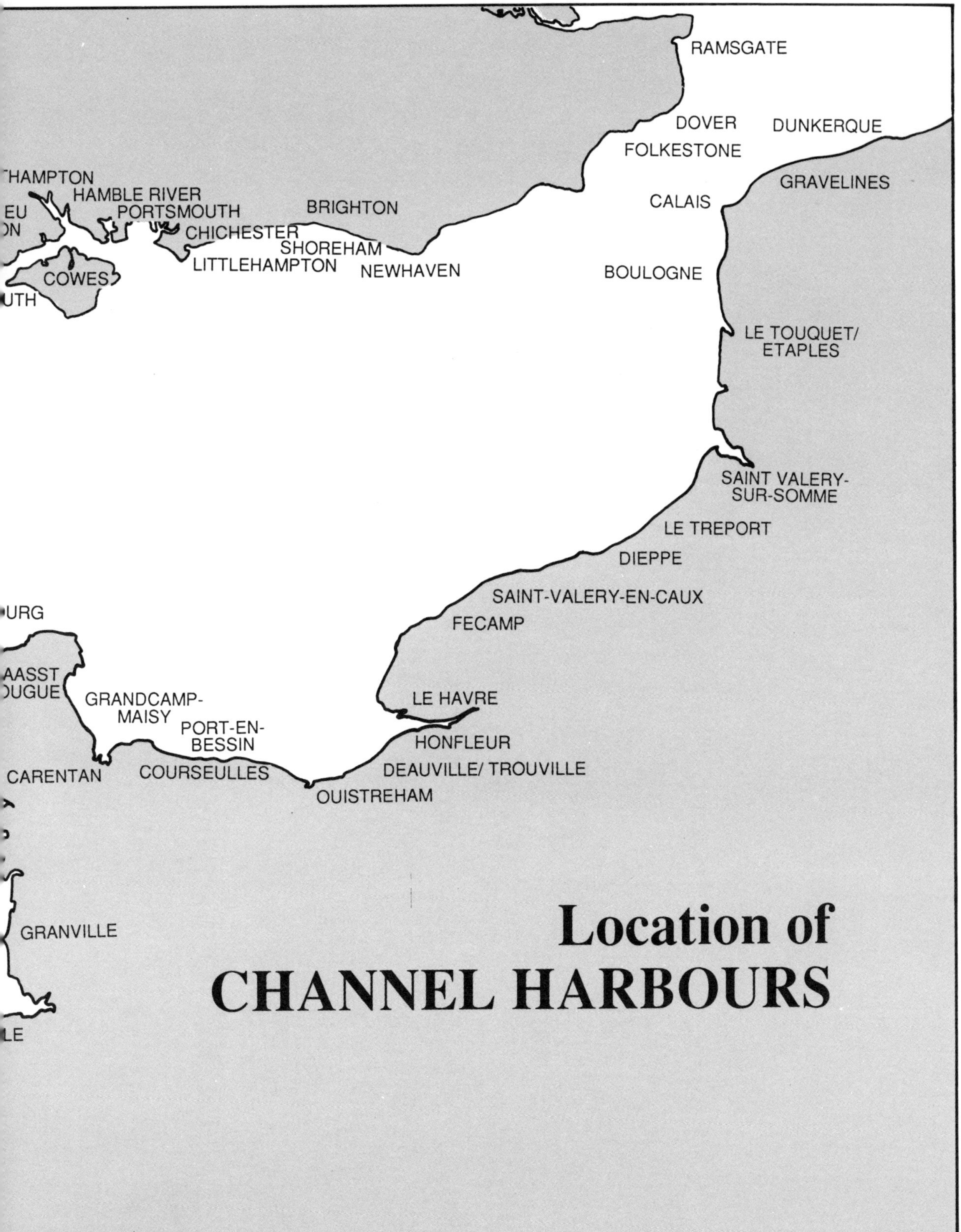

Location of CHANNEL HARBOURS

THE SOLENT

HARBOURS IN THE SOLENT

- SOUTHAMPTON, Southampton Water including Hythe Marina, Ocean Village, Shamrock Quay
- HAMBLE RIVER including Hamble Point Marina, Port Hamble, Mercury Yacht Harbour and Swanwick Marina
- Bembridge
- PORTSMOUTH including Camper and Nicholson's Marina, Gosport, and Port Solent
- Langstone
- CHICHESTER HARBOUR including Northney Marina
- COWES including Ancasta Marina
- YARMOUTH
- LYMINGTON including Lymington Yacht Haven, Lymington Marina
- BEAULIEU
- Christchurch

Southampton and the Solent is the base on which our book rests, the harbours from which our voyages of discovery are made to other harbours. Although they provide mainly outgoing yachting traffic they welcome ingoing as you will see on the following pages.

Because Southampton and The Solent are hosts to SHIPS first and to YACHTS second, the following words of wisdom are provided in full. They are produced with the approval of Associated British Ports

PORT OF SOUTHAMPTON

This information has been produced by Associated British Ports specifically for people who enjoy recreational activities afloat.

SOME FACTS YOU SHOULD KEEP IN MIND

1 The number of large commercial ships serving the Port of Southampton and the number of recreational craft afloat in local waters is increasing. It is essential that close quarter situations do not increase.

2 Most of the commercial vessels you meet will have a UK pilot on board regardless of the ship's flag. They will be listening to VHF R/T channel 12 or 14, the Port working frequencies.

3 Most large ships travel at a manoeuvring speed of between 10 to 15 knots whilst in the Solent and Southampton Water. The lower limit will vary from ship to ship and is "as safe navigation permits."

4 Ships often travel faster than you might expect in congested areas for various reasons.

5 Light, partially loaded or unevenly, trimmed ships may require to maintain a higher "as safe navigation permits" speed in order to remain under full control.

6 It takes less than 10 minutes for a fast ship to reach you from the visible horizon in clear weather, and in hazy conditions it takes a lot less. At 10 knots, a ship travels 1 nautical mile in 6 minutes: at 15 knots it takes only 4 minutes.

7 Large, deep draught ships cannot easily avoid small craft in narrow channels – it is up to you to stay clear. If one of these ships alters course to clear a yacht or small craft it is unlikely to regain track. The consequences can be disastrous.

8 A ship that is slowing down does not

steer very well; it needs the propeller action on the rudder to respond. If the Captain feels that a turn will save the situation, he may not slow down.

9 When the ship's engines are put "full astern" a captain will lose control of the ship. Single screw ships with engines going astern will, in most cases, swing the ship's bow to starboard. Therefore, if you have a choice, try to escape on his port side. Remember that it takes 4 to 6 minutes and 2,000 to 4,000 feet for a ship to stop after its engines are put astern.

10 There are numerous other small vessels operating within the Port of Southampton. Watch out for ferries, hydrofoils, tugs towing barges (especially at night, when unlit barges may remain invisible). Remember that a towing cable, which may be partly submerged, can cut a boat in two.

WHAT CAN YOU DO?

1 Avoid sailing in the big ship channels, especially in poor visibility. Obey Rule 9 of the ColRegs for conduct in narrow channels, by keeping to the starboard side of the channel and crossing only when this does not impede the passage of a large vessel that can safely navigate only within the narrow channel.

2 Do not underestimate the speed of ships. If your boat is slow, you might not be able to take effective evasive action if you find yourself on collision course with a large ship in visibility of a quarter of a mile or less.

IN THE TIME IT TOOK YOU TO READ THIS FAR, A SHIP CRUISING AT 15 KNOTS WOULD HAVE TRAVELLED ONE NAUTICAL MILE

3 Be visible. At night make sure your navigation lights can be seen. If you see the running lights of a vessel and you think you have not been seen, begin to get out of the way, using torches, search lights or a spotlight on sails, or fire a white flare to indicate your position. Carry a radar reflector high on your boat. Remember, from the bridge of a loaded container ship or large tanker, the captain or pilot will lose sight of you ahead a third of a mile, although you can see the ship at all times!

4 Be alert. Look around every so often, especially astern.

5 Keep watch at night. Even on a clear night you will have difficulty seeing a big ship approach. You might see it first as a black shadow against a background of shore lights, or as a growing shadow – at that point you are not far apart. Remember that your lights will not be easily spotted from the ship.

6 Watch the ship's lights. To determine whether you are in the path of a ship, pay attention to the sidelights rather than the masthead lights. If you see only one sidelight, or if one is much brighter than the other, you can be fairly sure that you are not in the direct path of the ship. This also gives an indication of which way to move in order to get clear altogether. If you see both sidelights, you are dead ahead – MOVE OUT FAST BUT be prepared for the ship to alter course at WEST BRAMBLE and CALSHOT. You may be SAFE or in GREAT DANGER, as ships turn through 100 degrees or so. You must be sure of your position. Learn to recognise the mastlights of a tug towing one or more barges and of a commercial fishing vessel, trawling, or fishing with outlying gear.

7 Know whistle signals. The captain of a ship will frequently not use the 'port' or 'starboard' whistle signals when passing small boats because he is afraid the signals will not be understood and might lead to erratic changes in course. Five or more short blasts on the whistle is the 'danger' signal. Check and see if it is for you – and if it is – MAKE AWAY FAST! Three short blasts means 'My engines are going astern.'

8 Know flag signals and shapes. Large ships proceeding seawards will fly International Code Flag 'E' over the answering pennant which indicates that the vessel will turn to port at the West Bramble buoy and make for the Nab (East). A vessel displaying the answering pennant over International Code Flag 'W' will indicate that the vessel will depart the Solent via the Needles (West). A large ship which displays a cylinder on her yardarm during the day or three red lights in a vertical line at night indicates that the ship is severely restricted in her manoeuvrability. Please give her a wide berth.

9 Keep your VHF R/T tuned to channel 12, the Port working frequency, and listen for traffic information from the Harbour Master's Operations Room, Call Sign VTS (Vessel Traffic Services).

If you believe you have not been seen or you are unsure of a ship's intentions, call them on channel 12, then shift to a working frequency (6 or an agreed alternative) for intership safety messages.

COLLISION AVOIDANCE CHECK LIST

Avoid ship channels. Cross them quickly and at right angles.

- Be alert. Watch for ship traffic
- Be seen, especially at night
- Know whistle signals – five or more mean DANGER
- LISTEN to VHF R/T Channel 12 – if you have to transmit keep your message brief, say what you have to say, then remain listening
- Use up-to-date navigation charts – read Local Notices to Mariners at your club or local marina
- Keep in mind, that FEW survive collisions with ships
- When in doubt, keep clear

And always be prepared for the unexpected: lifejackets do not help if you are not wearing them.

SOUTHAMPTON WATER

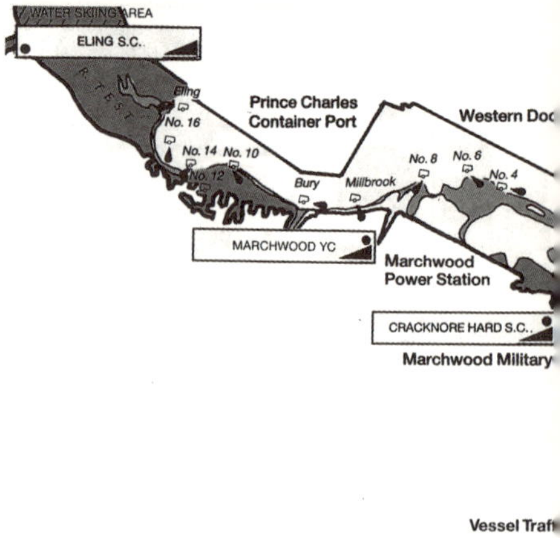

DESCRIPTION: Southampton has many attractions for the visiting yachtsman and his family. There is regular transport to all parts from the marinas shown, even from Hythe Marina a regular ferry runs across to a point not far from the main shopping centre, the new Bargate Shopping Centre. Yachting visitors to Ocean Village have their own Canute's Pavilion. There is a big selection of pubs and restaurants and you can safely visit Southampton in the knowledge that there will be plenty of interesting things to see and do.

The yacht harbours in the Southampton area are obviously harbours to sail FROM rather than harbours to sail TO. It is asking a lot to expect yacht harbours to be near to the sea and near to shore attractions. Transport convenience is irrelevant since everybody comes by car, everybody that is, except the visitor by boat to whom my book is addressed. The following notes should not be taken as a criticism, therefore, since all the harbours described fulfil splendidly the purpose for which they were intended.

Standard Port
SOUTHAMPTON

Harbour Entry
At all times

Admiralty charts 394/1905/2040/2041/2045

R/T: Marinas VHF Ch 80/37

Weather Centre: (0703) 228644

Visitors moorings available: At Hythe Marina (32323). Ocean Village, Shamrock Quay.
See also Hamble River

Telephone Code	0703
Customs	☎ 330330
Tourist Office	☎ 221106
Taxi	☎ 223450/466339
Hire Cars	Avis 226767 Budget 38833
Doctor	☎ 435355/335151
Dentist	☎ 228363/476001
Hospital	☎ 777222
Chemist	Boots, Above Bar
Post Office	59 High Street
Bank	High Street
Yacht Clubs	Royal Southern, Hamble

Laundrette All marinas

Shops/supermarkets
Shopping centre Above Bar

Pubs/restaurants
Pearl Harbour, 86 Above Bar; Geddes, Town Quay; Golden Palace, 17 Above Bar; Around the World, Town Quay; Pinocchio, 36 Oxford Street, Taps, Shamrock Quay.
At Hythe: Capers; Mr. Jacobs; The Observant Admiral.
At Ocean Village: Los Marinos; Oceans Wine Bar; Dolphins

Tourist attractions:
Maritime Museum, Hall of Aviation, Concerts, Theatres, Night Clubs, Discos, Gardens, Sport, visiting liners

KEY TO SYMBOLS

- Yacht Marina
- Visitors' mooring
- Fuel
- Slipway
- Crossing points

CAUTION

ABP NOTICE TO MARINERS NO. 19 OF 1989

Restriction Area of use by yachts and other craft under 20m LOA.

The transit and movement of small craft under 20m (66 feet) LOA through the area shown when vessels of over 100m (320 feet) LOA are navigating the Western Approach Channel (including the Thorn Channel and Calshot Reach) between West Bramble Buoy and Hook Buoy will not be permitted

SOUTHAMPTON WATER

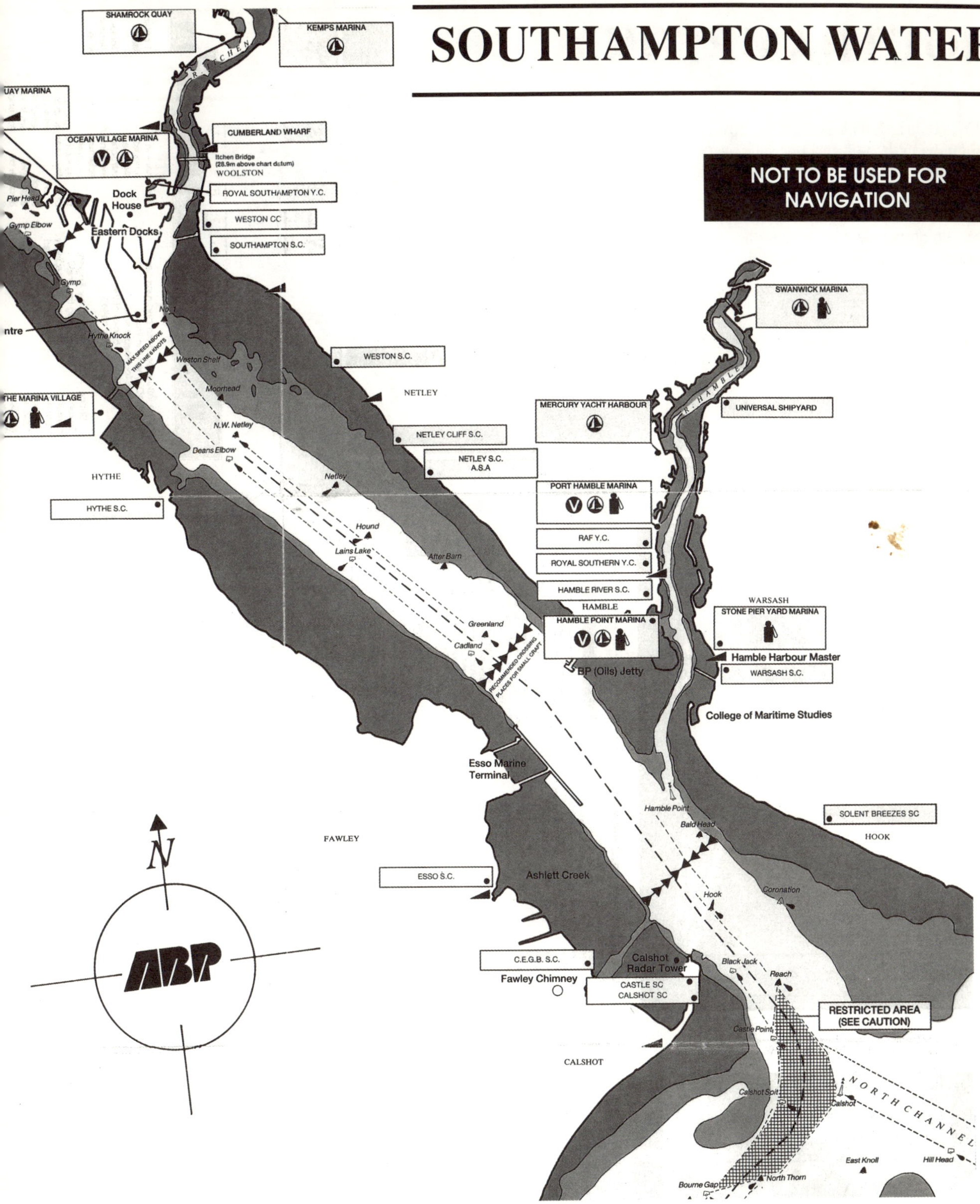

SOUTHAMPTON

HYTHE MARINA There are shops and pubs in the village a fair walk away and a regular Tuesday market in this New Forest village. Downstream is Fawley Refinery, with vast tankers secured alongside most of the time. From Hythe you certainly have the best view of the traffic of boats in Southampton Water and there is always something to see, from ferries and hydrofoils to container ships and the occasional liner.

Visitors welcome. VHF Ch 80

Charges:

Daily	£1 per metre
Weekly	£5 per metre

Available:

Water✓	Electric✓	Showers✓	
Petrol✓	Diesel✓	Chandler	
Repairs:	Yacht 840460	Engine 840460	
	Electrical	Sail	

Hythe Marina entrance

OCEAN VILLAGE MARINA
Ashore is what was once part of the dock area of Southampton but it is not too far to the shopping centre, also many pubs and restaurants.

Visitors welcome. VHF Ch 80

Charges:

Daily	£1 per metre
Weekly up to 12m	£5.75 p.m.
12lm to 24m	£6.50 p.m.
over 24lm	£9.00 p.m.

Available:

Water✓	Electric✓	Showers✓
Petrol✓	Diesel✓	Chandler✓
Laundrette✓		
Repairs:	Yacht✓	Engine
Electrical	Sail✓	

Shop, bar and restaurant in Canute's Pavilion shopping area

Ocean Village Marina

SHAMROCK QUAY

From a shore-going point of view the immediate area is semi-industrial but it is not too far to buses to take you into the city. Apart from the marina, Shamrock Quay is now a village of various yachting interests including a restaurant. It is created on the site of the old Camper and Nicholson yard, indeed, some of their old buildings, in a converted state, add charm to the place.

Builders of yachts for over two hundred years, including some of the most famous racing yachts in the world, Camper and Nicholsons left Shamrock Quay when Northam Bridge was built across the river downstream of them.

Visitors welcome.
VHF Ch 80 or (0703) 331709.

Charges:

Daily	£1 per metre
Weekly up to 12m	£4.60 p.m.
12ml to 24m	£4.90 p.m.
over 24ml	£5.60 p.m.

Available:

Water✓	Electric✓	Showers
Laundrette✓	Petrol	Diesel
Chandler.		
Repairs:	Yacht✓	Engine✓
	Electrical✓	Sail

Shamrock Quay

HAMBLE RIVER

Standard Port
SOUTHAMPTON

Harbour Entry
Navigable at all times to Bursledon Bridge

HM 0489 576387

Lat: 50° 49' N **Long:** 1° 18' W

Admiralty charts 1905

DESCRIPTION: There are probably more yachts in the Hamble River than in any other similar area in the UK, around 3,500 in fact. You can seek moorings in the river from the Harbour Master or, if you prefer being alongside, go in to one of the four marinas. Port Hamble and Swanwick have pubs and restaurants within walking distance.

There are Harbour Board pile moorings available in the river and you can come ashore at public hards at either Hamble or Warsash. Navigation in the river is easy, the various marks being clear. The entrance channel is marked by beacons and entry is along the lines of the leading transits. Least depth, at MLWS of about 2m7, is near Spit Pile Beacon. Until the early 19th century large wooden ships were built at Bursledon and at Warsash.

R/T: Hamble Harbour Radio Ch 16 68 (0830-1700 weekdays); (0900-1830 weekends, summer months). Marinas Ch 80 37

Yachting facilities: All available

Visitors moorings available: Piles B1 to B4 off Warsash, 9 to 16 off Port Hamble, also Hamble Point Marina, Port Hamble, Mercury Yacht Harbour and Swanwick Marina

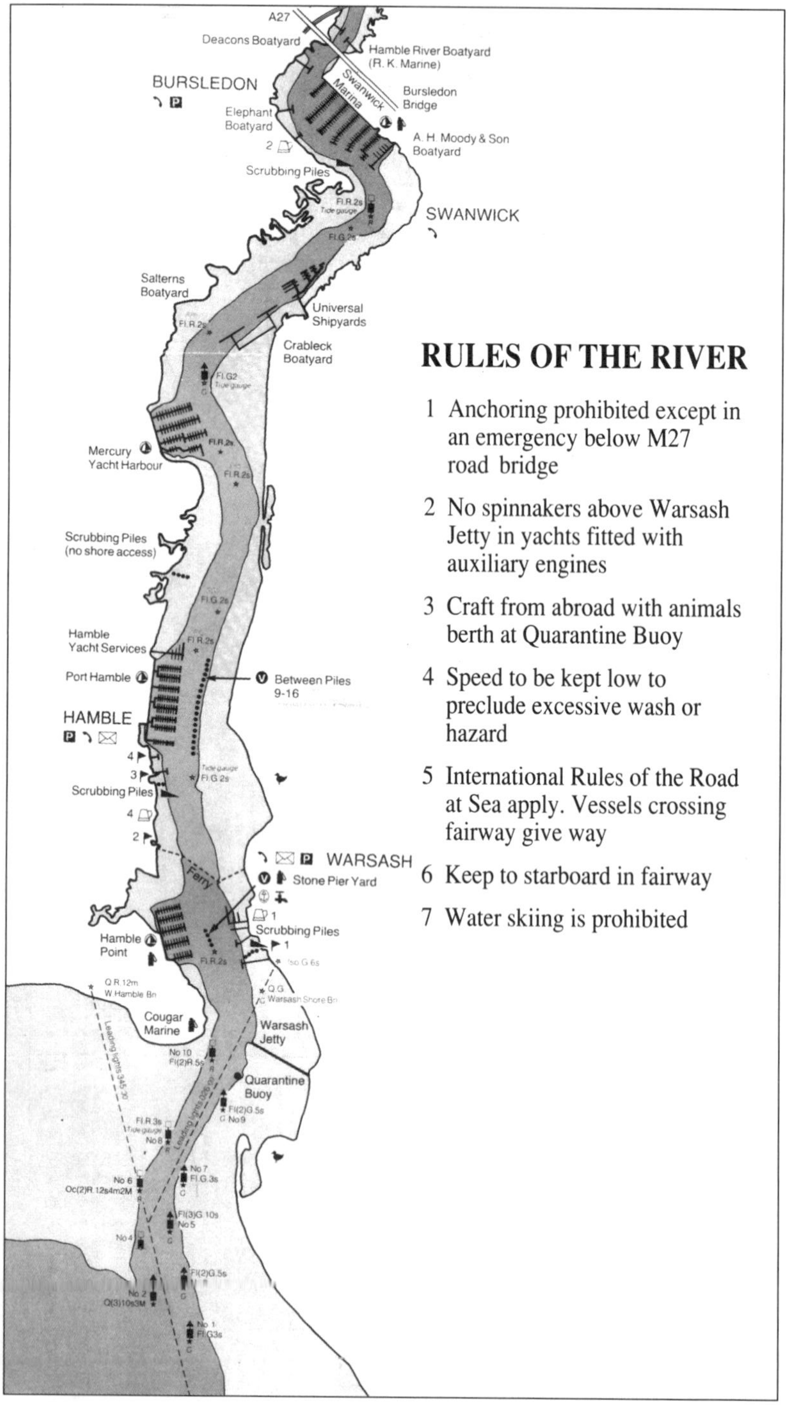

RULES OF THE RIVER

1. Anchoring prohibited except in an emergency below M27 road bridge
2. No spinnakers above Warsash Jetty in yachts fitted with auxiliary engines
3. Craft from abroad with animals berth at Quarantine Buoy
4. Speed to be kept low to preclude excessive wash or hazard
5. International Rules of the Road at Sea apply. Vessels crossing fairway give way
6. Keep to starboard in fairway
7. Water skiing is prohibited

Telephone Code
Bursledon 042121
Locksheath 04895

Customs Freephone Customs Yachts

Weather ☎ 0703 228844

Tourist Office ☎ 0703 832615

Taxi ☎ 04895/82222

Hire Car
☎ Sparshotts 04892 5111
☎ Oaktree 042121 3033

Doctor ☎ 04895 83777

Dentist ☎ 04895 2308

Hospital ☎ 0703 634288

Chemist ☎ 04895 3001

Post Office Warsash Road, Warsash

Bank High Street

Yacht Clubs
Hamble River SC
Royal Southern

Laundrette Marinas

Shops/supermarkets
Tesco, Bursledon. Shops at Warsash and Hamble

Pubs/restaurants
The Bugle; The King and Queen at Hamble; The Jolly Sailor; The Old Ship at Bursledon; Rising Sun; Nook and Cranny at Warsash

Tourist attractions:
The Hamble has always been a delightful river and it manages to retain its charm despite the increasing deluge of yachts it is asked to endure. Whether you come ashore at Hamble, to "The Bugle," or Warsash, to the "The Riser," or Bursledon, to "The Jolly," you are swallowed up by the ghosts of nautical memories past, the atmosphere seizes you. A more recent affectation is the arrival of the "Howards' Way" saga, and if it gives you pleasure to soak up the atmosphere of a television soap, the "Jolly Sailor" awaits you.

Hamble River at Bursledon Bridge

HAMBLE RIVER

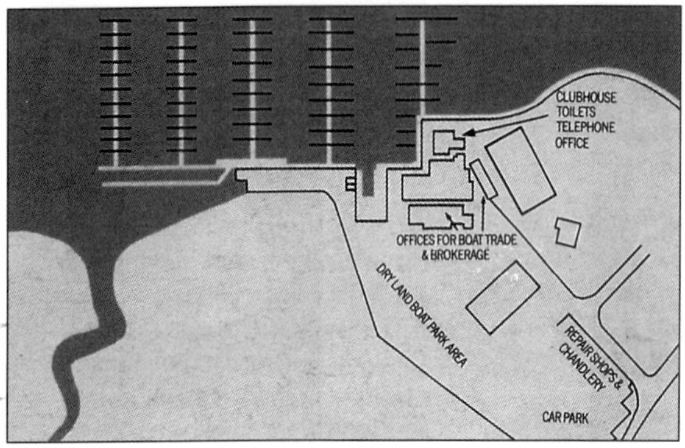

HAMBLE POINT MARINA

First in the Hamble River. Visitors welcome. Channel M (80) VHF

Charges:

Daily £1.40 p/metre + VAT   Weekly £8.00 p/metre + VAT

Apart from the club in the marina there is nothing ashore. It is a very long walk to Hamble Village.

Available:			
Water✓	Electric✓	Showers	Laundrette
Petrol	Diesel✓	Chandler✓	
Repairs:			
Yacht✓	Engine✓	Electrical✓	Sail 453109

PORT HAMBLE

Port Hamble was the first marina to be built in Britain. Channel M (80) VHF

Charges:

Daily £1.50 p/metre + VAT   Weekly £8.50 p/metre + VAT

PORT HAMBLE

It is a reasonable walk to Hamble Village which has a number of pubs and restaurants, also a bus service to Southampton. Street names here recall the days of wooden ship building on the Hamble, e.g. "Copperhull Terrace" and " Ropewalk."

Available:			
Water	Electric✓	Showers	Laundrette
Petrol✓	Diesel✓	Chandler 452388	
Repairs:	Yacht✓	Engine✓	Electrical✓
Sail 553623/582444			

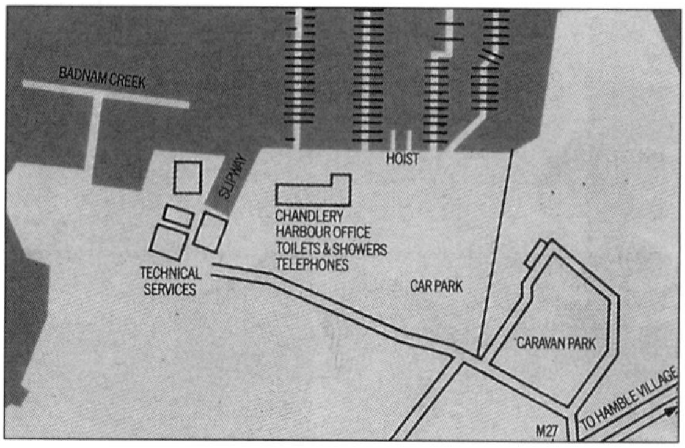

CHARGES FOR USE OF HARBOUR AUTHORITY FACILITIES
(Effective from 1st April 1990) All charges inclusive of VAT

VISITORS' PILE MOORINGS

Per Night	6 nights	1 week
Up to 25ft.	£2.00	£12.00
Over 25ft. up to 35ft.	£2.50	£15.00
Over 35ft. up to 40ft.	£3.00	£18.00
Over 45ft. up to 60ft.	£3.50	£21.00
Over 60ft. up to 80ft.	£4.00	£24.00
Over 80ft	£6.00	£36.00

VHF – INFORMATION ASSISTANCE

HARBOUR MASTER – (Call sign – Hamble Harbour Radio)

Office	Ch 68	**Mon-Fri** (0830-1700)
Boats	Ch 16,68	**Sat** 0900-1300 (Nov-Mar)
		0900-1830 (Apr-Oct)
		Sun 0900-1830 (Apr-Oct)
MARINAS	Ch 80	24 hour
SOLENT COASTGUARD		
Calling	Ch 16, 67	24 hour
Working	Ch 67, 73, 6, 10	

Mercury Yacht Harbour

MERCURY YACHT HARBOUR
Visitors welcome. Channel M (80) VHF.

Charges:

Daily	£1.20 per metre + VAT
Weekly	£7.50 per metre + VAT

MERCURY YACHT HARBOUR
It is a long walk from here to Hamble Village. The yacht harbour is named after *T.S. Mercury,* an old hulk used as a training ship for poor boys, and a familiar sight in the river until 1968 when it was closed through lack of money.

Available:
Water✓ Electric✓ Showers
Laundrette Petrol✓ Diesel✓
Chandler 452388
Repairs: Yacht✓ engine✓
electrical✓ sail 553623/453109

SWANWICK MARINA
Visitors welcome, Dockmaster 885262
Charges:
Daily 35p per ft. + VAT
Weekly £2.25 per ft. + VAT

SWANWICK MARINA
There are a number of attractive pubs and restaurants ashore, also bus services passing the entrance and a railway station nearby.

Available:
Water✓ Electric✓ Showers✓ Laundrette
petrol✓ diesel✓ Chandler Bursledon 6349
Repairs:
Yacht✓ engine✓ electrical✓ sail Bursledon 3914

Swanwick marina looking over the roof of "The Jolly Sailor"

PORTSMOUTH ☆☆☆☆

Standard Port
PORTSMOUTH

Harbour Entry
At all times subject to restrictions. See Pilot NP 27

Lat: 50° 47' N **Long:** 1° 06' W

Admiralty charts 394/2045/2050/2625/2628/2629/2631

R/T: QHM VHF Ch 11. Marinas VHF 80/37 (office hours)

Yachting facilities: All available

Visitors moorings available: Commercial port offers limited moorings in the Camber, apply berthing Master 0705 297395 x 310. Camper and Nicholsons Marina have 20, but 70 overnight: 524811. Port Solent have 20: 210765

Distances: Cherbourg 78, Nab Tower 10, Le Havre 95, St. Malo 150, Caen 80, Guernsey 110, Jersey 140

DESCRIPTION: A naval, commercial and ferry port with good facilities for yachts. Rightly advertised as the Flagship of Maritime England, Portsmouth has many fascinating tourist attractions, a huge selection of pubs and restaurants, mostly within a fairly compact area. On show is H.M.S. *Victory,* Lord Nelson's flagship at the Battle of Trafalgar in 1805 and the world's oldest surviving ship of the line. Also the *Mary Rose,* Henry's VIII's favourite warship, built 250 years before *Victory.* You can board H.M.S. *Warrior,* the world's first iron hulled, armoured warship. These are just a few of the naval attractions that Portsmouth has to offer.

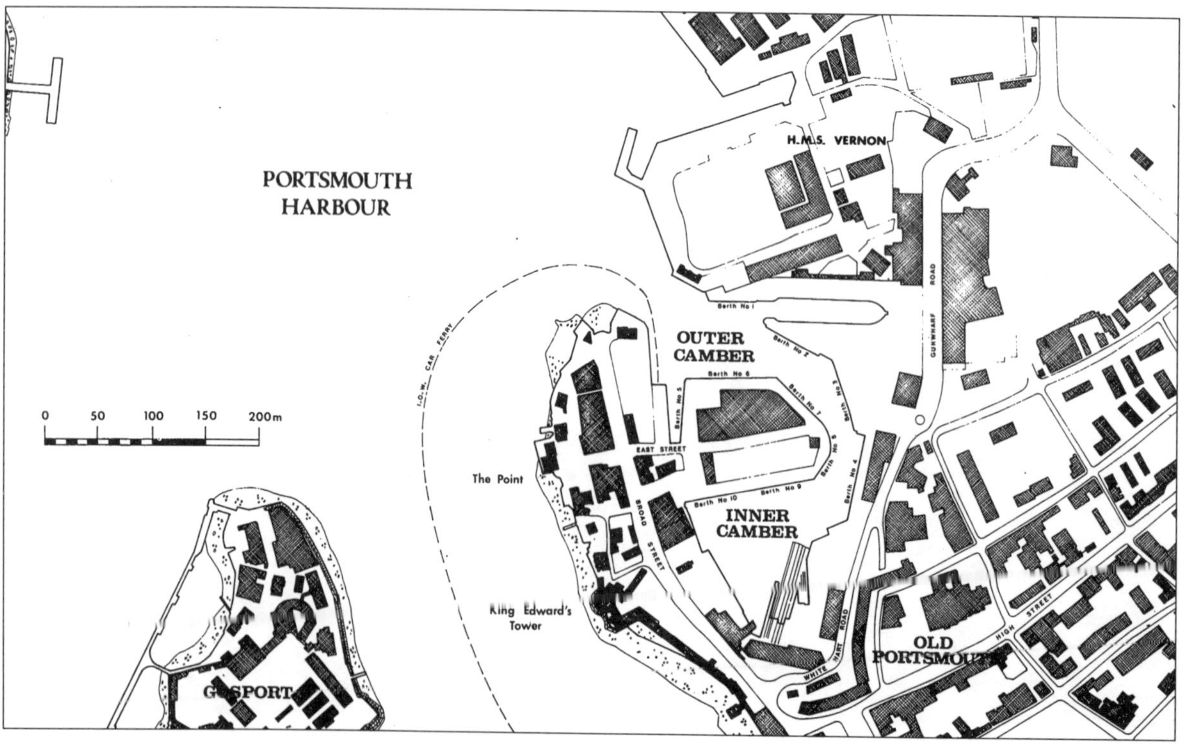

Telephone Code	0705
Customs	Freephone Customs Yachts
Weather	☎ 500457
Tourist Office	☎ 826722
Taxi	☎ 811111/824466
Hire Cars	☎ Avis 694851 ☎ Mitchell 664249
Doctor	☎ 821371
Dentist	☎ 824839
Hospital	☎ 822331/379451
Chemist	☎ 825245/821046
Post Office	☎ 835317/8
Bank	☎ Barclays 754500
Yacht Clubs	Portsmouth SC 820596 Waterside Club 370164
Police	☎ 321111
Laundrette	☎ 822643/822793

Shops/supermarkets
Waitrose, Tesco, Allders

Pubs/restaurants
Chimes 755411; Sally Port opp. the Cathedral 821860; Bridge Tavern, 58 East Street, 752992; Seagull 824866; Still & West, Bath Square 82157

Tourist attractions:
HMS "Victory," "Mary Rose," D-Day Museum, Charles Dickens Birthplace Museum, Sea Life Centre, HMS "Warrior," Royal Naval Museum, Submarine Museum, King's Theatre, Royal Marines Museum

PORTSMOUTH HARBOUR

Once through the harbour entrance, under power, the harbour opens out and vessels may safely proceed under sail. Note the small boat passage on your working chart.

The Gosport Ferry crosses the harbour at frequent intervals just north of Ballast buoy.

Keep to the west thus avoiding the main hazards in the east, which are the Isle of Wight ferry berths, the Naval Base and the International Continental Ferry Port. Camper and Nicholsons Marina is to port and a look-out should be kept for craft entering or leaving the Marina.

Proceed up the harbour heading north. If sailing at night beware of several unlit mooring buoys immediately south of the ammunition barges moored on the west side of the channel, also unlit pleasure craft moorings.

The harbour now broadens out considerably but most of this area is mud which dries at low water.

On the eastern side of the harbour is Fountain Lake (continental ferry port). The mud in the centre is bounded by two channels. The one to the NW leads to Fareham, while the other channel to the NE, called Portchester Lake, leads to Port Solent.

Port Solent

PORTSMOUTH ☆☆☆☆

CAMPER & NICHOLSON'S: GOSPORT

Charges Daily Rate:

Up to 7.6 metres	£9.00 inc. VAT
7.7 metres-9.1 metres	£12.00 inc. VAT
9.2 metres-10.7 metres	£15.00 inc. VAT
10.8 metres-12.2 metres	£18.00 inc. VAT
12.3 metres-13.7 metres	£20.00 inc. VAT
13.8 metres-15.2 metres	£22.00 inc. VAT
15.3 metres and above	Price on application

KEY

1. Main Gate
2. Public Telephones
3. Marina Office
4. Laundrette
5. Toilets/Showers
6. Club (Shores)
7. Yacht Stores
8. Fuel Barge
9. Repairs Office
10. Upperdeck Chandlery
11. Brokerage
12. Sail Repair Depository
13. Scrub off Berth (book at Marina Office)
14. Tourist Information Office
15. Gosport – Portsmouth Ferry
16. Town Centre
17. Waste Oil Depository
18. Waste Containers
19. Weather Forecasts
20. Taxis

A convenient marina in which to leave the boat and take the frequent ferry across to town and its attractions.

Camper & Nicholson's
Available: Water✓ Electric✓ Showers✓ Laundrette Petrol✓ Diesel✓ Chandler✓
Repairs: Yacht✓ Engine✓ Electrical✓ Sail✓

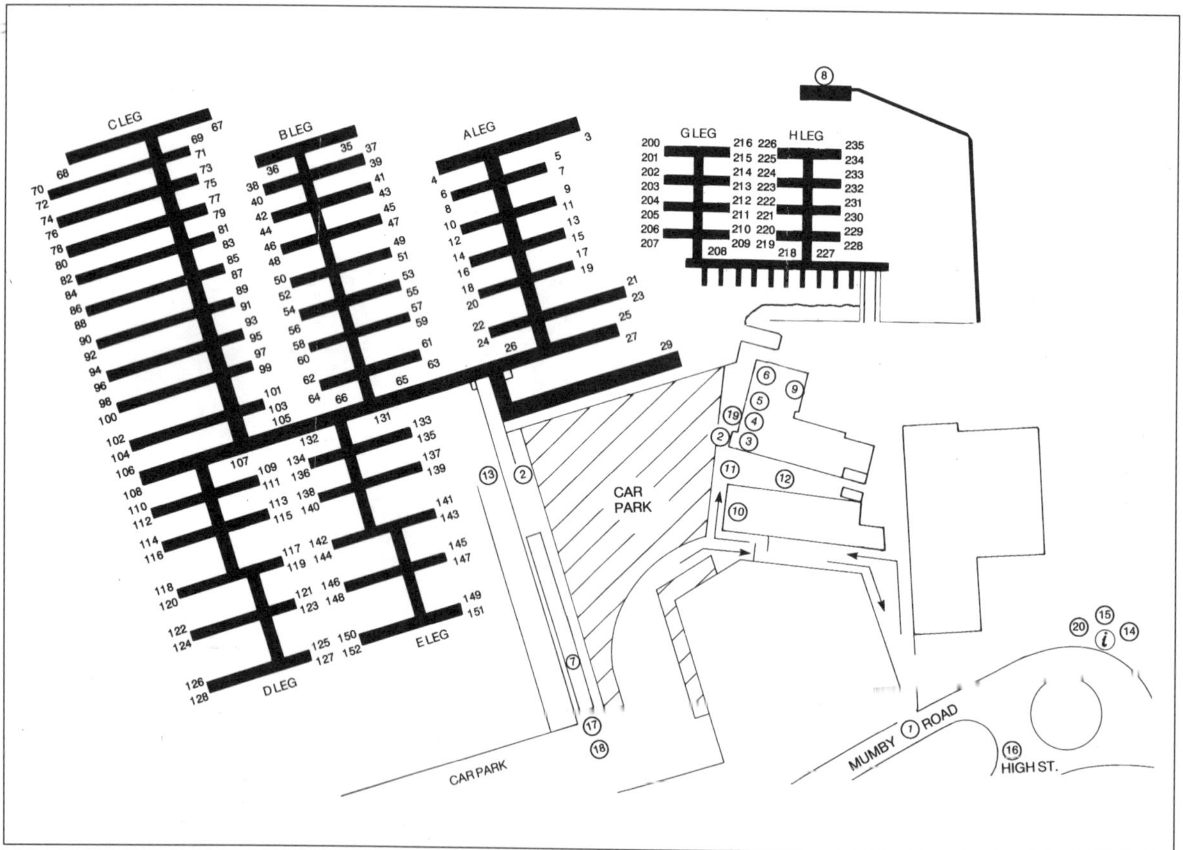

Camper & Nicholson's Marina

FACILITIES AVAILABLE

- Lock gates allowing full tidal access 24 hours a day
- Marina Control building manned 24 hours a day
- Waiting pontoons both extenal and internal
- Petrol and Diesel fuel
- Calor Gas and Camping Gaz available from fuel jetty
- Bertholders car parking
- Security bridgeheads
- Access controlled shower and toilets
- Coin operated laundrette, drying room
- Private Members Club
- Terraced Marina Cafe
- Travel Hoist, Mobile Crane and Boat Mover
- New boat sale centre
- Brokerage
- Full boat repair facilities including rigging
- Winter storage
- Selection of licenced premises

Port Solent

Available:	Water✓	Electric✓
Showers✓	Laundrette	Petrol✓
Diesel✓	Chandler	
Repairs:	Yacht	Engine
Electrical	Sail	

PORT SOLENT

Charges:

Daily	£1.00 per metre + VAT
Weekly	£5.82 per metre + VAT

Although Port Solent is some way from Portsmouth, it has a number of shore attractions. Shops, restaurants and bars on the quayside serve the visitor as well as the resident, for this is a marina complex with quality accommodation. For the yachtsmen there is a chandlery and boat repair facility. Access is available 24 hours a day

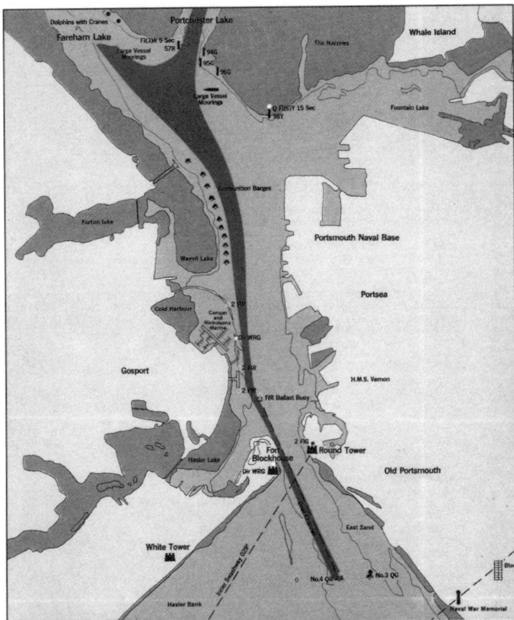

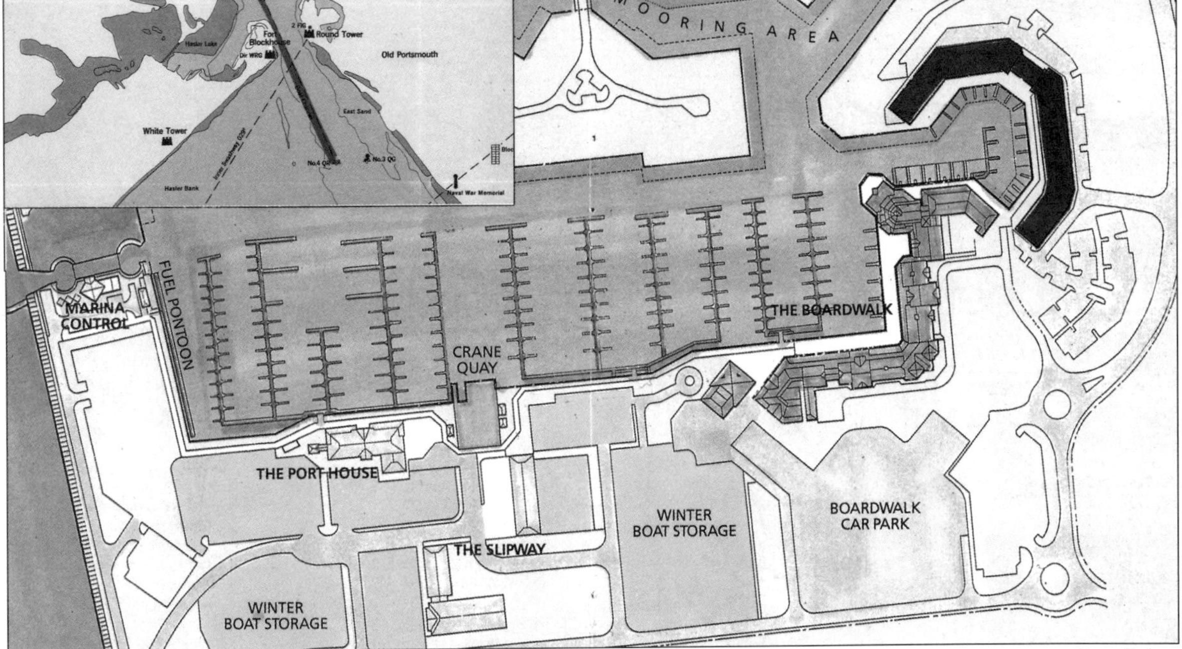

Port Solent

CHICHESTER HARBOUR *****

Standard Port
PORTSMOUTH

Harbour Entry
The entrance lies between Eastoke Point, Hayling Island and West Wittering

HO Itchener 512301

Lat: 50° 48 N **Long:** 0° 52' W

Admiralty charts 3418

Approach visual navigation aids: Leave Chichester Bar Beacon (half a mile offshore), to port when entering

R/T: The Harbour keeps a VHF Radio Listening watch on Ch 16 and 14 during office hours. Easter to end September. Marinas Ch 80/37

Yachting facilities: See next page

Visitors moorings available: Visitors moorings are available at Itchener and Emsworth through the Harbour Office. Chichester Yacht Basin 512731 has 40 berths for visitors; Northney Marina

Distances: Brighton 37, Cherbourg 74, Le Havre 90, Nab Tower 6

DESCRIPTION: Once inside the entrance to Chichester Harbour the channel divides into two main branches, the Chichester channel leading northeastwards and the Emsworth Channel northwards.
Chichester Harbour is special, a special yachting experience. A little challenge to your nautical skill with a natural beauty and peace, safeguarded to the best of their ability by the Chichester Harbour Conservancy, you will enjoy your visit here. And wherever you choose to come alongside there are facilities available. With fresh southerly winds the entrance is rough and becomes dangerous against Spring ebbs. Enter 3h-HW-1h. Once in, the harbour offers superb sailing in sheltered water, plus good beaches for the family.

Northney Marina

Mooring charges:

Chichester Harbour	Daily
Alongside Itchenor	£6.87
Pontoons	39p per metre
Conservancy Quays	
6m-12m	£3.00
12m-18m	£6.87
Chichester Yacht Basin	
Daily	£1 per metre
Weekly	£5.95 per metre

Northney Marina
£1.10 per metre per day
£5.50 per metre per week

☆☆☆☆☆ CHICHESTER HARBOUR

Telephone Code 0243

Customs
Freephone 100 'Customs Yachts'

Weather ☎ Portsmouth 8033

Tourist Office ☎ 775888

Yacht Clubs
At Birdham, Chichester

Police ☎ 0243 784433

Pubs/restaurants
Millstream, Bosham Lane, Bosham 573234; Micawbers, South St., Chichester 786989; Thompsons, Southgate, Chichester 528832

Tourist attractions:
The town of Chichester is a little way away needing transport, but it is a charming area to explore. With transport you could see: Apuldram Roses, Dell Quay, Arundel Castle, Hollycombe Steam Collection, Royal Military Police Museum, Roman Palace, Fisbourne and Chichester itself, of course, with the Cathedral, Festival Theatre, Fishbourne Roman Palace and Museum, the Mechanical Music and Bell Collection also Bosham Walk Art & Craft Centre at Birdham, Earnley Butterflies and Gardens

There are about 7,500 yachts based in Chichester Harbour which has seen boating activity since before Roman times. The Romans themselves used it, landing at Fisbourne. It is said that King Canute failed to repel the tide at Bosham. In the 17th Century Charles II kept a yacht at Itchener. Some of Nelson's ships were built on the shores of the harbour, as were 'D' Day landing craft. The tide in Chichester Harbour has a range of about 4 metres between high and low water. As there are considerable areas of mudland on each side of the main channels, this is all covered to a depth of 1 to 2 metres at high tide. At high tide the harbour has water area of 11 sq. miles, at low water ther are 12 miles or deep water channels, but as in places these are only a couple of hundred metres wide the sailing area is severely restricted.

Chichester Yacht Harbour

Chichester Yacht Basin
Available: Water Electric Showers Laundrette Petrol✓ Diesel✓ Chandler 784572
Repairs: Yacht 512731/512606, Engine 512731, Electrical 512731/512995, Sail 533622

Bosham
Repairs: Sail 572149

Emsworth
Available: Water✓ Electric✓ Showers Laundrette Petrol✓ Diesel✓ Chandler 374242
Repairs: Yacht 375211/374242
Engine 375211/374242
Electrical 375211/378314

Hayling Island
Available:
Water Electric Showers Laundrette Petrol Diesel Chandler 466321
Repairs: Yacht 466321
Engine 463592/466321
Electrical 466321/465051

CHICHESTER HARBOUR ☆☆☆☆☆

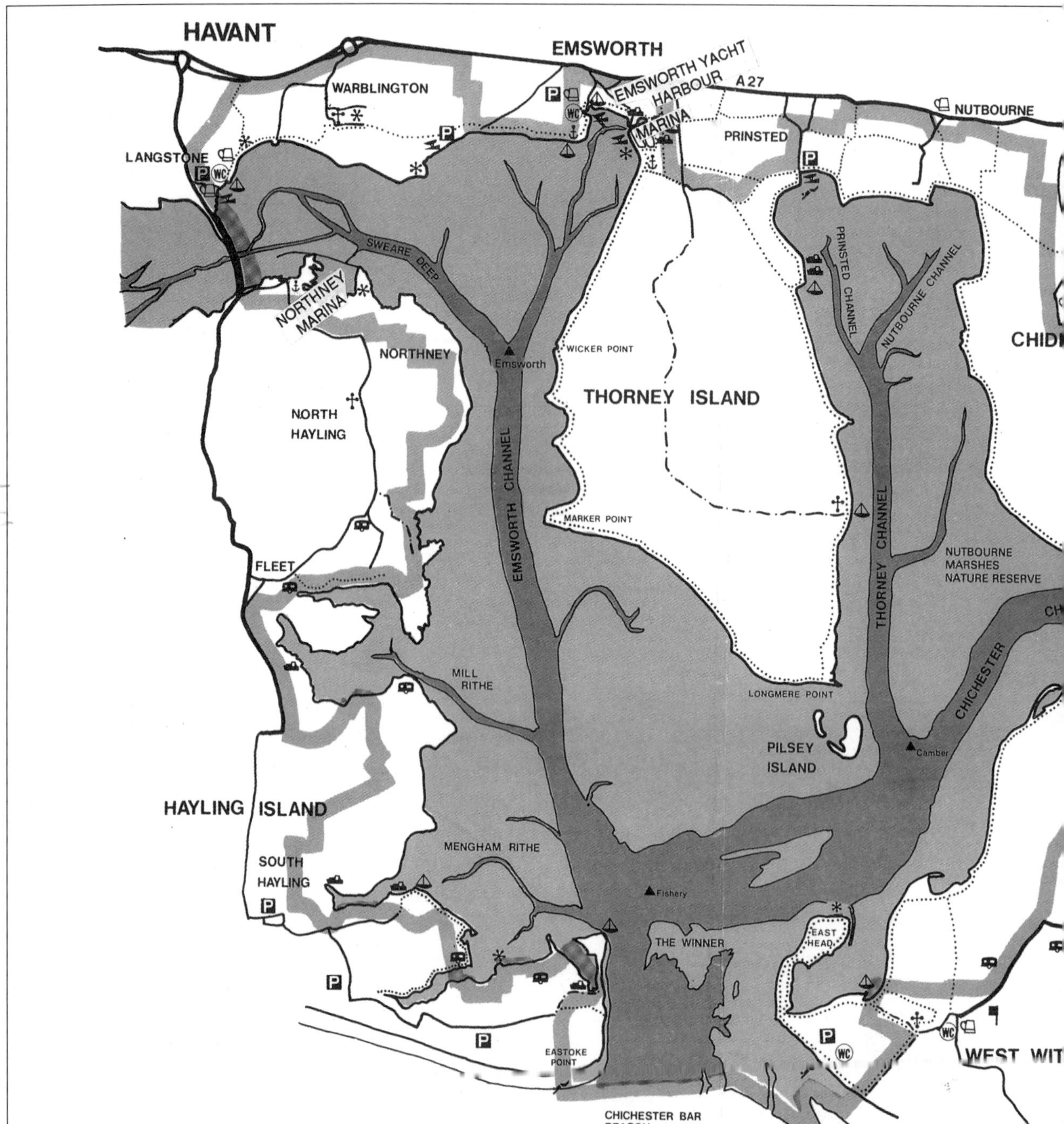

Chichester Harbour

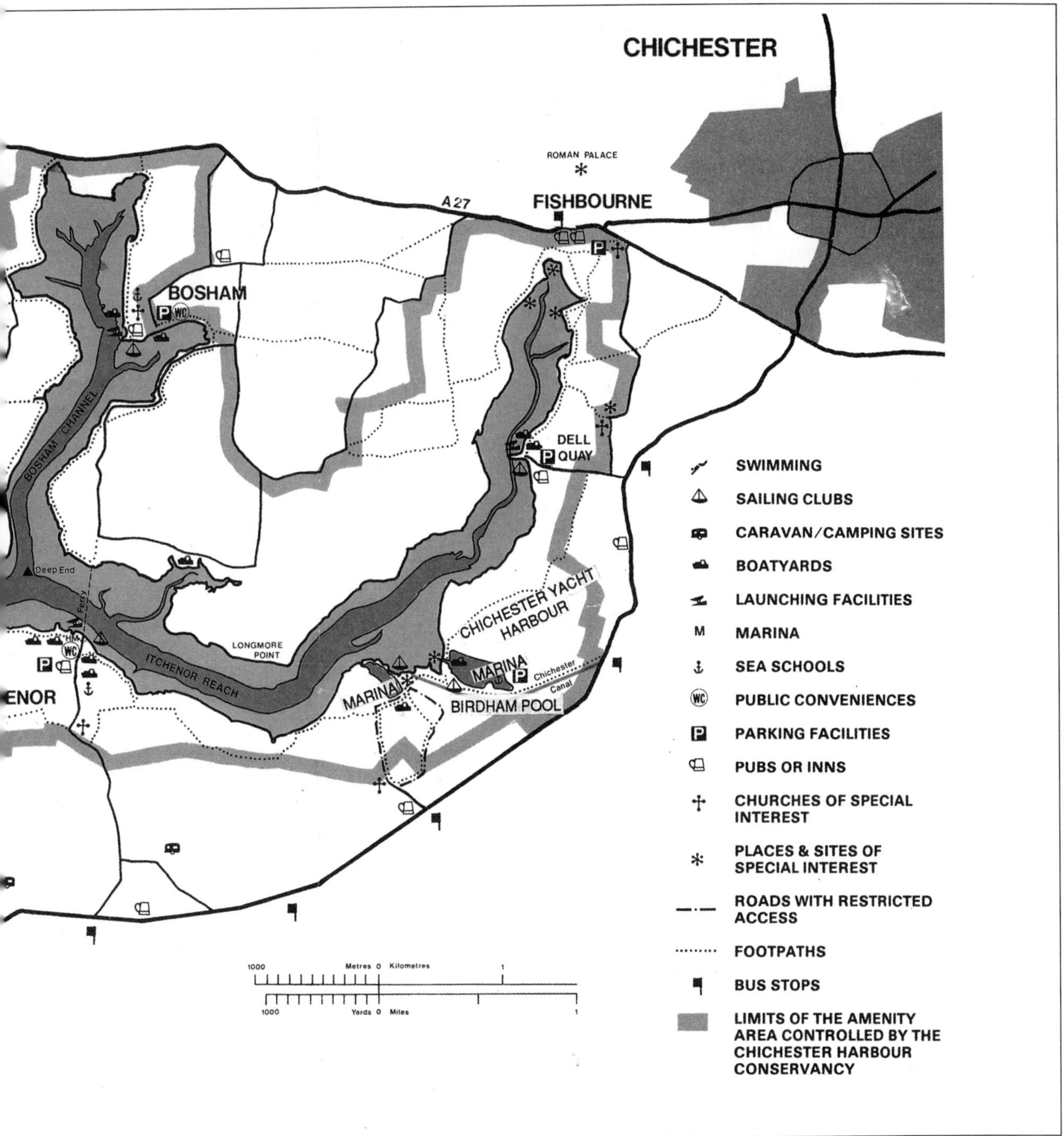

REPRODUCED BY KIND PERMISSION OF CHICHESTER HARBOUR CONSERVANCY

COWES ☆☆☆☆☆

Standard Port PORTSMOUTH	**Approach visual navigation aids:** Cowes Harbour and River Medina Admiralty Chart 2793
Harbour Entry At all times	**R/T:** Cowes Harbour radio VHF Ch 16; 11 12 14 69. Marinas 80/37
HM 293952	**Yachting facilities:** All available
Lat: 50° 46' N **Long:** 1° 18' W	**Visitors moorings available:** From Harbour Master, Ancasta Marina and Cowes Marina. See below
Admiralty charts 394/1905/2040/2793	**Distances:** Nab Tower 15, Portsmouth 10, Cherbourg 73, Brighton 45, Plymouth 115, Poole 27

DESCRIPTION: The Mecca of Yachting! The traditional image of Cowes centres on Cowes Week when almost 1,000 yachts compete in 200 races over a hectic nine day period in early August. Even at this time the Harbour Master offers a friendly welcome in managing to pack everyone in even if it entails the slight inconvenience of rafting up here and there.

At other times there is plenty of room. There are visitors' mooring buoys off Parade (West Cowes), mooring piles off Lallows Yard, Thetis Public Landing Pontoon, North of Thetis Wharf, mooring piles off UK Sailing Centre. At East Cowes there are mooring piles off Clarence Boatyard. Further upstream there is a visitors' pontoon off the Folly Inn. Admiralty Chart 2793 shows the location of moorings with the usual symbol. Although moored in the stream there is no need to worry about getting ashore because there is an efficient launch, or water-taxi service, originally instituted by the magazine, Yachting World, and these launches seem to be flying about all over the place, even up as far as the Folly Inn. Ancasta Marina is easily recognisable at West Cowes, as is Cowes Marina, a little further up at East Cowes.

There is certainly a welcome for yachtsmen at Cowes.

Harbour Master (Cowes Harbour Radio VHF Ch 69/16)

Mooring charges:
ANCASTA MARINA
(Ch 80 37 280013)
20p per foot LOA up to 4 hours
50p per foot LOA per night

Cowes Ancasta

Available:	Water✓	Electric✓
Showers	Laundrette	Petrol✓
Diesel✓	Chandler	
Repairs:	Yacht✓	Engine✓
Electrical	Sail	

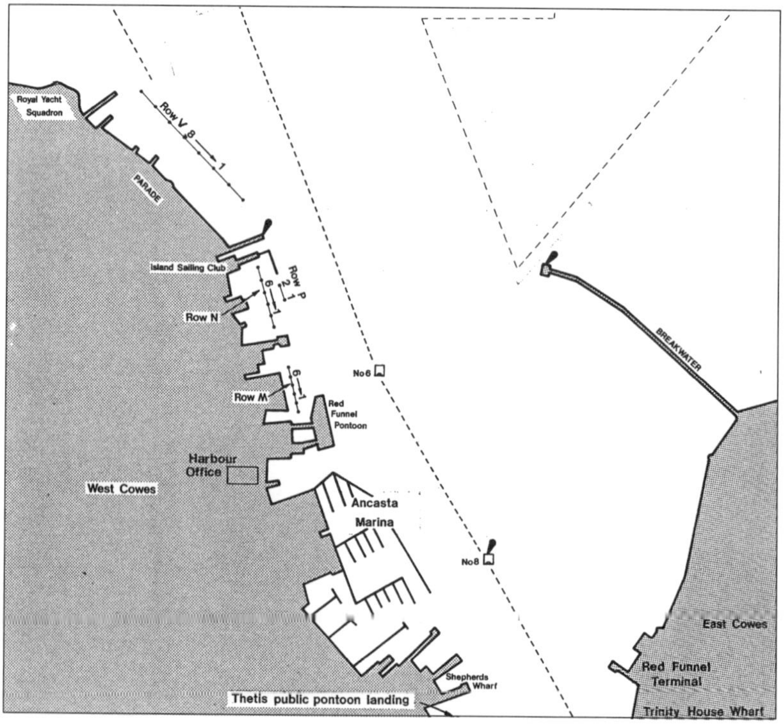

Entry showing Harbour Office and Ancasta Marina

☆☆☆☆☆ COWES

Telephone Code	0983
Customs	☎ 293132
Weather	Southampton 228844
Tourist Office	High Street
Taxi	☎ 293352/292083
Hire Cars	☎ 822247
Doctor	☎ 295251
Dentist	☎ 298769/291863
Hospital	☎ 63311
Chemist	Birmingham Road
Post Office	High Street
Bank	High Street
Yacht Clubs	Castle Rock 293581 Cowes Corinthian 296333 Island SC 293061
Police	☎ 295241
Laundrette	Mill Hill Road

Shops/supermarkets
Nearby

Pubs/restaurants
Murrays; Sullivans; Capri; Fastnet; Fountain; Harbour Lights; Globe

Tourist attractions:
Osborne House, where Queen Victoria sought seclusion after the death of the Prince Consort. Maritime Museum.

COWES MARINA
(Ch 80 37 293983)
30p per foot LOA

Cowes Marina

Available:	Water✓ Diesel✓	Electric Chandler	Showers	Laundrette	Petrol✓
Repairs:	Yacht✓	Engine✓	Electrical✓	Sail✓	

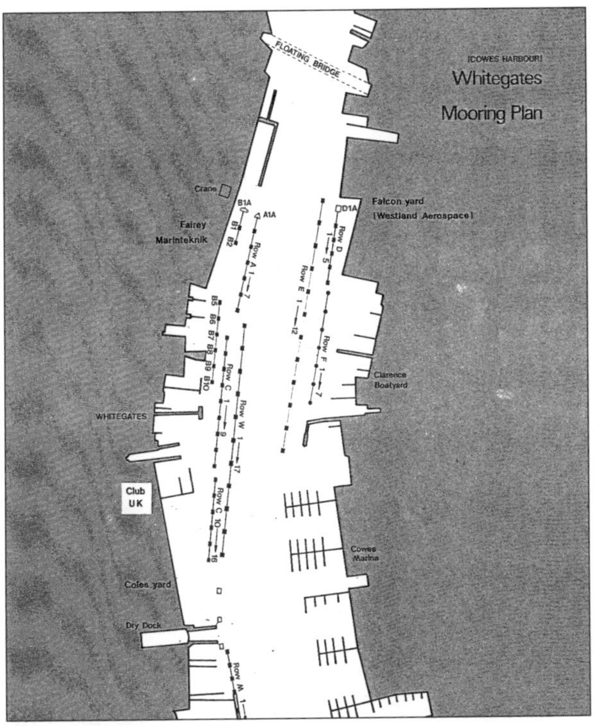

Middle reach showing Cowes Marina

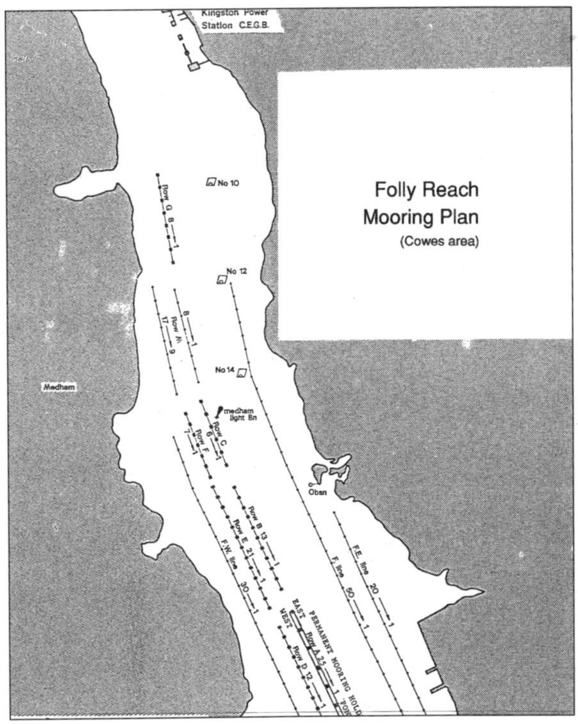

Folly Reach

YARMOUTH ☆☆☆☆☆

Standard Port
PORTSMOUTH

Harbour Entry
At all times. As directed at harbour entrance ot call VHF

HM 760321

Lat: 50° 42' N **Long:** 1° 30' W

Admiralty charts 2040/2021

Approach visual navigation aids: Leading markers bearing 188°. See plan

R/T: H.M. VHF Ch 16 (0800-1700); Ch 80 for berthing

Yachting facilities: All available

Visitors moorings available: 160 for visiting yachts; Water taxi

Distances: Weymouth 37, Torquay 75, Dover 111

DESCRIPTION: A charming harbour, surrounded by charming streets of pubs and a small selection of shops. Because of its attraction it is a favourite harbour amongst Solent Yachtsmen, particularly at weekends when the red flag (lights by night) "Full Up" has sometimes to be exhibited to late-comers. An ideal spot to lay up afloat for the winter. Until recently visiting yachts were met by Waterbourne harbour staff and directed to a berth; but the new Harbour Master intends to provide this information on entry. Yacht mooring buoys are laid outside harbour. Ferries to Lymington on mainland.

VISITING CRAFT – CHARGES PER DAY

Craft up to and inc. 20ft. length overall	£4.50
Craft over 20ft. up to and inc. 25ft.	£5.00
Craft over 25ft. up to and inc. 30ft.	£5.50
Craft over 30ft. up to and inc. 35ft.	£6.00
Craft over 35ft. up to and inc. 40ft.	£6.50
Craft over 40ft. up to and inc. 45ft.	£7.50
Craft over 45ft. up to and inc. 50ft.	£9.00
Craft over 50ft. up to and inc. 60ft.	£11.00
Craft over 60ft. up to and inc. 70ft.	£13.00
Craft over 70ft. up to and inc. 80ft.	£15.00
Craft over 80ft. up to and inc. 90ft.	£18.00
Craft over 90ft. up to and inc. 100ft.	£20.00
Craft over 100ft.	£23.00

Yachts of exceptional beam are charged extra namely: Trimarans and Catamarans at a rate of 1.5 times the length.

Yarmouth
Available: Water✓ Electric Showers Laundrette Petrol✓ Diesel✓ Chandle
Repairs: Yacht✓ Engine✓ Electrical✓ Sail✓

Entry to Yarmouth Harbour

YARMOUTH

Telephone Code 0983

Customs
First door on right in Quay St. 760406

Weather HM

Tourist Office Quay Street

Taxi ☎ 752784

Hire Cars ☎ 882301

Doctor ☎ 760434

Dentist ☎ 852189

Hospital Newport 525254

Chemist Quay Street

Post Office Quay Street

Bank The Square

Yacht Clubs
Royal Solent 760256
Yarmouth SC 761262

Police ☎ 528000

Laundrette No

Shops/supermarkets
Quay Street

Pubs/restaurants
The Kings Head; The Bugle; George Hotel; Wheatsheaf

Tourist attractions:
Yarmouth Castle

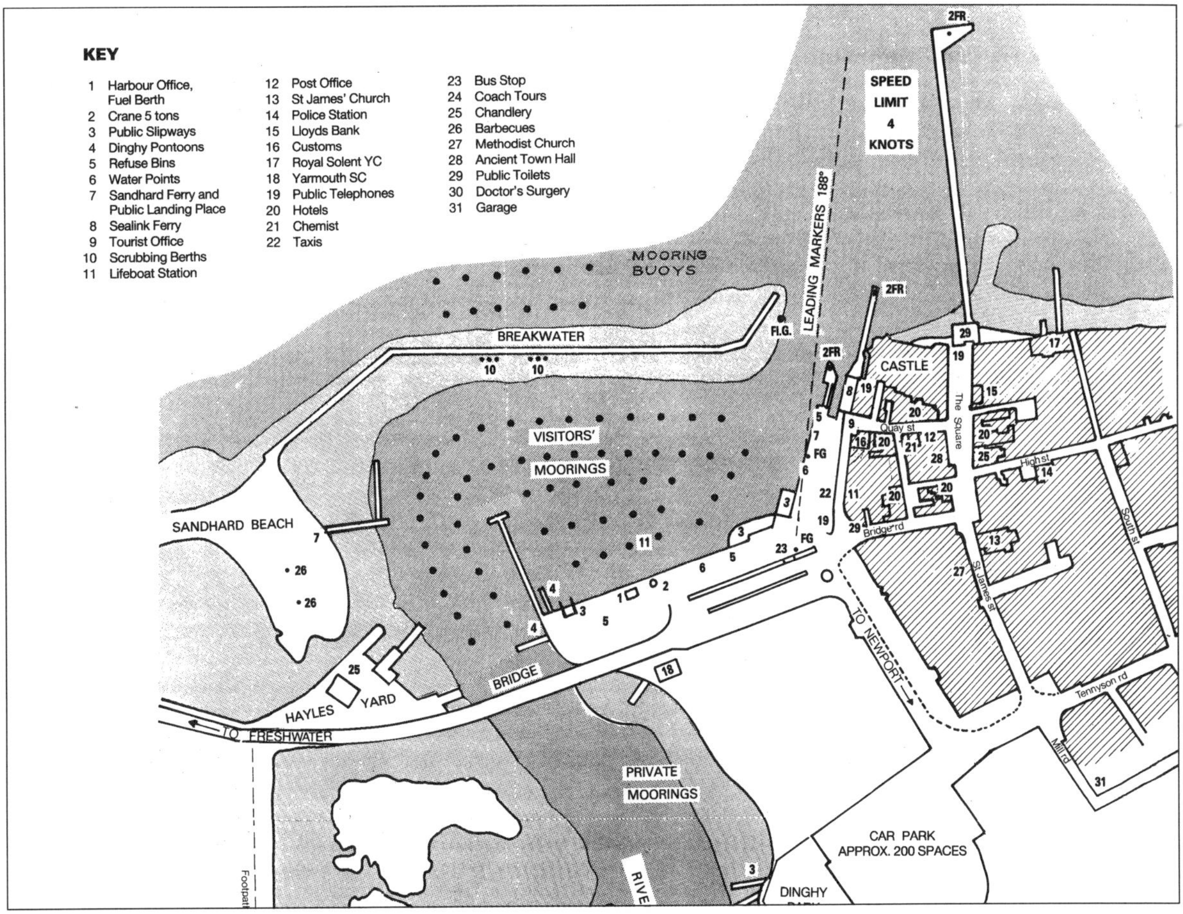

LYMINGTON ☆☆☆☆☆

Standard Port
PORTSMOUTH

Harbour Entry
Access at all times

HM 672014

Lat: 50° 45' N **Long:** 1° 32' W

Admiralty charts 2012/2040

Approach visual navigation aids: On entry leave Jack-in-the-Basket to port to clear Cross Boom

R/T: Marinas Ch 80 37 (office hours)

Yachting facilities: See next page

Visitors moorings available: Town Quay, Harbour Master 672014, Lymington Marina M (37) 673312 100 berths, Lymington Yacht Haven 677071

Distances: Brixham 75, Poole 17, Weymouth 39

DESCRIPTION: A very popular harbour for yachtsmen. There is always room for a visiting yacht on application to the Harbour Master, the marina or the Yacht Haven. Whichever you choose, you are within easy walking distance of the main shopping area of Lymington in which are many good pubs and restaurants. The Saturday market in the High Street is an attraction. About 6 miles away at Beaulieu is the National Motor Museum. Very crowded during the season. River much used by ferries to the Isle of Wight. Nearly 100 visitors' moorings off Town Quay, which also features alongside, pontoon berths. Train connections to London etc.

Mooring fees

	Daily	Weekly
Marina	50p per ft.	£2.30 per ft.
Yacht Haven	46p per ft.	£2.30 per ft.

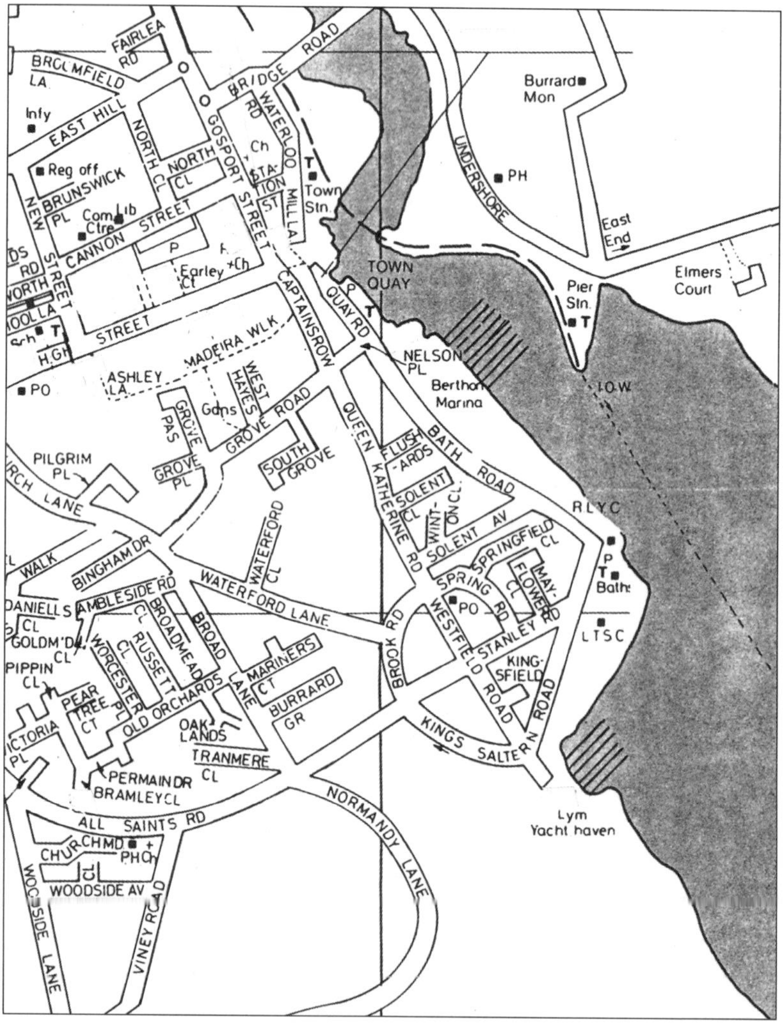

☆☆☆☆☆ # LYMINGTON

Lymington
Available: Water✓ Electric
Showers Petrol Diesel
Chandler 74266
Repairs: Yacht 79582
Engine 74266
Electrical 76511/71144
Sail 73797/73139

Lymington Marina
Available:
Water✓ Electric✓ Showers✓
Petrol✓ Diesel✓ Chandler✓
Repairs: Yacht✓ Engine✓
Electrical✓ Sail✓

Lymington Yacht Haven
Available: Water✓ Electric✓
Showers✓ Petrol✓ Diesel✓
Chandler✓ Laundrette✓
Repairs: Yacht✓ Engine✓
Electrical✓ Sail✓

Telephone Code	0590
Customs	Freephone Custom Yachts
Weather	☎ 98091
Taxi	☎ 671058/673827
Hire Cars	☎ 673227/676209
Dentist	☎ 74660
Hospital	☎ 677011
Chemist	High Street 672774
Post Office	☎ 672767
Bank	High Street
Yacht Clubs	Royal Lymington 672677 Lymington Town SC 672096
Police	☎ 675411
Laundrette	Marinas &New Street 672898
Shops/supermarkets	Tesco, High Street

Pubs/restaurants
Red Lion, High Street; Fisherman's Rest, All Saints Road 678931; The Railings, High Street 677123; Peelers Bistro 676165; Round House 679089; Mayflower 672160; Limpets 675595; La Piazza, Queen Street 675866

Town Quay

BEAULIEU ☆☆☆☆☆

Standard Port
PORTSMOUTH

Harbour Entry
At all times alongside Yacht Harbour Pontoons

HM 616200 or 616234

Lat: 50° 47' N **Long:** 1° 24' W

Admiralty charts 107/1905/2021/2040

Approach visual navigation aids: Beaulieu Spit Light Beacon

R/T: None

Yachting facilities: All available

Visitors moorings available: On piles or in marina 100 available

Distances: Chichester 25, Poole 25, Brighton 53

DESCRIPTION: The yacht harbour at Bucklers Hard is in a beautiful but remote, situation, but all facilities for the yacht are available at Bucklers Hard Yacht Harbour. There is good shelter from all winds.

Available:
Water✓ Electric✓ Showers
Petrol✓ Diesel✓ Chandler✓
Repairs: Yacht✓ Engine✓
Electrical✓ Sail✓

Charges:

Pile Moorings	
27-30 guide	£6.50 daily
	£32.50 weekly
Marina	
Up to 39ft	£16 per day
	£80 a week
40ft. to 50ft.	£19 a night
	£95 a week

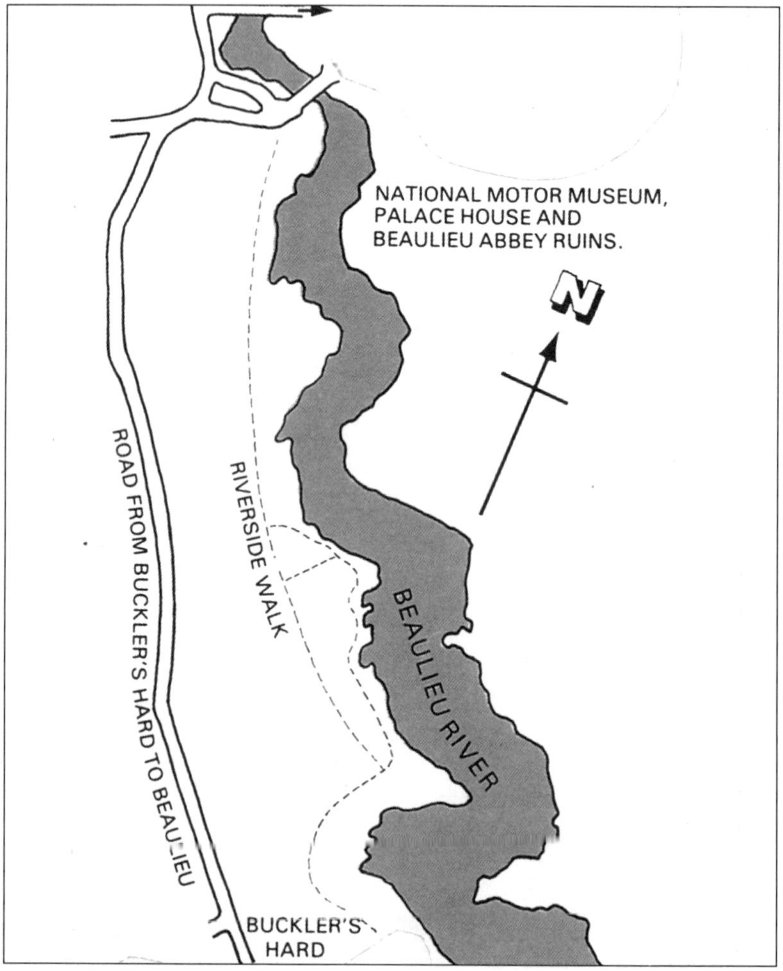

Telephone Code	0590
Customs	Nearest Lymington
Hospital	☎ Lymington 77011
Police	Lymington
Laundrette	Not available

Shops/supermarkets
Village shop in Bucklers Hard Village

Pubs/restaurants
The Master Builder, Bucklers Hard

Tourist attractions:
The surroundings are of such exceptional beauty that they should suffice for most visiting yachtsmen, indeed, this is all they come for. The Harbour Master is able to arrange for medical attention in an emergency. It is a short walk from the harbour to Bucklers Hard Village and the Master Builders House pub, buffet and restaurant. Adjoining are the Chapel and village shop. Across the road is the Maritime Museum, Bucklers Hard in the 18th Century, New Inn 1793 and Labourer's Cottage. There are riverside walks and only a few miles away is the National Motor Museum, well worth a visit since it is one of the largest collections of motor vehicles in the world.

Bucklers Hard

LESSER HARBOURS

BEMBRIDGE

Solent

Isle of Wight
50° 41' N, 1° 05' W
Admiralty chart 2022, 2050
Harbour Master: 872828

Access 3h-HW-2h to marina with limited facilities
An area of clean sand. A small town with not a great deal to offer.
Radio Telephone: Bembridge Marina VHF Ch 16 80.

CHRISTCHURCH

Between Lymington and Poole

Admiralty chart 2172
Christchurch Harbour Association: 478612

Difficult harbour entrance through which tide ebbs strongly. Vessels drawing in excess of 3' 6 should not attempt to enter. A lot of the harbour dries. Enter and leave during stand caused by double highs; ebb is fierce after 2nd HW.
Christchurch is a charming place, with most facilities available.

LANGSTONE

Solent

Admiralty chart 3418
Harbour master: 463419

Mudbank surroundings and more mudbanks. Moorings a fair way from landing places. Langstone Marina, VHF Ch 80, entry to marina 3h-HW-3h. Good shelter once inside but with fresh onshore winds the entrance can be dangerous especially against a Spring ebb.

Christchurch Harbour showing The Run (bottom of picture), Avon Beach (right hand side of picture), Mudeford, with Christchurch in background

CHANNEL EAST

LITTLEHAMPTON ☆☆☆☆☆

Standard Port
SHOREHAM

Harbour Entry
Nearly all berths dry at LW, port traffic signal

HM 721215

Lat: 50° 48' N **Long:** 00° 33' W

Admiralty charts 1991

Approach visual navigation aids: Ldg Lts sectored (white/orange), occ. lighthouse in line with fixed green front leading light.

R/T: Port Ch 16; Marinas Ch 80 or 37 (office hours)

Yachting facilities: Available

Visitors moorings available: Tie up alongside County Wharf on the East Bank next to the Harbour Master's Office (582613). Other moorings at Littlehampton Marina, but unsuitable for visiting yachts owing to restrictions imposed by footbridge. VHF Ch 37-713553. Arun Yacht Club has berths to port below footbridge.

Distances: Le Havre 86, Cherbourg 82, Dieppe 83

DESCRIPTION: With a history going back to 600 BC, Littlehampton has flourished as a port and become a popular seaside resort, indeed it has been recommended as a holiday destination since 1764. Connections with the past include "The Old House" in East Street and the "White Hart Inn" in East Street. The visiting yachtsman will find everything to hand, and a great deal of historical interest all around. Entry is between two piers, the West Pier extending further seaward than the East Pier. The harbour is difficult to enter with strong south easterly winds. Strong South Westerlies cause a nasty swell in harbour. The bar dries. Local beach polluted by short sewer outfall. Littlehampton Harbour is situated at the mouth of the River Arun and the town is on the east bank, a mile from the entrance.

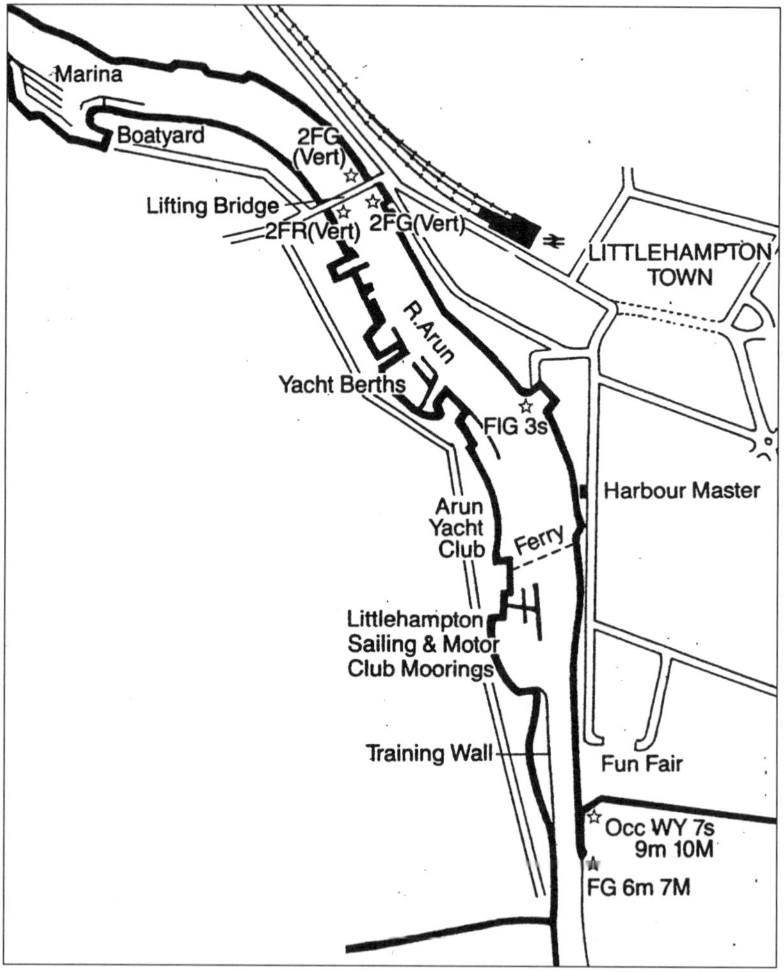

Mooring charges:
At the Marina the daily rate is 20p
Harbour Board:

	5-8 m.	8-11 m	Over 11m.
Daily	£1.80	£3.60	£4.50
Weekly	£3.60	£7.00	£9.00

☆☆☆☆☆ LITTLEHAMPTON

Telephone Code	0903
Customs	☎ 0273 592664
Tourist Office	☎ 713480
Taxi	☎ 717832
Hire Cars	☎ 723200/714367/ 726127/782087
Doctor	☎ 714113
Dentist	☎ 713456
Hospital	☎ 717101
Chemist	☎ 713516

Post Office	☎ 714444
Bank	High Street
Yacht Clubs	
Arun	☎ 716016
Littlehampton	☎ 715859
Sussex Motor	☎ 453078
Sussex YC	☎ 464868
Police	☎ 716161
Laundrette	☎ 722014

Shops/supermarkets
High Street; Gateways and Tesco within short walk adjacent East Bank

Pubs/restaurants
Cafeteria in Marina;
Arun View Inn;
Six Bells; Seagull; Pier Road;
Steam Packet; La Casita;
Seahorse Floating Pub;
The Balaton

Tourist attractions:
Covered market Friday and Saturday, also on Sunday in Summer. Maritime Museum, West Beach, Smarts Amusement Park

Littlehampton Harbour

SHOREHAM ☆☆☆

Standard Port
SHOREHAM

Harbour Entry
At any time subject to port traffic signals

HO 593801

Lat: 50° 49' N **Long:** 00° 17' W

Admiralty charts 1991

Approach visual navigation aids:
Ldg Lts Middle Pier Front F WR or G 10m W Watch house R base. 355°Rear Fl W 10s 15m Grey round stone tower.

R/T: VHF 14 16; 14 Lady Bee Marina Ch 80

Yachting facilities: Some available

Visitors moorings available: At Lady Bee Marina (a few) 593801 (in the eastern part of the harbour). Locks 4h-HW-4h; 110 berth marina with 10 for visiting yachts

Distances: Nab Tower 30, Cherbourg 85, Dieppe 75, Brighton 10

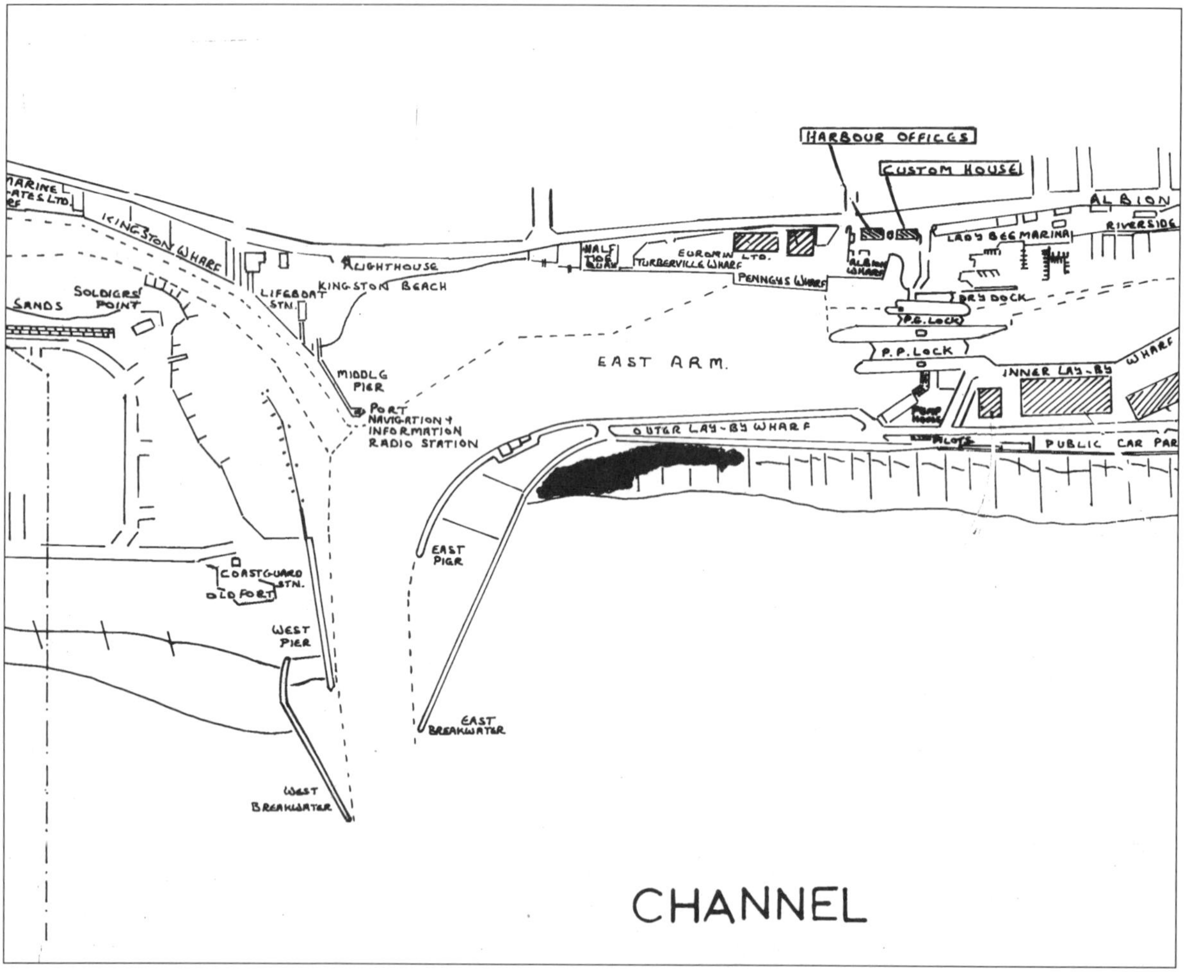

☆☆☆ SHOREHAM

DESCRIPTION: Shoreham is a successful commercial harbour in a commanding position, according to its brochure, for the increasing development of European trade. Amongst the industrial activity ashore there is the Lady Bee Marina with a few moorings for visitors but no one would pretend that this is in any way a pleasure resort. How different it all would have been in 1651 when Charles II escaped from here to Fecamp, after his defeat by Cromwell at Worcester. Situated near the mouth of the River Adur, Shoreham was an important port in the 13th and 14th centuries but was later much reduced. It has achieved considerable importance today. Centred between two breakwaters it extends over four miles and is divided into three sections. In the Aldrington Basin the two schooners *Malcolm Miller* and *Winston Churchill* are based. Ships sail from Shoreham to every quarter of the globe, even providing a regular service from here to the Falkland Islands. Lock into Lady Bee Marina. Opens 4h-HW-4h. Entrance rough in strong onshore winds. Visiting yachts are charged a minimum of one month's dues – even for an overnight stay!

Yacht Clubs

Sussex Yacht Club

Sussex Motor Yacht Club

Available:
Water✓ Electric✓ Petrol✓
Diesel✓ Chandlery✓

Repairs: Yacht✓ Engine✓

BRIGHTON ☆☆☆☆☆

Standard Port
SHOREHAM

Harbour Entry
At all times

HM 693636

Lat: 50° 49' 5.N **Long:** 00° 06' 0 W

Admiralty charts 1652 1991

Approach visual navigation aids: E Breakwater Fl(4) W R 20s 10m W pillar G band S

R/T: Brighton Control VHF Ch 16; 68 11. Marina Ch 80

Yachting facilities: See below

Visitors moorings available: In Brighton Marina 1600 with 200 for visiting yachts (Pontoon 10). Apply Harbour Office on end of W Jetty

Distances: Chichester 37, Newhaven 8, Dover 63, Fecamp 65, Dieppe 68, Cowes 45, Dinard 68, Ramsgate 80, Nab Tower 35

DESCRIPTION: Brighton claims to be the entertainment capital of the South Coast, with year round leisure facilities, splendid architecture, grand squares, quality shopping and a cosmopolitan life. But all this is a few miles away from the marina; there is a regular bus service between the marina and the town, also a quaint electric railway. The marina itself has a lot to offer though, with supermarkets, shops, restaurants all presented in a stylish way with the addition of a new Brasserie and 8-screen cinema – and Brighton is there when you want it. Brighton Marina claims to be Britain's largest marina, enclosing a total area of 126 acres and providing easily accessible berthing for up to 2,000 craft. Easy access to the sea is available at any state of the tide. In strong southerly winds the entrance and approaches can be difficult and very rough.

Mooring charges:
Mooring fees per 1/2 metre LOA (min. 8m)

1 day	63p
1 week	£3.15
1 month	£11.75
3 months	£52

Available:
Water✓ Electric✓ Showers✓
Laundrette✓ Petrol✓ Diesel✓
Chandler✓

Repairs: Yacht✓
Engine✓
Electrical 684385/693258
Sail✓

Brighton Marina

Telephone Code	0273
Customs	☎ Marina 697936 823177
Weather	☎ 0898 500 456
Tourist Office	☎ 23755
Taxi	☎ 24555
Hire Cars	☎ 202426/Avis 773233 Europcar free telephone
Doctor	☎ 600103
Dentist	☎ 692444/604451
Hospital	☎ 696955

Chemist	☎ 207461
Post Office	Ship St. ☎ 573209
Bank	North Street
Yacht Clubs	Brighton Marina ☎ 697049
Police	☎ 606744
Laundrette	Marina

Shops/supermarkets
In Brighton Marina Village, Asda Superstore

Pubs/restaurants
Master Mariner, Village Square; Leonardos. There are 400 restaurants in Brighton. Try Bartons, 7 Prince Albert St. 729474; Browns 4 Duke St. 23501; Cafe de Paris, 40 St. James St. 603740; Cannings, 100 Marine Parade 606311; Fudges, 127 Kings Rd. 205852; Taverna Sorrentina, 45 Kings Rd. 25229

Tourist attractions:
The Royal Pavilion, Brighton Race Course, shops in The Lanes, Theatre Royal, Palace Pier, Sunday Market

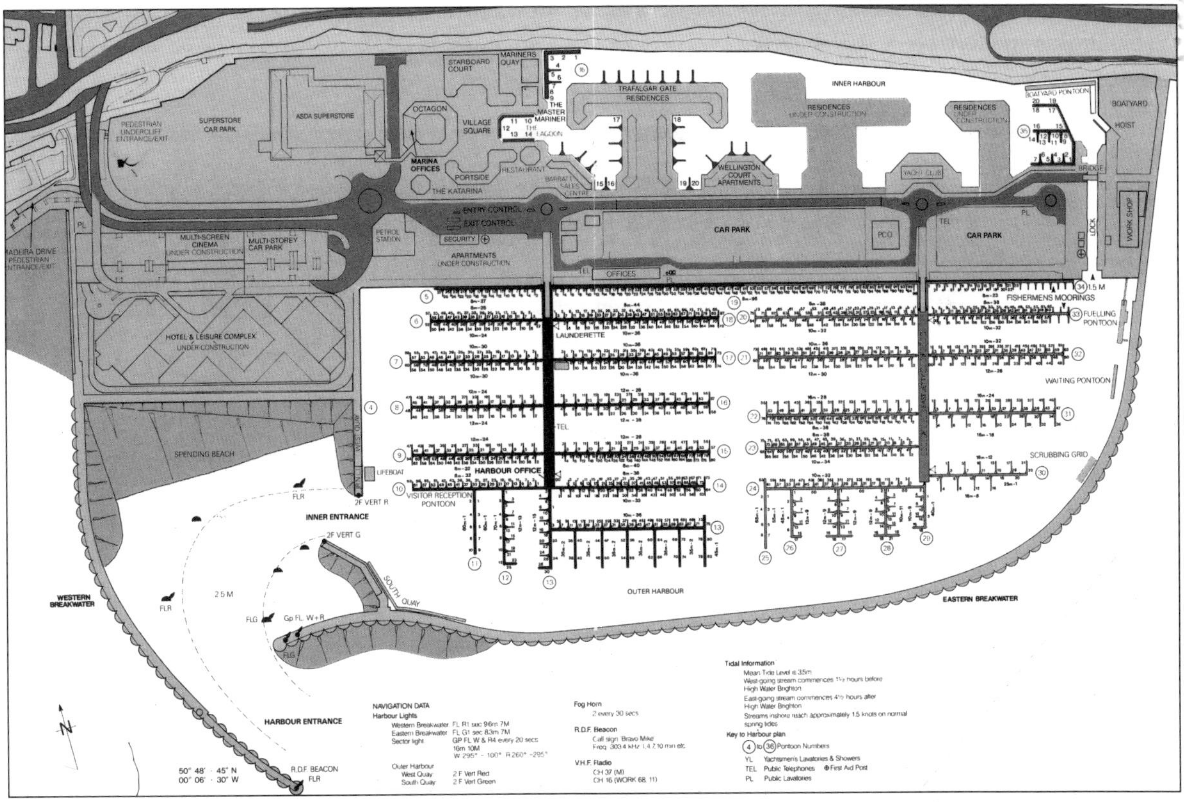

FOLKESTONE ☆

Standard Port
DOVER

Harbour Entry
At any time subject to traffic signals

Lat: 51° 05' N **Long:** 1° 12' E

Admiralty charts 1991 1992

Approach visual navigation aids:
Ldg Lts No. 1 Berth Front F R
267° Rear FG

R/T: VHF Ch 16; 22 (occasionally)

Yachting facilities: See below

Visitors moorings available: See remarks

Distances: Dieppe 70, Nab Tower 91, Brighton 60

DESCRIPTION: I have included Folkestone because you would probably be surprised if I didn't – but it does not claim to be a yachting port. Visiting yachts are not really welcome because there is a great deal of commercial traffic; and what welcome there is – is a on a temporary basis. But, in any case, the harbour dries and the mud is unpleasant; a visiting yacht will compete for space with fishing boats and will need to keep out of the way of cross-Channel ferries. One day, maybe there will be a yacht marina here. There is good shelter except in strong winds from the east. It is a busy ferry terminal.

Available:
Water at South Quay Slipway
Electric Showers Laundrette
Petrol/Diesel nearby garage
Chandler 55752

Repairs: Yacht Engine
Electrical Sail

Restaurants:
India, 1 Old High St. 59155;
Paul's, 2a Bouverie Rd. West 59697.

Folkestone Inner Harbour (courtesy Clive Boiardini Yachts)

NEWHAVEN ☆☆☆☆☆

Standard Port
SHOREHAM

Harbour Entry
At all times subject to harbour traffic signals

HM 514131

Lat: 50° 47' N **Long:** 0° 04' E

Admiralty charts 1652/2154

Approach visual navigation aids: Breakwater Head Oc (2) W 10s 12m concrete tower

R/T: Port Control VHF 16; 12. Marina 80/37

Yachting facilities: See below

Visitors moorings available: Newhaven Marina (513881). 50 berths out of 300

Distances: Nab Tower 40, Dieppe 65, Cherbourg 92, Dover 57

DESCRIPTION: Newhaven claims to be the gateway to Europe, yet lying in the heart of the Sussex Downs it is attractive to visitors. Lying at the mouth of the River Ouse, in the north west part of Seaford Bay it is a commercial port and cross-Channel ferry terminal, Newhaven town is on the west bank, about $\frac{1}{2}$ mile above the entrance. Easily recognisable from seaward is the concrete breakwater protecting the harbour. Keep close to breakwater in strong onshore winds. When entering river, watch out for ferries warping off using wire cables across the harbour. As the only port open to shipping at all states of the tide between the hundred miles of coastline between Folkestone and Portsmouth, the port handles over one million passengers and $1\frac{1}{2}$ million tonnes of cargo a year. There is a modern shopping complex built around a pedestrian precinct and shops, pubs and restaurants are conveniently to hand. Obviously Newhaven is more of a commercial harbour than a yachting centre but all facilities are available for the yachtsman. The marina is subject to silting.

Mooring fees per 24 hours

Up to 25ft.	£10
26 to 40ft.	£15
41 to 60ft.	£25
61ft. and over	£35

Available:
Water✓ Electric✓ Showers
Laundrette Petrol Diesel
Chandler✓

Repairs: Yacht 514118
Engine 514118
Electrical 693258

KEY
1 Marina Office, 2 Showers & Toilets, 3 Chandlery, 4 Cafe, 5 Brokerage, 6 Supermarket, 7 Laundrette, 8 Fishing Tackle Shop, 9 Marine Engineers & Shipwrights, 10 Public Toilets, 11 Showers & Toilets, 12 Yacht Club

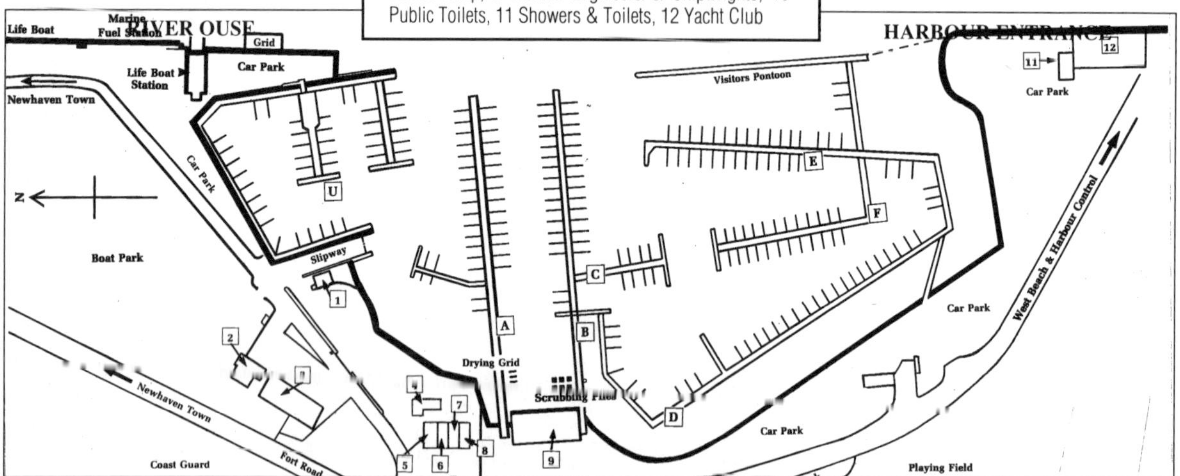

Newhaven Marina

☆☆☆☆☆ NEWHAVEN

Telephone Code	0273
Customs	☎ 513177
Tourist Office	☎ 515712
Taxi	☎ 514764/514450
Doctor	☎ 515076
Dentist	☎ 514406
Hospital	☎ 513441
Chemist	High Street
Post Office	High Street
Bank	High Street

Yacht Clubs

Newhaven Marina
Newhaven & Seaford

Police	☎ 515801
Laundrette	Marina

Shops/supermarkets

High Street shopping precinct. At West Quay you can buy fresh fish

Pubs/restaurants

Bridge Hotel, High St.; Shenfield Arms, Fort Rd.; Crown Inn, 16 Bridge St.; Newhaven Marina Restaurant; Buttemers, 18 Chapel St.

Tourist attractions:

Newhaven lies between two famous seaside towns, Brighton nine miles along the coast to the west and Eastbourne, 12 miles to the east. Newhaven Flea Market. The new traffic-free central shopping centre is convenient, with the usual selection of shops and supermarket. At the West Quay, where the town's fishing fleet is moored, there are several shops selling fish at low prices.

Newhaven Harbour

DOVER ☆☆☆☆

Standard Port DOVER	**Approach visual navigation aids:** Admiralty Pier. Extension Head Fl W 7.5s 20m White Tower
Harbour Entry At all times subject to traffic signals	**R/T:** Dover Port Control VHF Ch 12 74
HM 240400/206560	**Yachting facilities:** See next page
Lat: 51° 07' N **Long:** 1° 20' E	**Visitors moorings available:** Visiting yachts are normally berthed on the south and western side of Wellington Dock
Admiralty charts 1698/180/1892	**Distances:** Calais 23, Brighton 63, Boulogne 25, Nab Tower 96, Dieppe 75, Newhaven 57, Cherbourg 145

DESCRIPTION: Nearest port to mainland Europe. Large enclosed harbour offers yachtsmen a safe anchorage. There is an attractive sea front and promenade, a small but bustling town with a wide range of shops. It will be noted that although the traffic control signal may be exhibited for entry (departure) every vessel manoeuvring to enter or leave the Port is required to obtain specific permission to enter or leave.

Vessels awaiting permission to enter should keep at a safe distance of at least 1½ miles clear of the Entrances until so authorised. Responsibility for entering or leaving with caution and the safe navigation of each vessel subsequent to the receipt of permission to proceed continues to remain the responsibility of the Master.

Vessels not equipped with VHF may establish contact with Port Control by lamp using the following local signals:

Signal	Meaning
Morse SV	I wish to enter Port
Morse SW	I wish to leave Port

Port Control will reply either OK or WAIT.

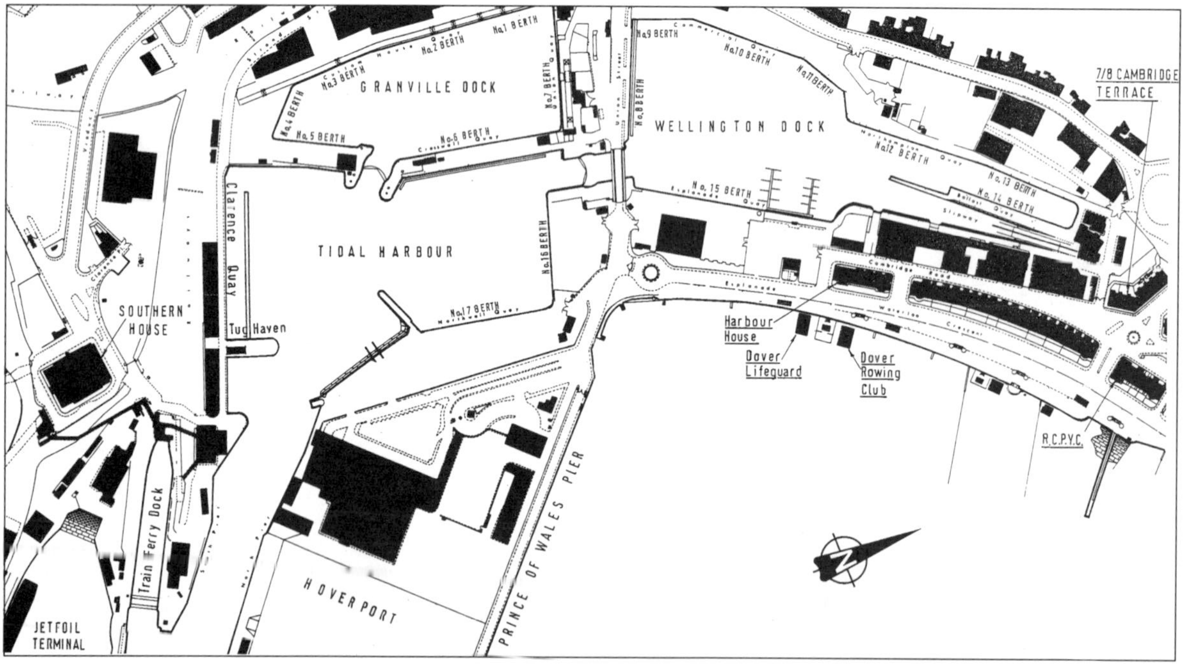

☆☆☆☆ DOVER

Telephone Code	0304	**Hospital**	☎ 201624	**Shops/supermarkets** All available
Customs	☎ 206789 x 312	**Chemist**	Boots nearby	**Pubs/restaurants** Monte Bianco. Numerous selection nearby
Tourist Office	☎ 205108	**Post Office**	Biggin Street	**Tourist attractions:** Old Town Gaol, Dover Castle, Dover Museum, Roman Painted House, Crabble Mill, The White Cliffs Experience
Taxi	☎ 207423/204420	**Yacht Clubs** Royal Cinque Ports	☎ 206262	
Hire Cars	☎ 206265/211200	**Police**	☎ 240055	
Doctor	Health Centre nearby	**Laundrette**	In town	

Mooring fees

Under 5m LOA £2.80 per day per yacht. 5m and over 70p per metre per day. Vessels over 27 metres should make prior arrangements.

Wellington Dock Available:

Water✓	Electric	Showers✓	Laundrette	Petrol
Diesel 201073/201677		Chandler		
Repairs:	Yacht 201073/ 201677	Engine 201073 201677	Electrical 201073 201677	Sail

Wellington Dock

RAMSGATE ****

Standard Port
DOVER

Harbour Entry
Subject to harbour signals.
Lock in 2h-HW-2h

HM 586251/HO592277

Lat: 51° 20' N **Long:** 1° 25' W

Admiralty charts 1827/1828

Approach visual navigation aids:
Ldg Lts Western Marina. Front Dir Oc WRG 10s 5m Black Δ Orange stripe W mast 270° Terminal Rear Oc W 5s 5m Black ∇ Orange stripe on W mast

R/T: Port Control VHF Ch 14; Marina Ch 14

Yachting facilities: See next page

Visitors moorings available: Inner and outer basin. Yachtsmen are welcomed but Ramsgate is a busy port so take care

Distances: Dover 13, Dieppe 91, Nab Tower 111, Cherbourg 160, Brighton 80

DESCRIPTION: Because it is the closest yacht marina to the European coast, Ramsgate is a natural port of call for yachtsmen who are crossing the English Channel. Many visitors spend their holiday periods in the marina at Ramsgate, with others from several different countries because every effort is made to make visiting yachtsmen feel welcome and because it is in the centre of the town, close to shops, restaurants and entertainments, and because of easy access and good sailing areas. From this harbour in June 1815, Wellington set out with his army for Europe, and the final victory over Napoleon at Waterloo. Six years later, following his coronation, George IV chose Ramsgate as his port of embarkation when making a return visit to Hanover. Impressed with his reception he commanded that Ramsgate be called "Royal" henceforth. A busy ferry and commercial port. Yachts should contact Port Control before arrival and also obey traffic signals.

Ramsgate Yacht Marina

☆☆☆☆ RAMSGATE

Telephone Code	0843
Weather	Canterbury 8091
Customs	Thanet 225511
Tourist Office	☎ 591086
Taxi	☎ 585585
Doctor	☎ 591758/593252
Dentist	☎ 591694/592423
Hospital	☎ 225544

Post Office	Nearby
Bank	Queen Street
Yacht Clubs	Royal Temple ☎ 592737
Police	☎ 581724
Laundrette	Marina

Shops/supermarkets
Adjacent to marina

Pubs/restaurants
Captains Table, 80c Harbour Parade; Alexandra, 80 Harbour Parade; Marians, 14 Harbour St. 591809; Harrys Crab & Oyster Bar, Harbour Parade 591110; The Lazy Fox, 12 Westcliff Arcade 583039

Tourist attractions:
Maritime Museum, Model Village, Motor Museum

Mooring fees:

Inner Basin	per day	per week
Up to 12 metres	£10	£43
12 to 18 metres	£11	£53

Available:

Water✓	Electric✓	Showers	Laundrette✓	
Petrol 592662	Diesel 592662	Chandler 597158/591733		
Repairs:	Yacht 593140	Engine 593140	Electrical 593140	Sail

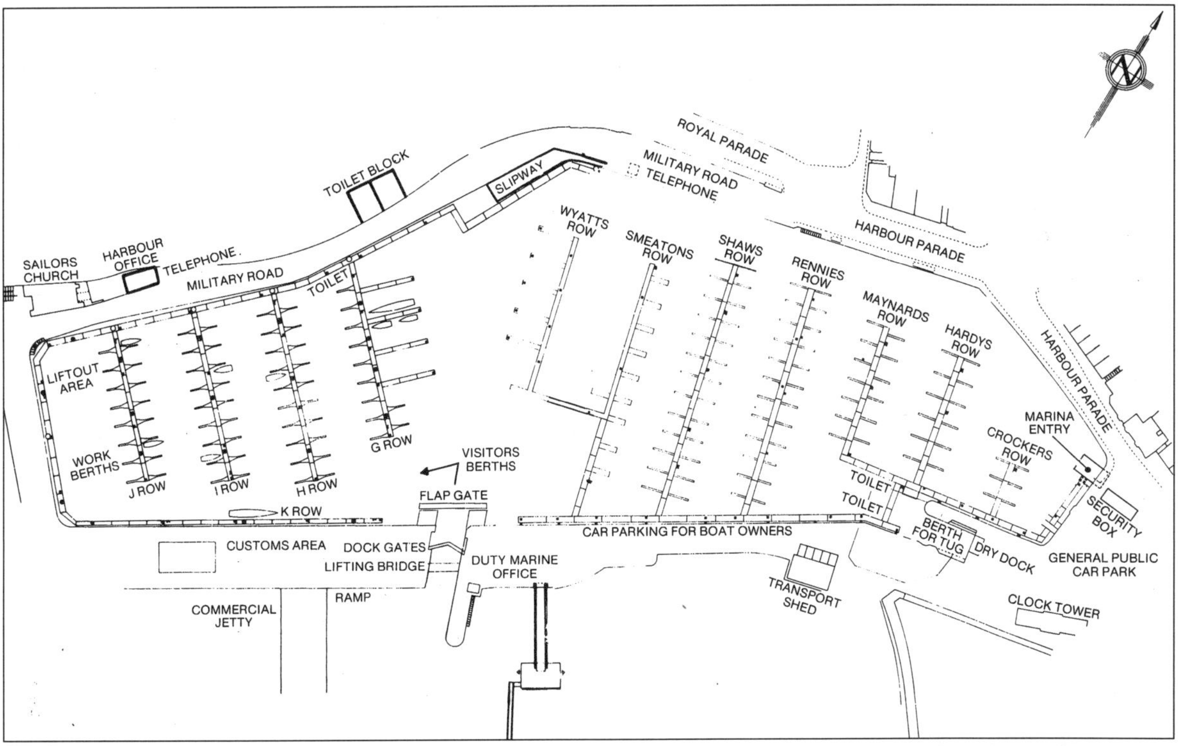

Royal Harbour of Ramsgate

LESSER HARBOURS

RYE

Between Newhaven and Folkestone

50° 56' N, 0° 46' E
Admiralty chart 1991
Harbour Master: 0797 225225

Harbour dries. Tie up at catwalk and piles near Harbour Master's office or if directed, go upriver to yacht moorings alongside Strand Quay. Entrance difficult in strong winds from SE to SW. Best time to enter 2h-HW-3h but stream runs hard on a Spring ebb.
The town of Rye is several miles from the harbour but is a charming town, well worth a visit, with quiet streets of 15th-16th century houses. Rye is the senior Cinque Port. Maybe there will be a marina here one day.

CABOURG, DIVES

Between Deauville and Ouistreham

49° 19' N, 0° 07" E
Admiralty chart 1892, 2146
Bureau du port: Cabourg Yacht Club
Telephone 31.91.23.55

Harbour dries.
Access to port 2½h-HW-2½h
A town with a certain old fashioned charm, a promenade, casino, gardens. Mooring area dries, quays occupied by fishing boats, an "adventurous" anchorage.
River dries to soft mud.

LE TOUQUET/ETAPLES

Between Boulogne and St. Valery-sur-Somme

Admiralty chart 2451
SHOM 6795
Capitainerie 21.05.12.77
Entrance not easy to find. Yacht moorings dry.

Le Touquet is well known as a fashionable resort at the mouth of the Canche River, which runs across the Artois plateau. Etaples is a fishing port favoured by artists. With brightly painted houses it is a market town of great charm. A new marina is planned.

LE CROTOY

Between le Touquet and Saint Valery-sur-Somme

50° 13' N, 1° 38' E
Admiralty chart 2612
Capitainerie: Cite Mercier
Telephone: 33.22.2781.44
Bassin a Flot 1½-HW-2h

A small village with a yacht harbour offering most facilities. There is a splendid beach, also a casino. Shoal draft boats may remain afloat in Bassin but beware of being neaped.

GRAVELINES

Between Dunkerque and Calais

50° 59' N, 2° 08' E
Admiralty chart 323
Capitainerie: 20 Bassin Vauban
Telephone: 33.28.23.13.42
H.M. VHF 28
Yacht Club Gravelines
Bar dries, harbour dries
Bassin a Flot 1½-HW-1½.

An inshore fishing port which provides entry to the French canal system through the River Aa, (see my "Through The French Canals"). The fortifications here are well preserved. There is also a massive nuclear power station. Dries in the offing, entrance possible 3h-HW, and is difficult in fresh onshore winds.

DUNKERQUE ☆☆☆

Standard Port
DIEPPE

Harbour Entry
At any time subject to port entry signals

Cap 28 66 79 90

Lat: 51° 03' N **Long:** 02° 22' E

Admiralty charts 323/1350
SHOM 6500, 6501, 6651

Approach visual navigation aids:
Ldg Lts Front Dir FVi 3m W metal col R top.
185° Rear Dir FVi 4m Grey pylon

R/T: Ch 12 16 73; Trystram Lock Ch 73; Yacht Club Ch 09

Yachting facilities: See next page

Visitors moorings available: Port de Plaisance 40 moorings for visitors. Municipal Marina in the Bassin du Commerce (through Trystram Lock) 35 places

Distances: Dover 42, Needles 163, Nab Tower 135

DESCRIPTION: A commercial harbour, but the yacht basin is right in the middle of the town, with shops, churches, museums, sport, numerous restaurants and a casino all within easy distance. It is, nevertheless a large industrial centre which you will no doubt observe as you approach and the vast commercial port installations will convince you. Nearby, at Gravelines is a massive nuclear power station. Dunkerque also provides entry to the French canal system through the Canal de Bergues. It is the country's third largest port with oil refineries and steel works on an impressive scale. Sometimes the cloud of chemical smog is somewhat disturbing and there is not much temptation to linger. The Port de Plaisance is on the west side of the Port d'Echouage. A warm welcome will be found in the Municipal Marina with its DIY Club.

Dunkerque Harbour: Port de Plaisance centre, Municipal Marina lower right

☆☆☆ DUNKERQUE

Telephone Code 28

Customs Rue de l'Yser 28 66 87 14

Weather Meteo 28 66 46 26

Tourist Office Le Beffroi 28.66.79.21

Taxi 28.66.73.00

Hospital ☎ 28.29.59.00

Chemist Quai des Hollandais

Post Office Rue du President Poincare

Bank Place Jean-Bart

Yacht Clubs
de la Mer du Nord, quai des Monitors,
de Dunkerque, quai des Risbans

Police ☎ 28.64.51.09

Shops/supermarkets Nearby

Pubs/restaurants
Pelle á Tarte, 20 Digue de Mer; La Meunerie, 174 Rue des Pierres; La Sourbise,49 Route de Bergues; Le Richelieu; Hirondelle, 46 Avenue Faidherbe; Grand Morien, 35 Place Jean-Bart; Aux Halles, 35 Rue a l'Amiral-Ronarc'h; Auberge du Flamand, 11 Place Ch-Valentin.

Tourist attractions:
In the Musée des Beaux-Arts, by the Post Office there is a display depicting the withdrawal of Allied soldiers from the beaches of Dunkerque in May 1940 (and Flemish, and French paintings, too)

Available:
Water✓ Electric✓ Showers
Laundrette Petrol✓ Diesel✓ Chandler 28.65.02.11

Repairs:
Yacht 28.66.49.62 Engine 28.66.82.37 Electrical Sail✓

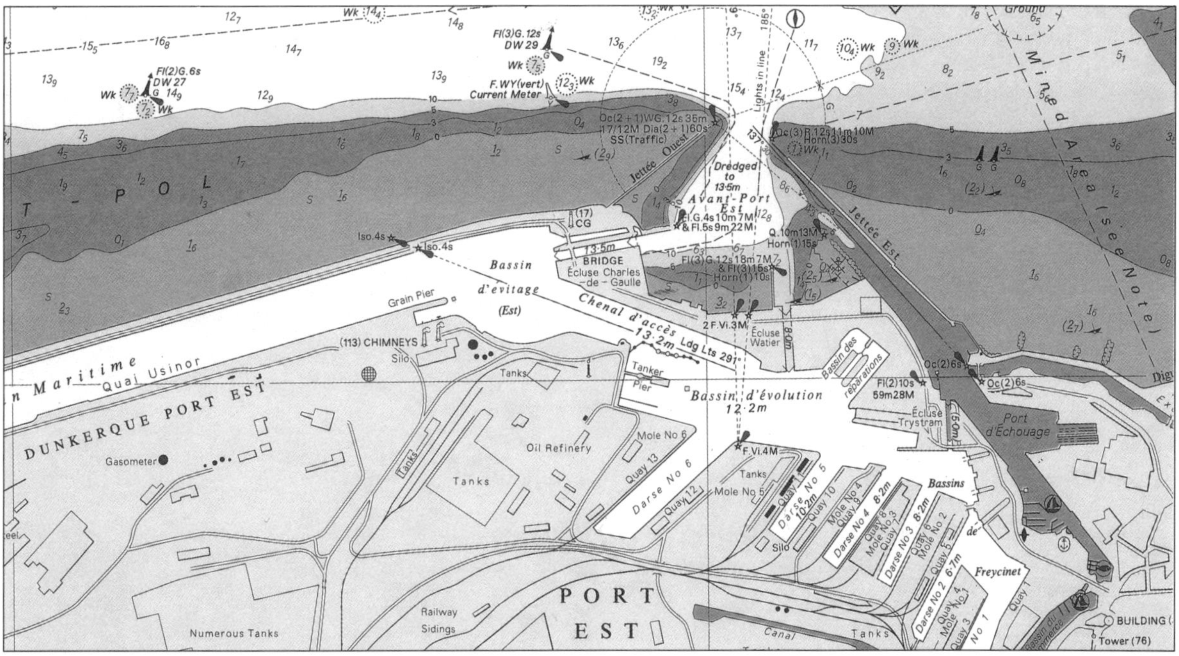

Crown Copyright. Reproduced from Admiralty charts with the permission of the Controller of Her Majesty's Stationery Office

CALAIS ☆☆☆☆☆

Standard Port
DIEPPE

Harbour Entry
Lock in to Bassin Ouest– Weekdays $1^1/_2$-HW-$^1/_2$h Weekends 2h-HW-1h

Cap 21.96.31.20

Lat: 50° 58' N **Long:** 01° 51' E

Admiralty charts 1352/1892
SHOM 6474/6651/6681

Approach visual navigation aids: Main light N side town Fl (4) W 15s 23m W 8-sided tower B top

R/T: Ch 12/16 (H24)

Yachting facilities: See below

Visitors moorings available: Port de Plaisance (access to canals). Harbour Office 21.96.31.20, Quai de Marée

Distances: Needles 140, Nab Tower 112, Dover 23, Fecamp 95, Le Havre 120, Boulogne 20

DESCRIPTION: Busiest of the cross channel passenger ports Calais is dominated by its port, thus for the visiting yachtsmen all is around, and how pleasant to hasten for that first bottle of duty free, how much better than anything bought in England it tastes (more so since it will end from 1992). Calais is a very pleasant harbour in which to buy your first, and subsquent, bottle of wine and may it continue to be so for the visiting yachtsmen, unaffected by what is happening just down the road, *underneath* our passage from England. Calais also provides entry to the French canal system through the Canal du Calais. Entrance to this busy ferry port is difficult in fresh NW-NE winds. The Avant Port develops an uncomfortable surge.

Available:
Water✓ Electric✓ Showers
Laundrette✓ Petrol✓ Diesel✓
Chandler✓

Repairs: Yacht✓
Engine 21.96.29.97
Electrical✓
Sail✓

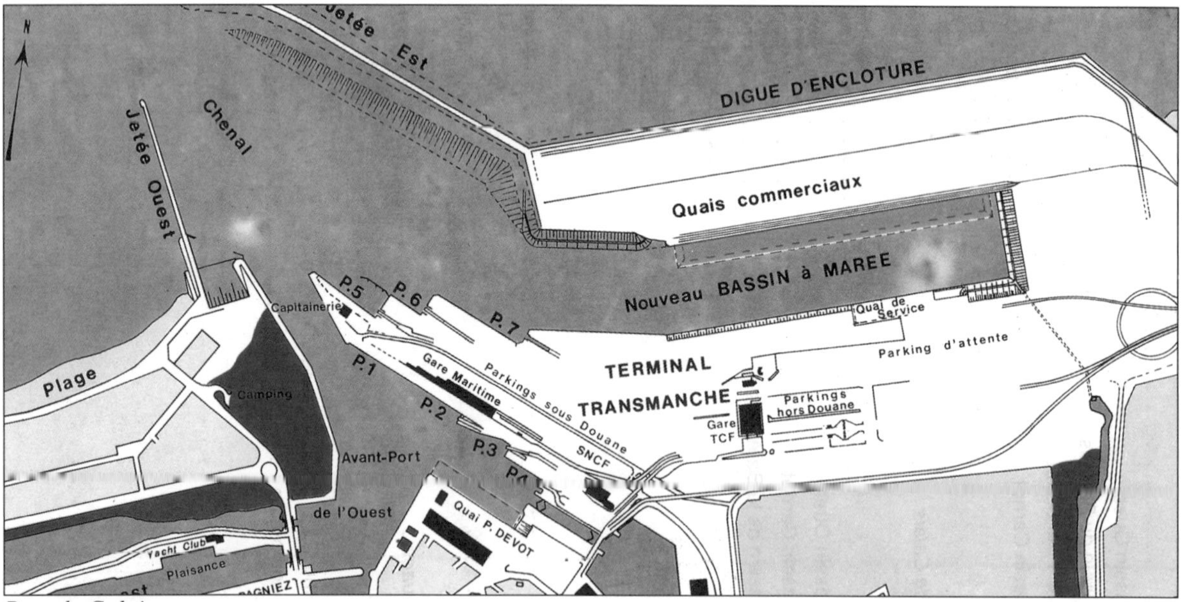

Port de Calais

☆☆☆☆☆ CALAIS

Telephone Code 21

Customs 2 rue Lamy 21.34.75.40

Weather ☎ 21.31.52.23

Taxi 21.97.05.22/21.97.13.14

Hospital ☎ 21.97.99.60

Chemist Rue Jean Quehen

Bank Barclays, rue Lafayette

Yacht Clubs
Calais. Societé des Régates de Calais

Police ☎ 21.96.74.17

Laundrette Marina

Shops/supermarkets
Continent, Mammouth, Printemps, Prisunic

Pubs/restaurants
L'Atre, Bd. des Alliés; Le Channel, 3 Bd. de la Résistance; Sole Meuniere, (menus from 65-200F) Bd. de la Résistance; Le Touquet, Cafe de Paris, George V, 36 rue Royale

Tourist attractions:
Musée des Beaux-Arts et de la Dentelle, Musée de la Guerre, Rodin's Burghers of Calais. There are Wednesday and Saturday markets off the Place d'Armes and Thursday and Saturday markets at Place Crévecoeur

Le Port de Plaisance de Calais

BOULOGNE ☆☆☆☆

Standard Port
DIEPPE

Harbour Entry
Access at all times subject to harbour traffic signals

Cap 21.30.10.00

Lat: 52° 44' N **Long:** 01° 37' E

Admiralty charts 438/1892
SHOM 6436, 6682, 6795

Approach visual navigation aids:
Ldg Lts Gare Maritime Eperon NW Front 3 FG 5m W Col R bands G lantern. 123° Quai Gambetta Rear Dir FR 11m grey building

R/T: VHF 12/16

Yachting facilities: See below

Visitors moorings available: In Port de Plaisance (21.80.72.00)

Distances: Calais 21, Dunkerque 42, Dieppe 56, Needles 126, Nab Tower 100, Dover 25

DESCRIPTION: The commercial and port areas are in the Low Town. The High Town includes the Castle Museum, Convent of the Annonciades, Imperial Palace and the historical past. The High Town, or Haute Ville, rises above the port as you might imagine. Boulogne claims to be the largest fishing harbour in Europe. You do your shopping in the Low Town and when you have done that and want to meet up with a few ghosts from the past you climb up to the Haute Ville, with its cobbled streets and ramparts, around which you should walk.
Julius Ceasar crossed from Boulogne to conquer Britain in 53 BC. Historical Boulogne can be visited by regular organised tours from 15th June to 15th September, every Saturday at 3 pm starting from the Castle Museum. There are other guided tours and the Syndicat d'Initiative, on the Quai de la Poste will be pleased to give you details. The Port de Plaisance is alongside Quai Chanzy. Limited facilities, unpleasant smells at low water. Superb fish stalls on Quai Gambetta. Busy ferry, fishing and commercial quay; signals must be obeyed. There is a reasonably clean beach inside Digue Nord. Trains to Paris and Europe.

Mooring fees:

May-Sept	Oct-April	
Up to 5m	51.51	30.79
5m to 7.99m	55.701	33.30
8m to 10.99m	89.69	47.29

Available:

Water✓	Electric	Showers	Laundrette
Petrol✓	Diesel✓	Chandler ✓	

Repairs:

Yacht✓	Engine✓	Electrical✓	Sail

Crown Copyright. Reproduced from Admiralty charts with the permission of the Controller of Her Majesty's Stationery Office

Customs Bd. Daunou 21.30.14.24

Weather 21.33.82.55

Tourist Office
Quai de la Poste ☎ 21.31.68.38

Taxi 21.91.25.00

Hire Cars
Hertz ☎ 21.31.53.14
Europcar ☎ 21.30.59.45

Doctor ☎ 21.80.15.15

Hospital ☎ 21.99.33.33

Chemist Rue Victor Hugo

Post Office pl Frederic Sauvage

Bank Rue Victor Hugo

Yacht Clubs
Le Yacht Club Boulonais

Police ☎ 21.30.12.34

Laundrette rue Nationale

Shops/supermarkets
Good food shops in the Low Town or Ville Basse. Shopping is centred near the harbour. Champion Supermarket on the pier. The best shopping streets are Grande-Rue, Nationale, Faidherbe and Thiers

Pubs/restaurants
de la Haute Ville, 60 Rue de Lille; Bouquet, 4 Rue Charles Cazin; L'Aquarium, 1 Rue Coquelin; La Paix, 12 Rue Faidherbe; Chez Jules, Place Dalton; La Matelote, 80 Bd. Ste Beuve; La Liegeoise, 10 rue Mousigny; L'Huitriere, 11 Place de Lorraine

Tourist attractions:
Casino, rue Felix Adam, The Châteaux at Pont-de-Briques, The Stele of the Legion d' Honneur, Napoleon's Column, Notre-Dame. Street markets at weekends and mid-week.

Small local boats in Bassin Fréderic Sauvage

ST. VALERY-SUR-SOMME ***

Standard Port
DIEPPE

Harbour Entry
Lock in 2h-HW-2h

Cap 22.26.91.64

Lat: 50° 11' N **Long:** 01° 39' E

Admiralty charts 2612
SHOM 3800

Approach visual navigation aids: Channels in to the Somme are difficult, W Head of embankment 1S0 G 4s 9m W pylon G top

R/T: Ch 9 (2h-HW-2h)

Yachting facilities: See next page

Visitors moorings available: Pontoon berths for visitors

Distances: Boulogne 35, Dieppe 22

DESCRIPTION: A small town at the mouth of the river, giving access to the French canal system via the Canal de la Somme, a pleasant harbour amidst a pleasant town. From here William of Normandy left to conquer England. The date will be familiar to you.
The difficulties of the Baie de Somme are caused through frequent changes of the banks, in fact pilotage is compulsory for vessels over 75 grt. If you cannot reach the ports of Baie de Somme (Le Hourdel, Le Crotoy or Saint-Valery-sur-Somme) before high water you should proceed to seaward of the sandbanks, or make for Dieppe. At Le Hourdel you can moor alongside on dry or hard sand. (For Le Crotoy see Lesser Harbours).
The channel to the inner part of Baie de Somme is marked by port and starboard hand buoys (which are moved as the banks change); the approach channel to St. Valery, which dries, is also so marked. The harbour dries but on the east side is the yacht marina with depths of 2m.
As you stroll along the shady promenade to the pleasant and peaceful town you get a good view of the bay. The entrance is dangerous in fresh onshore winds.

Port de Plaisance

☆☆☆ ST. VALERY-SUR-SOMME

Telephone Code	22
Weather	Meteo 21.31.52.23
Tourist Office	☎ 22.60.93.50
Taxi	☎ 22.26.93.59
Doctor	☎ 22.26.92.25
Dentist	☎ 22.26.90.07
Hospital	☎ 22.60.82.17
Chemist	☎ 22.60.82.27
Post Office	Place Guillaume le Conquerant
Bank	Quai Perrée
Yacht Clubs	Sport Nautique Valéricain
Police	☎ 22.60.82.08

Pubs/restaurants
Le Relais des Quatre-Saisons, 2 Place de la Croix-l'Abbe (5 menus 50-240F); Restaurant du Port de Plaisance; Hotel des Pilotes, Quai Perée

Tourist attractions:
A town with an amazing past, renamed Saint Valery in the tenth century. Many historic sites remain.

Through the lock at the end of the harbour you can proceed up the Canal de la Somme to Abbeville (minimum depth 3m4). The two locks and four bridges will open for you if you sound your hooter or siren. Once in the French canal system you can, of course, proceed much further than Abbeville, to Paris or the Mediterranean, subject to your height above the waterline and draught, but you see coasters navigating up to Abbeville.

Available:

Water	Electric	Showers
Laundrette✓	Petrol✓	Diesel✓
Chandler ✓		

Repairs:

Yacht✓	Engine✓
Electrical✓	Sail

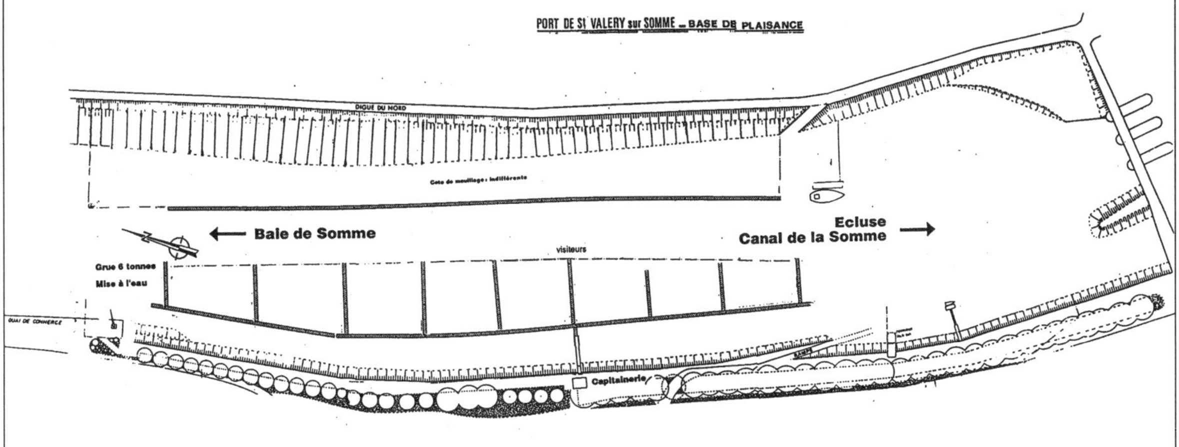

LE TREPORT ☆☆☆

Standard Port
DIEPPE

Harbour Entry
Lock in to Bassin á Flot 1½h-HW (outer harbour dries)

Cap 35.86.17.91

Lat: 50° 04' N **Long:** 01° 22' E

Admiralty charts 1351/2147
SHOM 934, 5928

Approach visual navigation aids: Jetée Ouest head Fl (2) G 10s 20m W tower G top Jetée Est Oc R 4s 6m W col R top

R/T: Call "Ovaro" Ch 16; 12 (2h-HW)

Yachting facilities: See below

Visitors moorings available: On entry report Capitainerie to (P) on Quai Bellot. Sometimes limited

Distances: Dieppe 14, Boulogne 41, Calais 53

DESCRIPTION: You imagine you are approaching Dover with the backdrop of white cliffs; at one time quite a number of fishing boats used to sail in here until the river started to silt up. It certainly dries a long way offshore but once inside the Bassin á Flot the facilities are good, there are many restaurants and a pleasant promenade.
Popular because it is probably the nearest seaside resort to Paris.
The entrance channel dries, as does the Avant Port and the Arriere Port. You can secure alongside the quays in the Avant Port at high water but not in the Arriere Port which you enter over a sill 1m5 above chart datum. A difficult entrance in fresh onshore winds, entry should not be attempted except at one hour either side of local HW.

Available:

Water✓	Electric	Showers
Laundrette	Petrol✓	Diesel✓
Chandler✓		
Repairs:	Yacht✓	Engine✓
	Electrical	Sail

Quai Bellot to port on entry

☆☆☆ LE TREPORT

Customs
quai Edouard-Gelée 35.86.15.34

Weather Meteo 21.05.13.55

Tourist Office ☎ 35.86.05.69

Hire Cars ☎ 35.86.13.34

Doctor ☎ 35.86.03.79/35.86.16.23

Dentist ☎ 35.86.02.46/35.86.25.12

Hospital ☎ 35.86.04.33

Chemist ☎ 35.86.25.99

Post Office rue Abbe-Vincheneux

Bank Quai Francois

Yacht Clubs
de Bresle 35.86.60.52

Police ☎ 35.86.14.66

Shops/supermarkets
Mammouth

Pubs/restaurants
Le St. Louis, 43 Quai Francois 1er (4 menus 95-200F); La Marée, 34 Quai Francoise Ler; Le Maritime, 3 Avenue des Canadiens; Le Grill de la Plage, 10 Esplanade de la Plage; Restaurant du Casino et de la Plage, Esplanade de la Plage

Tourist attractions:
Casino, Cable car

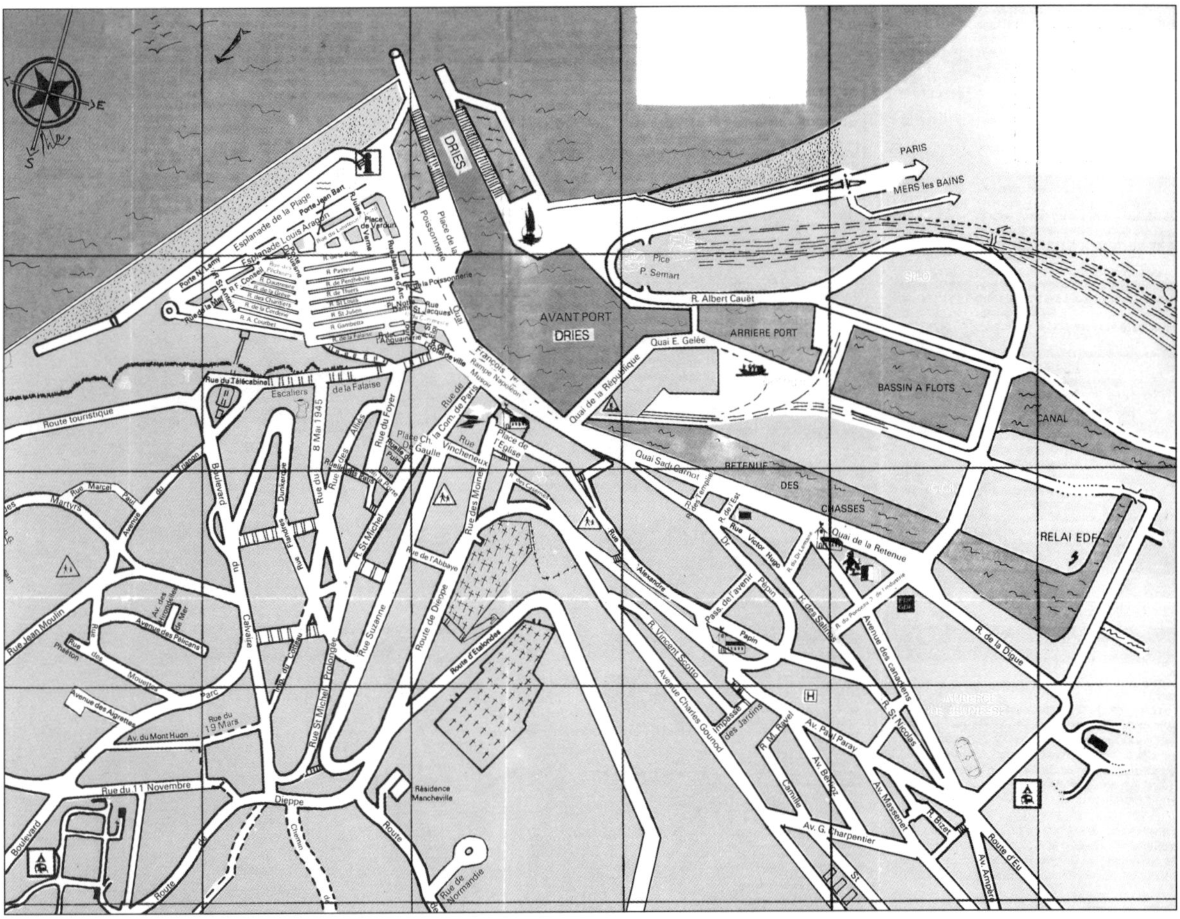

DIEPPE ☆☆☆☆☆

Standard Port
DIEPPE

Harbour Entry
At any time subject to harbour signals. Lock in to Bassin Duquesne 2h-HW-1h

Cap 35.84.10.55

Lat: 49° 56' N **Long:** 01° 05' E

Admiralty charts 2147
SHOM 934/5927

Approach visual navigation aids:
Ldg Lts Old Jetée Est Front Q R 9m W pylon R top
138° Chapelle de Bon-Secours Rear Q R 9m R & W structure

R/T: Dieppe Port VHF 12 16

Yachting facilities: See below

Visitors moorings available: In Port de Plaisance 35.84.32.99

Distances: Le Treport 14, St. Valery-en-Caux 15, Newhaven 65, Boulogne 56, Fecamp 31, Needles 115, Nab Tower 92

DESCRIPTION: Although it is busy commercially the commerce does not seem to intrude into the charm of Dieppe; set between the headlands you easily identify it with anticipation. It is tempting to buy fish from the markets if there is sufficient expertise available in the galley but when you experience a meal at one of the restaurants your DIY economy falters. There are a large number of bars and restaurants lining the quay of this attractive harbour.
FERRY PORT: It can be a rough entrance in NW-NE winds when a heavy surge develops, making the Port de Plaisance uncomfortable.

Mooring fees:

Day	7m	8m	1.0m	12m
	55	60	75	95

Available:
Water✓ Electric Showers
Laundrette Petrol✓ Diesel✓
Chandler

Repairs: Yacht✓ Engine✓
Electrical✓ Sail

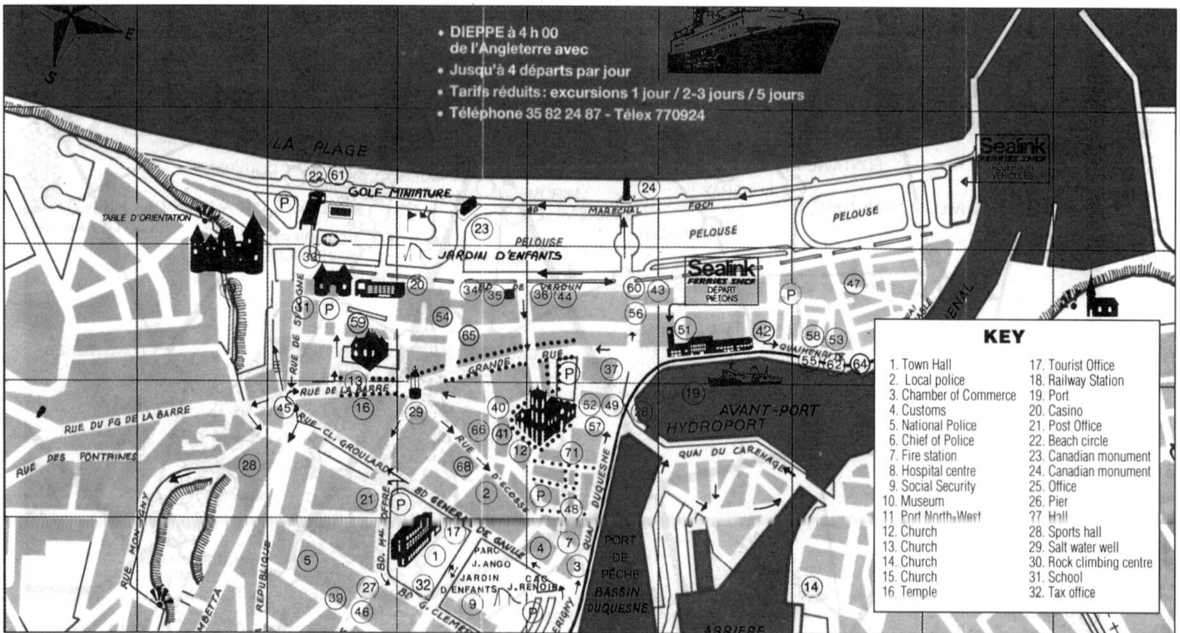

Lock in to Bassin Duquesue

☆☆☆☆☆ DIEPPE

Customs	☎ 35.82.05.62
Weather	☎ 35.80.11.44
Tourist Office	☎ 35.84.11.77
Taxi	☎ 35.84.20.05
Hire Cars	☎ 35.04.97.10
Doctor	☎ 35.84.14.91
Hospital	☎ 35.82.20.75
Chemist	Quai Henri-IV

Post Office	Bd. Marechal Joffre
Bank	Quai Henri-IV-Grande Rue
Yacht Clubs	Cercle de la Voila de Dieppe Dieppe Nautique
Police	☎ 35.82.04.35

Shops/supermarkets
Mammouth, Intermarche. All shops nearby. The pedestrianised Grande Rue leads from the port

Pubs/restaurants
La Marmite Dieppoise, 8 Rue St. Jean (2 menus 110 and 180F); Le Sully, 97 Quai Henri IV; Le Peshett, 79 Quai Henri IV; L'Armorique, 17 Quai Henri IV; Normandy, 16 Rue Duquesne; Le St. Jacques, 12 Rue d l'Oranges, La Mélie, 2 Grande-Rue du Pollet. You must try La Sole Dieppoise

Tourist attractions:
Saturday market, Musée de Dieppe (in medieval castle), Casino, Le Centre Jean Renoix, War Musuem

The Harbour, Dieppe

ST. VALERY-EN-CAUX ☆☆☆☆☆

Standard Port
DIEPPE

Harbour Entry
Lock in outer harbour access 3h-HW-3h; marina lock 2h-HW-2h. Port signals. Harbour dries and bar dries

Cap 35.97.01.30

Lat: 49° 52' N **Long:** 0° 43' E

Admiralty charts 2612
SHOM 6794

Approach visual navigation aids:
Jetée Ouest Oc (2 + 1) G 12s 14m G tower
Jetée Est Head Fl (2) R 6s 4m W mast R top

R/T: VHF Ch 9

Yachting facilities: See below

Visitors moorings available: Officially there are about 20 visitors berths in this 550-berth marina but, once you lock in, a berth seems to be found easily

Distances: Dieppe 15

DESCRIPTION: Situated in a valley between two white cliffs and not easily identified, St. Valery-en-Caux seems to be diverting its energies to tourism rather than its former role of a fishing harbour. It was destroyed in WW2 but you see timber houses and remnant of an old convent. On the east cliff is a memorial to the 51st Highland Division, and on the west cliff a monument to the French Cavalry Division who fought with sabres against Rommel's tanks. The harbour is situated very conveniently in the town. Although St. Valery is principally a yachting harbour it is used by coasters. The harbour bar dries, as does the Avant Port, and visiting yachts lock in to the Bassin á Flot where there are finger berths. Seas in the entrance can be rough in E-N winds. Traffic signals control entry/exit. Green light, enter only – Red light, leave only. Red and green, no movement.

Available:

Water	Electric✓	Showers
Laundrette	Petrol✓	Diesel✓
Chandler✓		
Repairs:	Yacht✓	Engine✓
	Electrical✓	Sail✓

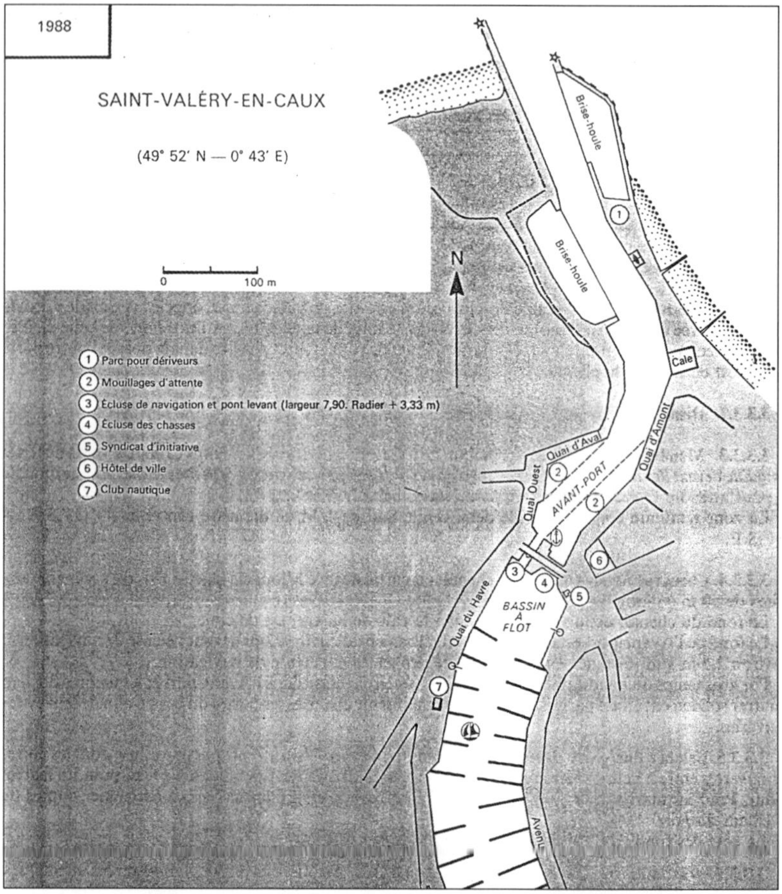

"Extrait des I.N. C. 21 (ou C. 22) du SHOM, reproduit avec son aimable autorisation"

☆☆☆☆☆ ST. VALERY-EN-CAUX

Customs	☎ 35.28.19.40
Weather	Meteo 35.80.11.44
Tourist Office	☎ 335.97.00.63
Taxi	☎ 35.97.01.32/35.97.19.07
Hire Cars	☎ 35.97.10.54
Doctor	☎ 35.97.05.99
Dentist	☎ 35.97.00.01
Hospital	☎ 35.97.00.11
Post Office	Rue de la Poste
Bank	Place de la Chapelle
Yacht Clubs	Club Nautique Valeriquais
Police	☎ 35.97.05.27

Shops/supermarkets
Holiday resort facilities, shops nearby

Pubs/restaurants
La Barcarole, 22 Quai du Havre (3 menus 58-96F); Le Restaurant du Port, 18 Quai d'Aumont (2 menus 110-195F); Le Port, 18 Quai d'Amont; Hotel des Terrasses

Tourist attractions:
Ancient houses on Quai du Havre, Casino. It is difficult to believe that St. Valery-en-Caux is virtually a rebuilt town, having been destroyed fifty years ago.

FECAMP ☆☆☆

Standard Port
DIEPPE

Harbour Entry
At any time if drawing less than 1m 20 subject to traffic signals

Cap 35.28.13.58

Lat: 49° 46' N **Long:** 00° 22' E

Admiralty charts 1352/2612
SHOM 932/6765

Approach visual navigation aids: Jetée Nord Fl (2) W 10s 16 grey tower R top in line with Jetée Sud Light bearing 085°

R/T: VHF 12 16 (2½h-HW-½h); Yacht harbour 09 (0800-2000)

Yachting facilities: See below

Visitors moorings available: In Avant Port, or lock in to Bassin Bérigny 30 berths in this 500 berth port. Lock opens 2h-HW

Distances: Dieppe 31, Calais 95, Brighton 65, Le Havre 25

DESCRIPTION: A fishing port with a claim to fame not connected with fish. In the narrow streets running parallel to the port you will find the Benedictine Distillery on rue Alexandre-le-Grand. Open for visitors between 9.30 and 11.30 am and in the afternoon from 2 pm till 5.30, tours last almost an hour. The smells, or perfumes should one say, are out of this world.
There is a pleasant promenade and Fecamp attracts quite a number of tourists. Entry to the harbour can be difficult in moderate winds from the W-NW direction. Best time about one hour either side of local HW.
The yacht harbour is immediately to starboard on entering, in the Avant Port, although sometimes there is a swell here and it is more comfortable to lock in to Bassin Berigny. There is a boatyard in the Bassin Freycinet.

Marina Avant Port
Available: Water✓ Electric
Showers Laundrette Petrol
Diesel✓ Chandler

Repairs: Yacht ✓ Engine✓
Electrical Sail

Avant Port
Available: Water✓ Electric
Showers✓ Laundrette Petrol
Diesel✓ Chandler

Repairs: Yacht Engine
Electrical Sail

Bessin Berigny
Available: Water✓ Electric
Showers Laundrette Petrol
Diesel✓ Chandler✓

Repairs: Yacht 35.28.28.15
Engine 35.28.28.15
Electrical 35.28.28.15
Sail

The harbour at Fecamp (courtesy of Christian Sappa C.E.D.R.I.)

☆☆☆ FECAMP

Telephone Code 35

Customs ☎ 35.28.19.40

Weather Port de Plaisance 21.16.11

Tourist Office Place Bellet 28.20.51

Taxi 35.28.17.50

Hire Cars ☎ 35.28.16.04

Doctor ☎ 35.28.15.11

Dentist ☎ 35.28.00.39

Hospital ☎ 35.28.05.13

Chemist Place Nicolas

Post Office Place Bellet

Bank Place Général Charles de Gaule

Yacht Clubs Société des Régates de Fécamp

Police ☎ 35.28.16.69

Launderette Rue des Forts

Shops/supermarkets
Rue de President,
Coty near harbour

Pubs/restaurants
LeMaritime, 2 Place Nicholas Selles (4 menus 95-200F); Le Viking, 63 Albert Ler; Hotel de la Poste

Tourist attractions:
Benedictine Distillery, Eglise de la Trinité, Fete de la Mer first week in July

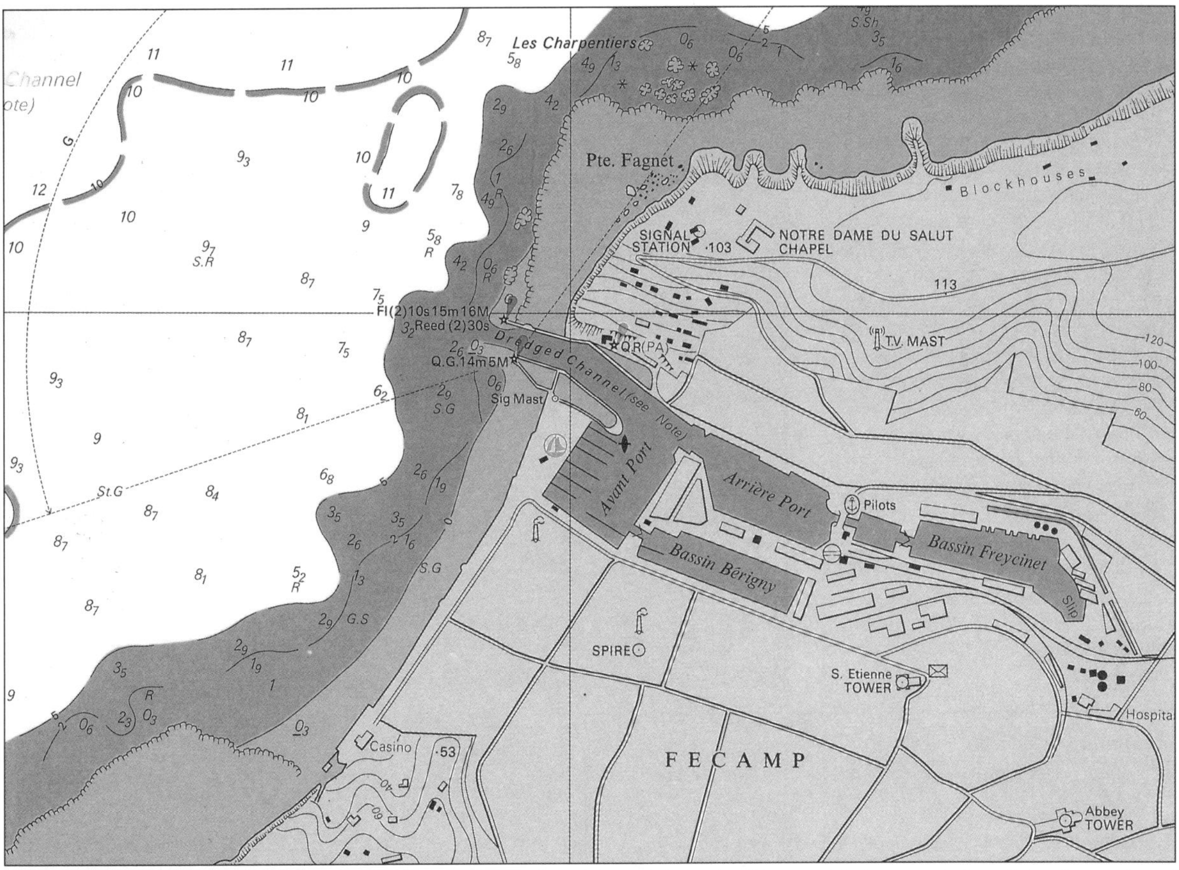

Crown Copyright. Reproduced from Admiralty Charts with the permission of the Controller of Her Majesty's Stationery Office

LE HAVRE ☆☆☆☆

Standard Port
LE HAVRE

Harbour Entry
At any time subject to port signals

HM 35.22.72.72

Lat: 49° 29' N **Long:** 0° 27' E

Admiralty charts 2990/266/2146
SHOM 6683, 6796

Approach visual navigation aids:
Ldg Lts Front F Vi on leading line only
106° Rear F Vi

R/T: Havre Port Ch 12 20; Marina Ch 09

Yachting facilities: See below

Visitors moorings available: Le Havre Plaisance 35.22.41.03. 1,000 plus berths immediately to Port on entering harbour

Distances: Needles 100, Nab Tower 85, Dover 120, Cherbourg 70, Fecamp 25

DESCRIPTION: The yacht harbour is rather a long walk from the town but the yacht clubs are on the quay. There are pleasant shops in the town and a selection of restaurants. Le Havre does not have the character that age brings because it has been rebuilt in the last fifty years, necessary following total destruction in World War Two. The main street, Avenue Foch runs almost to the yacht harbour and there are buses. Le Havre is also the most used port for entry to the French canal system. Most yachtsmen needing to unstep their mast before proceeding south do so here because it is most convenient but, you can proceed up the Seine to Rouen before doing so if you wish (non-tidal thence to Paris). For this purpose you come out of Le Havre harbour and cross to the entrance to the Seine at the beginning of the flood tide; thus you can reach Rouen on one tide. Or you can stay in Le Havre harbour, proceed through the commercial docks and up the Tancarville Canal, to lock out in to the Seine as the tide serves, just by the Tancarville Bridge. An important cross-channel port.

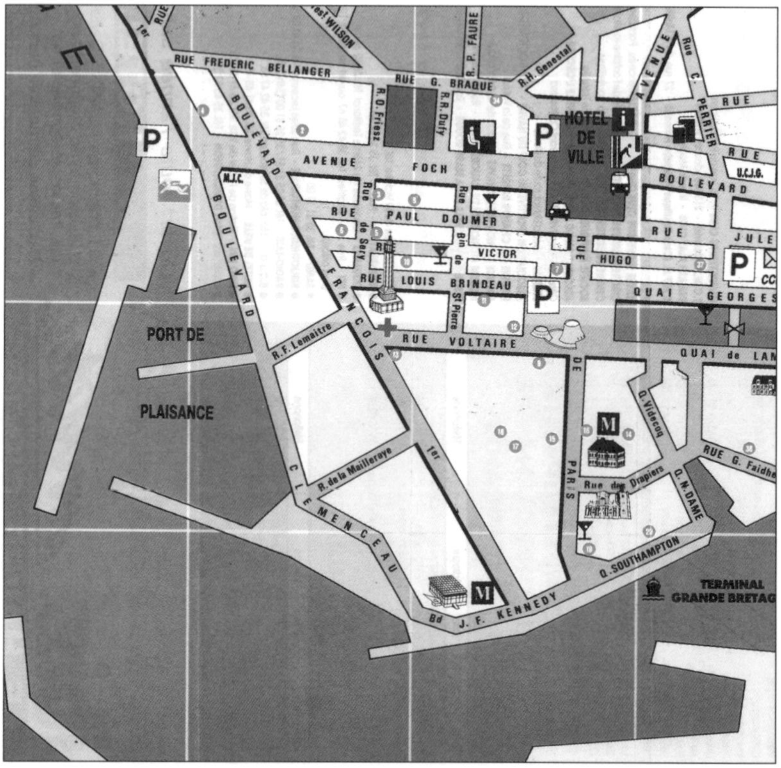

Available:			
Water✓	Electric✓	Showers	Laundrette✓
Petrol✓	Diesel✓	Chandler 35.21.08.06	
Repairs:	Yacht 35.21.08.06	Engine	
	Electrical 35.48.64.02	Sail	

Mooring fees:

	Day	Week
5m 51 to 8m 50	38F to 71F	235F to 382F
8m 51 to 11m 50	73F to 101F	406F to 568F
11m 51 to 16m 00	108F to 162F	623F to 855F

☆☆☆☆ # LE HAVRE

Telephone Code	35
Customs	☎ 35.42.38.79
Weather	Meteo 35.42.21.06
Tourist Office	☎ 35.21.22.88
Taxi	☎ 35.25.81.81
Hire Cars	☎ 35.24.44.44
Doctor	☎ 35.22.81.23
Dentist	☎ 35.42.57.57
Hospital	☎ 35.22.81.23
Chemist	Rue Louis Brindeau
Post Office	Rue Jules Siegfried
Bank	Boulevard de Strasbourg
Yacht Clubs	Societe des Regates du Havre 35.42.41.21; Sport Nautique du Havre
Police	☎ 35.21.77.00
Laundrette	rue Saint Michel

Shops/supermarkets
Quite a long walk away. Small shops nearby

Pubs/restaurants
Le Thalassa, 58 Rue des Sauveteurs (4 menus 95-345F); La Manche, 18 Bd Albert Ler; Guimbarde, 61 Rue Louis-Brindeau; Le Gascon, 83 Rue Dauphine; Nice-Havrais, 8 Pl Fredéric-Sauvage

Tourist attractions:
Beaux Arts Museum (with a splendid view of the harbour),

The mega-yacht harbour, Le Havre

HONFLEUR ☆☆

Standard Port
LE HAVRE

Harbour Entry
Lock in Vieux Bassin 1h-HW-1h and bridge

Cap 31.89.20.02

Lat: 49° 25' N **Long:** 00° 14' E

Admiralty charts 2146/270
SHOM 6683/6796

Approach visual navigation aids: From River Seine entrance by radar tower and channel well marked

R/T: Port VHF Ch 12 16 68 (Bassin) 73

Yachting facilities: See below

Visitors moorings available: Of the three harbours Bassin de l'Ouest or Le Vieux Bassin is reserved for yachts

Distances: Le Havre 11, Grandcamp Maisy 68, Portsmouth 105

DESCRIPTION: There are few more attractive places to tie up than the picturesque Vieux Bassin, situated in the old part of the town. Cobbled quays, 18th century buildings, in fact all the really attractive parts of Honfleur are concentrated round the basin. Of the old ports of Normandy, Honfleur is the best preserved. Fishing boats secure alongside the quay and sell fish, either direct from the boats or from stalls. Honfleur has been developed and extended with modern suburbs but the old slate-fronted tall houses provide the background for the harbour. Situated on the left bank of the Seine, Honfleur is approached through a channel between two high jetties. Preparing to turn out of the Seine one needs to be aware of passing traffic in the river. Entrance dries as does the Avant Port. Time entry 3h-HW-3h.

Available:

Water✓	Electric✓	Showers
Laundrette	Petrol	Diesel
Chandler		

Repairs:

Yacht	Engine✓
Electrical✓	Sail

Honfleur (courtesy of Erwan Quemer)

☆☆ HONFLEUR

Telephone Code	31
Customs	☎ 31.89.12.13
Weather	☎ 31.88.28.62
Tourist Office Place Arthur Boudin	31.89.23.30
Taxi	☎ 31.89.07.29
Hire Cars	☎ 31.89.08.01
Doctor	☎ 31.89.07.40
Hospital	☎ 31.89.07.74
Chemist	Place Hamelin
Post Office	Rue de la Republique
Bank	Quai Sainte Catherine
Yacht Clubs Club Nautique Honfleurais	31.98.87.13
Police	☎ 31.89.21.24
Laundrette	Rue Cachin
Shops/supermarkets	Nearby

Pubs/restaurants
L'Absinthe, 10 Quai de la Quarantaine; Le Crystal, 3 Rue Haute; Au Petit Marayeur, 4 Rue Haute; Le Cheval Blanc, 2 Quai des Passagers; Au Vieux Honfleur, 13 Quai St. Etienne (a la carte only)

Tourist attractions:
Musée Eugène Boudin, Ste Cathérines Wooden Church, Musée Maritime

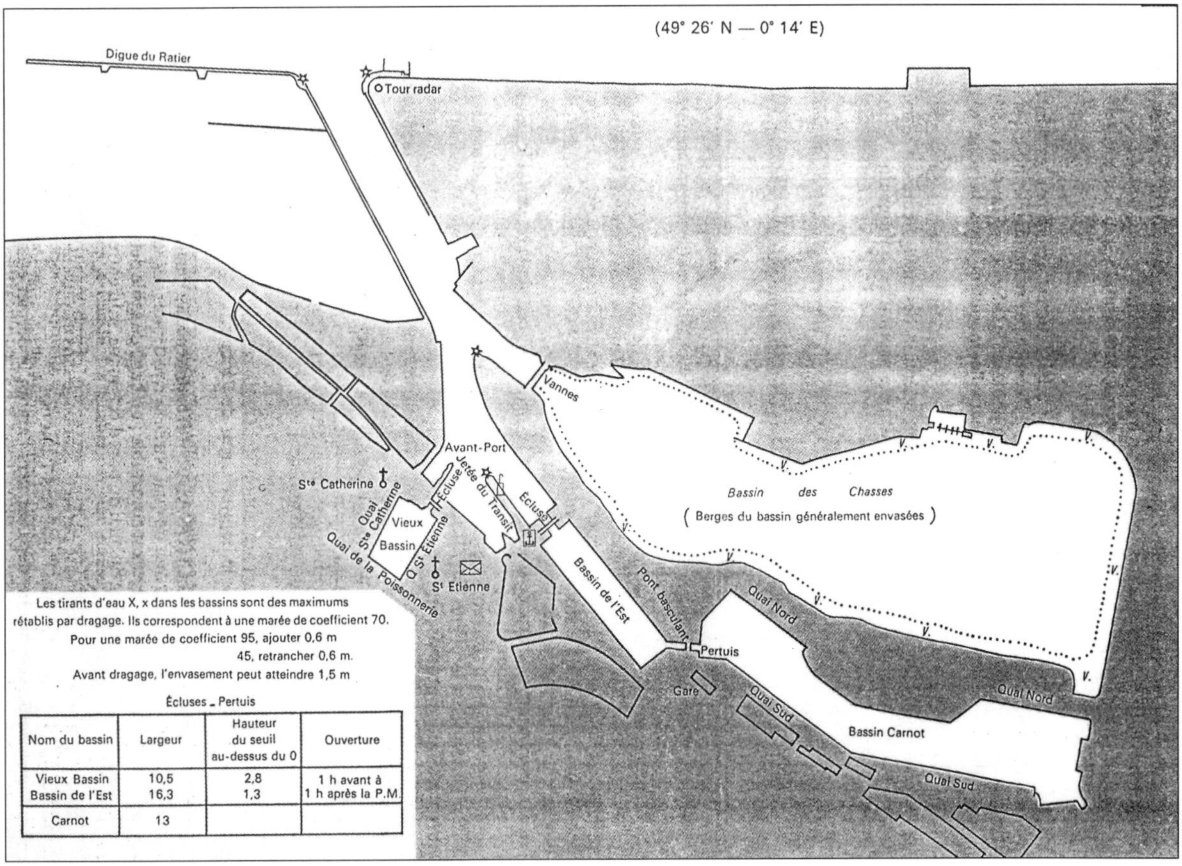

Les tirants d'eau X, x dans les bassins sont des maximums rétablis par dragage. Ils correspondent à une marée de coefficient 70.
Pour une marée de coefficient 95, ajouter 0,6 m
45, retrancher 0,6 m.
Avant dragage, l'envasement peut atteindre 1,5 m

Écluses – Pertuis

Nom du bassin	Largeur	Hauteur du seuil au-dessus du 0	Ouverture
Vieux Bassin Bassin de l'Est	10,5 16,3	2,8 1,3	1 h avant à 1 h après la P.M.
Carnot	13		

DEAUVILLE/TROUVILLE ☆☆☆☆

Standard Port
LE HAVRE

Harbour Entry
Yacht Harbour lock 2h-HW-2½h.
Harbour dries. Bassin de Plaisance.
Bassin des Yachts or Bassin Morny

Cap 31.88.28.71
Port Deauville 31.98.30.01

Lat: 49° 22' N **Long:** 0° 05' W

Admiralty charts 2146/1349/2613
SHOM 5530, 6928

Approach visual navigation aids:
Ldg Lts Front Pointe de la Cahotte Oc R 4s 12m W tower R top
150° Rear Oc R 4s 10m W pylon R Top

R/T: VHF Ch 09, 11

Yachting facilities: See below

Visitors moorings available: See note below.
Port Deauville Marina VHF Ch 09. Deauville Yacht Harbour Ch 11

Distances: Le Havre 8, Needles 100, Nab Tower 90

DESCRIPTION: It will be seen from the plan that Deauville Port is to the south on entry. Trouville Yacht Harbour and Bassin a Flot are less expensive than Deauville. Bassin a Flot (or Bassin Morny) is nearest the town but all amenities are near to the port.

Deauville is an expensive holiday town visited by many Parisiens. Trouville is a town with a life apart from tourism, a busy working port with an unspoilt character. Deauville was once a fashionable resort and still enjoys high class popularity in July and August. These neighbouring towns are situated on either side of the entrance to the Riviére la Touques. Entry can be difficult when the wind is onshore, fresh NW-N, and the sea then breaks in the channel. The best time for entering is at high slack water but you sometimes get eddies at the entrance to the Bassin des Yachts.

Deauville/Trouville Available:
Water✓ Electric✓ Showers
Laundrette Petrol✓ Diesel
Chandler

Repairs: Yacht✓ Engine✓
Electrical✓ Sail

Bassin des Yachts Available:
Water✓ Electric✓ Showers
Laundrette Petrol ✓ Diesel
Chandler

Repairs: Yacht Engine
Electrical Sail

Bassin Morny Available:
Water✓ Electric✓ Showers
Laundrette Petrol✓ Diesel✓
Chandler 31.88.65.55/31.98.50.92

Repairs: Yacht ✓ Engine✓
Electrical Sail

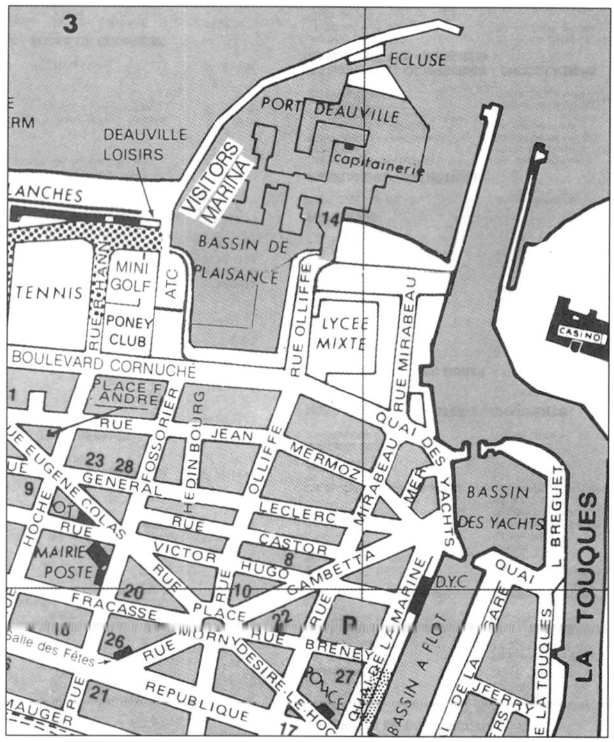

☆☆☆☆ DEALUVILLE/TROUVILLE

Telephone Code 31

Customs
2 Rue Eugéne-Decaens 31.88.25.29

Weather Meteo 31.88.84.22

Tourist Office
☎ 31.88.21.43 Deauville
☎ 31.88.36.19 Trouville

Taxi ☎ 31.87.15.15

Hire Cars ☎ Avis 31.88.16.73
Europcar 31.98.38.83

Doctor ☎ 31.88.24.64

Dentist ☎ 31.88.34.82/31.88.30.77

Hospital ☎ 31.88.12.07

Chemist ☎ Place de Morny

Post Office Rue Breney

Bank Place Morny

Yacht Clubs
Deauville Yacht Club
VHF Ch 9 31.88.38.19

Police ☎ 31.88.29.39/31.88.13.07

Shops/supermarkets
Printemps, Rue Eugéne-Colas. Good selection near Trouville Bassin des Yachts

Pubs/restaurants
L'Ambassade, D'Auvergne, 109 Bis Avenue de la Republique; Le Buccarius, 48 Rue Gambetta; L'Espérance, 32 Rue Victor Hugo; Le Nid D'Eté, 121 Avenue de la Republique; L'Océan (2 menus 95 and 135F), 1 Quai de la Marine. **Trouville:** Carmen, 24 Rue Carnot; Chez Maria, La Marine, 146 Bd. Fernand-Moureaux; Le Central, Bd. F Moureaux (2 menus 70 and 105F).

Tourist attractions:
Race Course, Casinos, Tuesday market, Friday market. **Trouville**: Aquarium, Sunday market, Wednesday market

Deauville Harbour

OUISTREHAM ***

Standard Port
LE HAVRE

Harbour Entry
Lock in Entry 1½h-HW-2¼h; Exit 2h-HW-1¾h observe signals

Cap 31.97.14.43

Lat: 49° 17' N **Long:** 0° 15' W

Admiralty charts 1821/2675/1349/2613
SHOM 6927, 7055

Approach visual navigation aids:
Ldg Lts Jetée Est head Front Dir Oc (3 + 1) R 12s 9m W pylon R top
185° Rear Dir Oc (3 + 1) R 12s 15m Tripod R top

R/T: Ouistreham Port Ch 12 16 18 (2h-HW-3h); Caen Port Ch 12 68; Marina Ch 09. Marina 31.97.13.05

Yachting facilities: See below

Visitors moorings available: Room for 60 in this 650 berth marina

Distances: Cherbourg 65, Nab Tower 87, Le Harve 19, Calais 136, Dieppe 68

DESCRIPTION: The yacht harbour is in a very pleasant situation but it is quite a walk to the town. Ouistreham is a cross-channel ferry port and the terminal is known as Caen. Actually it is 7½ miles on the Canal de Caen to the Bassin Saint-Pierre at Caen and there are three movable bridges en route. Maximum speed 7 knots. No overtaking. Bridges open for "convoy." Good marina in centre of Caen. There is a beautiful beach at Ouistreham. It is a commercial and fishing port and you can buy fish on the quay. Arriving from sea you should wait for the locks to open on pontoon temporary berths. Unless directed to the contrary use East lock, and make sure you secure in anticipation of movement in the lock. With a dredged approach and entrance this is becoming a popular yachting harbour.

Ouistreham
Available: Water✓ Electric✓ Showers Laundrette Petrol✓ Diesel✓ Chandler✓

Repairs:
Yacht 31.97.13.05
Engine 31.97.13.05
Electrical✓ Sail✓

Caen
Available:
Water✓ Electric Showers Laundrette Petrol✓ Diesel✓
Chandler 31.86.24.89

Repairs:
Yacht 31.86.24.89
Engine 31.86.24.89
Electrical✓ Sail

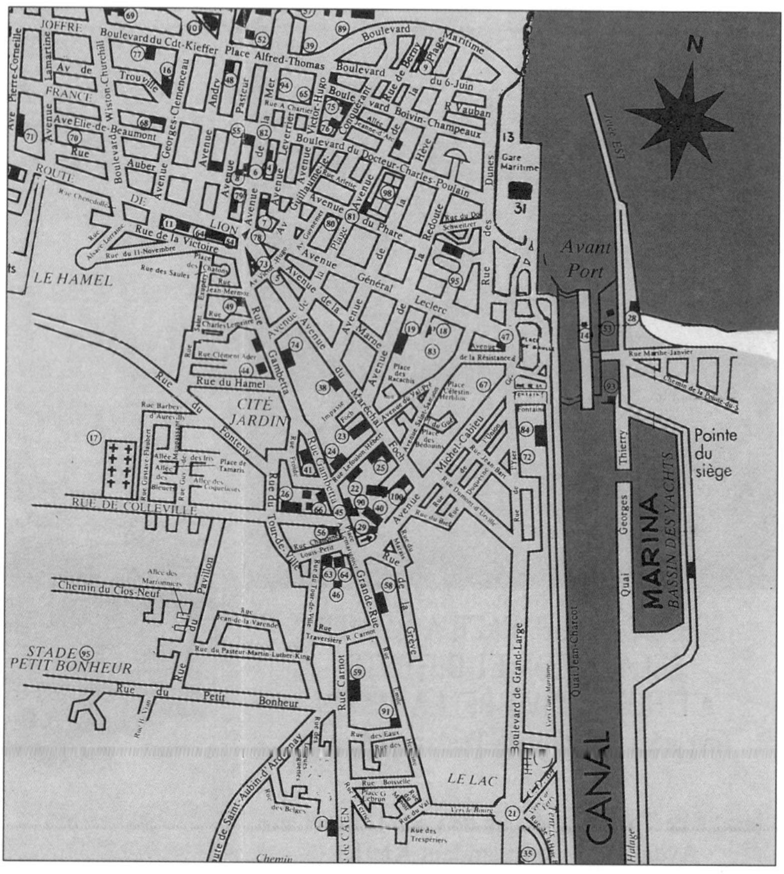

☆☆☆ OUISTREHAM

Telephone Code 31

Customs
Quai Vendome á Caen 31.86.61.50

Weather Meteo 31.74.48.11

Tourist Office
Jardin du Casino 31.97.18.63

Taxi ☎ 31.97.14.09/31.97.35.67

Hire Cars ☎ 31.97.14.09

Doctor ☎ 31.96.56.10/31.96.03.15

Dentist ☎ 31.97.39.27/31.97.13.41

Hospital Samu 31.44.88.88

Chemist 61 Ave de la Mer

Post Office Port de Plaisance

Bank Ave de la Mer

Yacht Clubs
Societé des Régates de Caen, Ouistreham 31.97.13.05

Police ☎ 31.97.13.15

Laundrette rue de la Mer Riva Bella

Shops/supermarkets
Wide selection, a little distance away. The centre of Caen now features one of the best shopping precincts, with Nouvelles Galeries, Printemps, Bon Marche, etc.

Pubs/restaurants
Le Clipper, 15 Av du Général-Leclerc (2 menus 48 and 75F); Au Coin du Port, 99 Avenue Michel Cabieu; Les Tisons, Avenue de la Mer; Broche d'Argent, Place du Général de Gaulle; La Racasse, 78 Avenue de la Mer. Caen: La Bourride, 15 Rue du Vauguex; Le Dauphin, 29 Rue Gémare; Le Pressoir, 3 Avenue Henry-Chéron

Tourist attractions:
Museum commemorating the Anglo-French Commando landing and the events of D-Day (Musée de Débarquement), Casino, Tuesday market
Caen: Musee des Beaux-Arts, Citidel

The sea locks at Ouistreham Riva-Bella

COURSEULLES-SUR-MER ☆☆

Standard Port
LE HAVRE

Harbour Entry
Lock in 2h-HW-2h to Bassin Joinville and swing bridge

Cap 31.37.51.69

Lat: 49° 20' N **Long:** 0° 27' W

Admiralty charts 259/1821/1349/2073
SHOM 5515, 5598

Approach visual navigation aids: Jetée Est head Oc (2) R 6s 7m Brown pylon R top. Jetée Ouest head 1S0 WG 4s 9m Brown pylon G top

R/T: VHF Ch 9

Yachting facilities: See below

Visitors moorings available: In Bassin Joinville; Marina 31.97.46.03

Distances: Ouistreham 9, Port-en Bessin 12, Grandcamp-Maisy 23

DESCRIPTION: If you like oysters you should be happy here because Courseulles is a fishing port famous for its oysters, said to be the best in Normandy. Courseulles is a popular holiday resort offering all the facilities expected. The harbour is surrounded by car parking and modern holiday flat developments but the town is near at hand. Courseulles is situated at the mouth of the Riviére la Seulles which flows to and from the sea through drying sandbanks. Difficult of approach when the wind is onshore, the best time of approach is at the HW stand. Marina depth is maintained by a sill. Basin lock operates 2h-HW-2h.

Available:

Water✓	Electric	Showers
Laundrette	Petrol✓	Diesel✓
Chandler 31.37.45.08		

Repairs:

Yacht ✓	Engine 31.37.42.34
Electrical✓	Sail

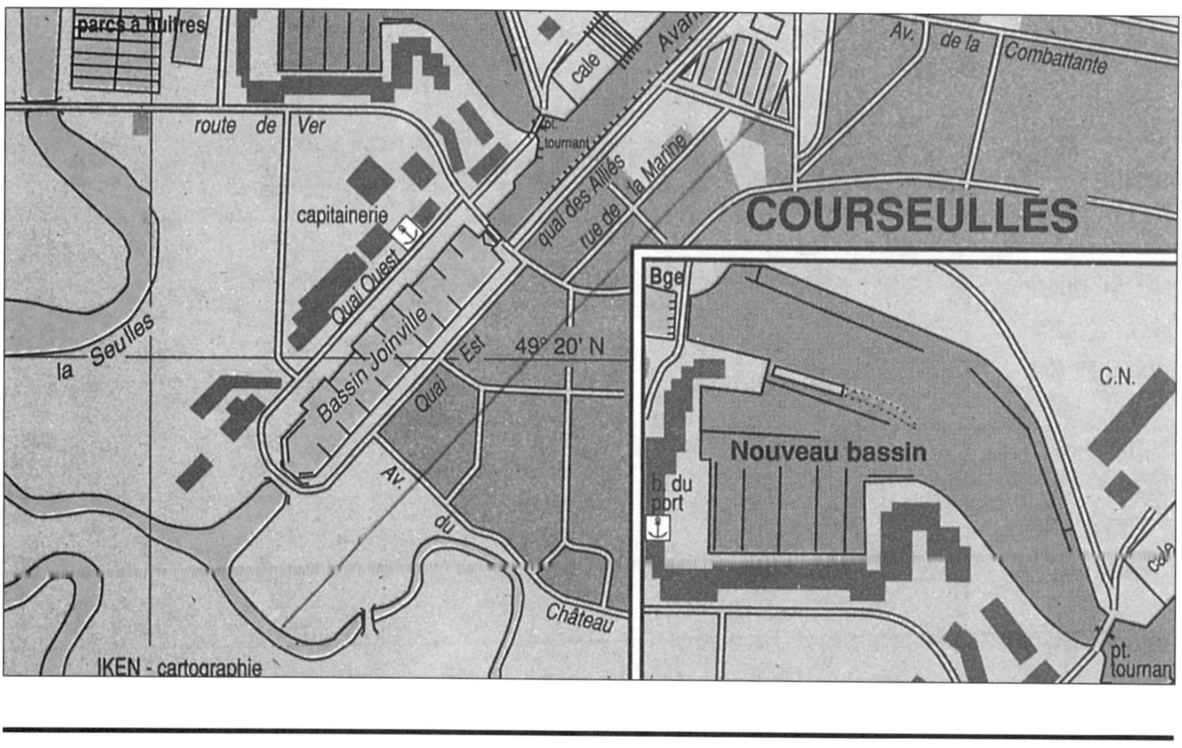

☆☆ COURSEULLES-SUR-MER

Telephone Code 31

Customs ☎ 31.37.46.19

Weather Meteo 31.74.48.11

Tourist Office
Rue de la Mer 31.37.46.80

Taxi ☎ 31.96.54.07

Hire Cars ☎ 31.37.94.13/31.37.97.21

Chemist Rue de la Mer

Post Office Rue de la Mer

Bank Rue de la Mer

Yacht Clubs
Sociéte des Régates 31.37.47.42

Police ☎ 31.37.07.13

Laundrette Apply Capitainerie

Shops/supermarkets
All available nearby in the town

Pubs/restaurants
Belle Aurore (a la carte), 32 Rue Maréchal Foch; Pécherie (4 menus 78-395F), 6 Place du 6-Juin

Tourist attractions:
Maison-de-la-Mer, La Croix de Lorraine, Aquarium, Tuesday market, Friday market

Port de Courseulles

PORT-EN-BESSIN ☆☆☆

Standard Port
LE HAVRE

Harbour Entry
Lock in 2h-HW-2h harbour dries

Cap 31.21.70.49

Lat: 49° 21' N **Long:** 0° 46' W

Admiralty charts 2073
SHOM 5515/6927

Approach visual navigation aids:
Ldg Lts Front Oc (3) W 12s 10m W plylon G top
240° Rear Oc (3) W 12s 11m W 8 grey house

R/T: VHF Ch 03 and Ch 18 when lock is operating

Yachting facilities: All available

Visitors moorings available: The outer harbour is a possibility if you are able to take the ground safely, since it dries completely. 10 berths are reserved for visitors in the deepwater basin. Contact HM on arrival. Waiting berth is alongside Quai de L'Epi.

Distances: Cherbourg 47, Le Havre71, Dieppe 108, Boulogne 140, Needles 60

DESCRIPTION: A busy fishing port, busy with fishing boats which limit the room available for yachts; the time, too, that one can stay might well be limited. You might have to lie outside of fishing boats. Between here and Grandcamp Maisy, about 20 miles away, is the large American War Cemetery at St. Laurent. This is where the Americans came ashore on the beaches under the codename of Omaha and 100,000 lives were lost. The remains of blockships and various other obstructions, which formed Omaha Beach, the artifical harbour created by the Allies, are dangers to navigation. They are marked to seaward by buoys and covered by the green sector of the light on the west mole of Port-en-Bessin Harbour.

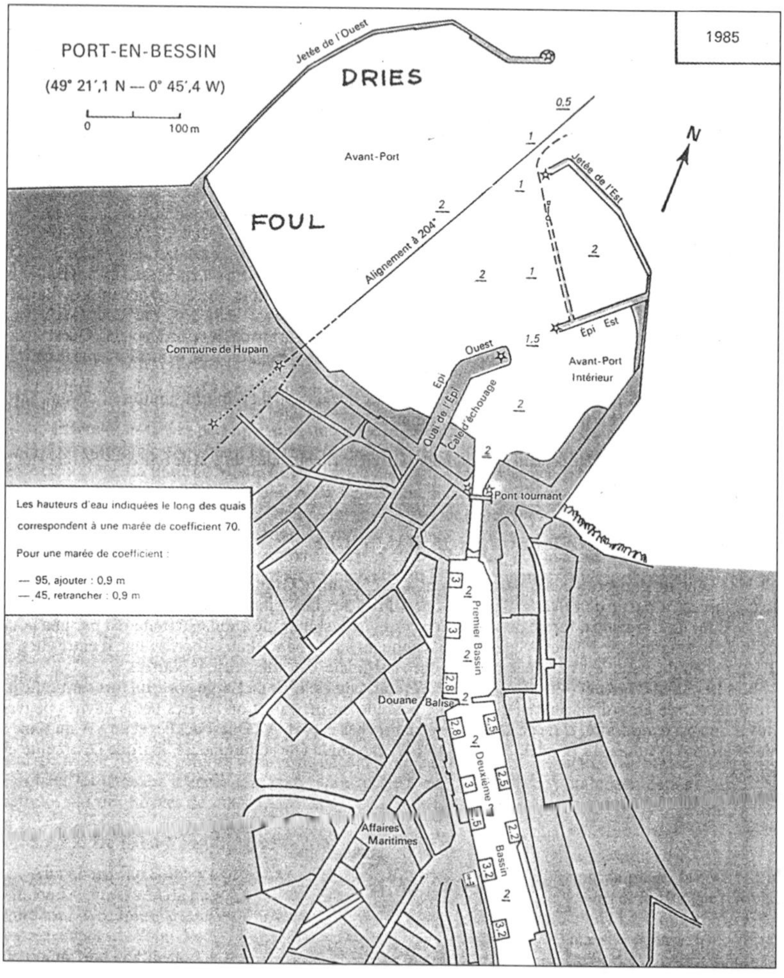

"Extrait Des I.N. C. 21 (ou C.22) du SHOM, reproduit avec son aimable autorisation"

☆☆☆ PORT-EN-BESSIN

Telephone Code 31

Customs ☎ 31.21.71.09

Weather Meteo 31.74.48.11

Tourist Office
Rue du Croiseur-Montcalm 31.21.92.33

Taxi ☎ 31.21.90.70

Yacht Clubs
Centre Nautique de Port-en-Bessin
31.21.72.12

Police ☎ 31.21.70.10

Shops/supermarkets
Shops nearby

Pubs/restaurants
Hotel de la Marine, Quai Letouruer;
La Foucée, 12 Rue Lefournier

Tourist attractions:
Sunday Market

Entrance to Port-en-Bessin

Port-en-Bessin

CHANNEL WEST

POOLE ☆☆☆☆

Sayls.
50 42 39   50 38 95
1 56 93   01 54 78

Standard Port
PORTSMOUTH

Harbour Entry
At all times (chain ferry across entrance)

HM 685261

Lat: 50° 39' N **Long:** 01° 54' W

Admiralty charts 2172/2611/2175

Approach visual navigation aids: Between South Haven Point and South end of Sandbanks

R/T: Poole Harbour Control VHF Ch 16 14 (H24)

Yachting facilities: Available in marinas

Visitors moorings available: Alongside Town Quay, Poole Harbour (Salterns) Marina Ch 80/37 Tel: 709971, Cobbs Quay Ch 80/37, Poole 674299

Distances: Lymington 17, Cowes 27, Cherbourg 65, Alderney 68

Poole Harbour (Salterns)
Available:
Water✓ Electric✓ Showers✓
Laundrette Petrol✓ Diesel✓
Chandler✓

Repairs: Yacht✓ Engine✓
Electrical✓ Sail✓

Poole Cobbs Quay
Available:
Water✓ Electric✓ Showers✓
Laundrette Petrol✓ Diesel✓
Chandler

Repairs: Yacht✓ Engine✓
Electrical✓ Sail✓

DESCRIPTION: Poole Harbour is one of the largest and most attractive natural harbours in the world. To berth alongside Poole Quay is most convenient from a going ashore point of view, the town being only a few minutes away from the quay. You may have other yachts alongside, however, and you may not lie as quietly as in a marina.
Salterns (Poole Harbour) Marina is easy to approach, but apart from the club and a few local shops there is little of interest ashore. The Marina is usually full during the summer months.
Cobbs Quay is approached as the tide serves, via the swing bridge and, here again, apart from the resources of the marina there is no interest ashore. Visitors' berths sometimes available at Poole YC, Hamworthy, Tel. 672687. Ferry port for Cherbourg (summer) and Channel Islands. Busy commercial port.

Mooring charges:	**Daily**
Cobbs Quay	£1 per metre

Telephone Code	0202
Customs	☎ 674567
Weather	☎ 0703 228844
Tourist Office	☎ 675151
Taxi	☎ 672251/678404
Hire Cars	☎ 745000/715655
Doctor	☎ 676111/672474
Dentist	☎ 673037/672810
Hospital	☎ 675100

Chemist High Street

Post Office High Street

Bank High Street

Yacht Clubs
Poole Harbour 707321
Poole 672687
Royal Motor 707227
Parkstone 743610

Police ☎ 552099

Laundrette
Adastral Square & Marina

Shops/supermarkets
Sainbsbury, Tesco in Poole.
All shops near Town Quay

Pubs/restaurants
Corkers, 1 High Street, The Quay; Fishnets, Old Mill Suite, The Quay; Jon B's, 20 High Street; Raj Poot, 43 High Street; The Warehouse, Poole Quay

Tourist attractions:
Poole Pottery, Waterfront Museum, Poole Park (near shops), Aquarium, Customs House, Natural World, Brownsea Island

Fuel barge in harbour.
Water taxi

Cobbs Quay

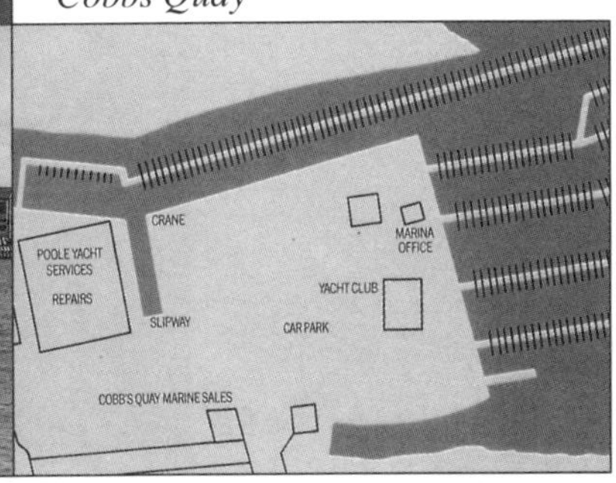

Town Quay

POOLE ☆☆☆☆

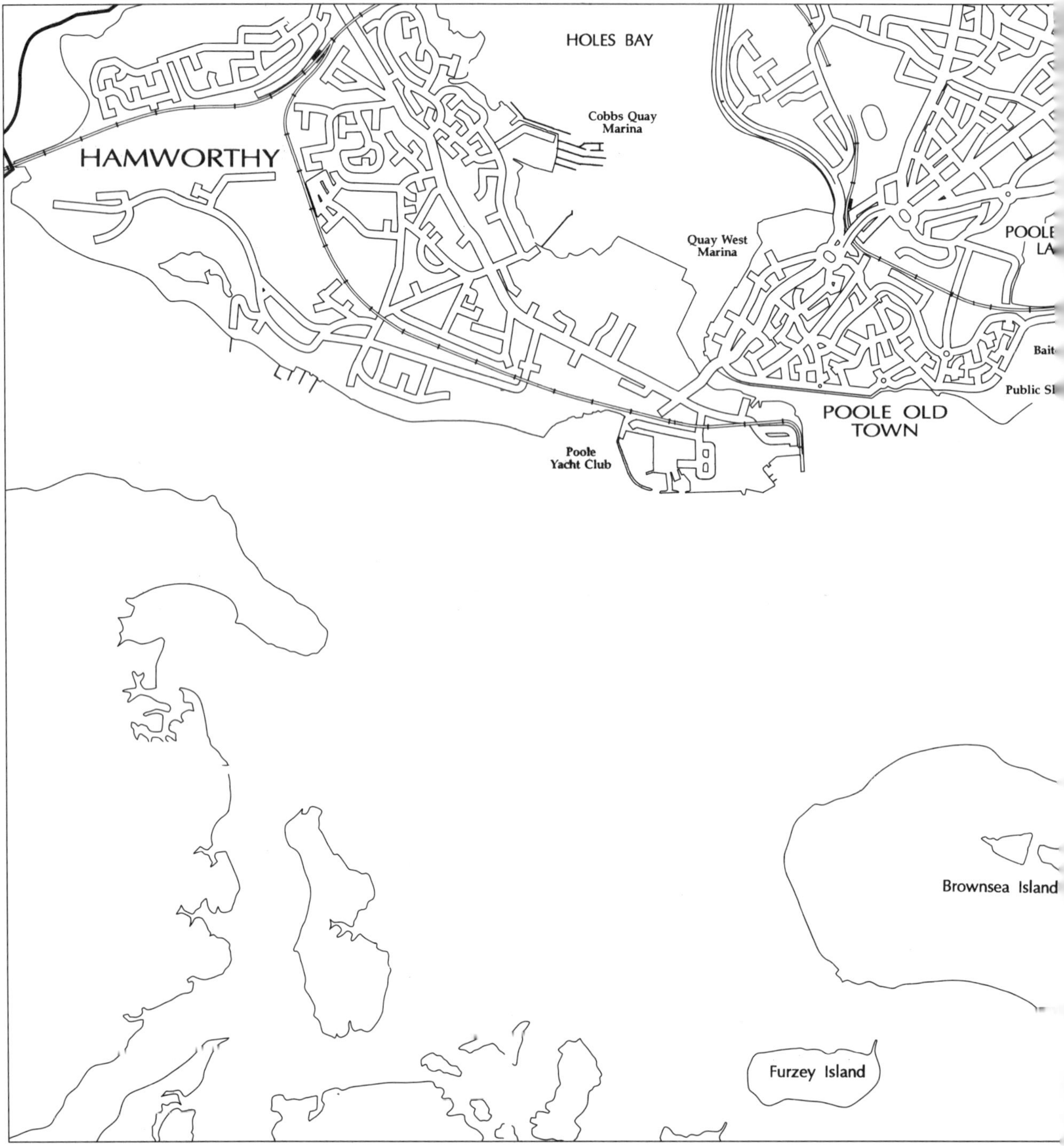
HOLES BAY
Cobbs Quay
Marina
HAMWORTHY
Quay West
Marina
POOLE OLD
TOWN
Poole
Yacht Club
Brownsea Island
Furzey Island

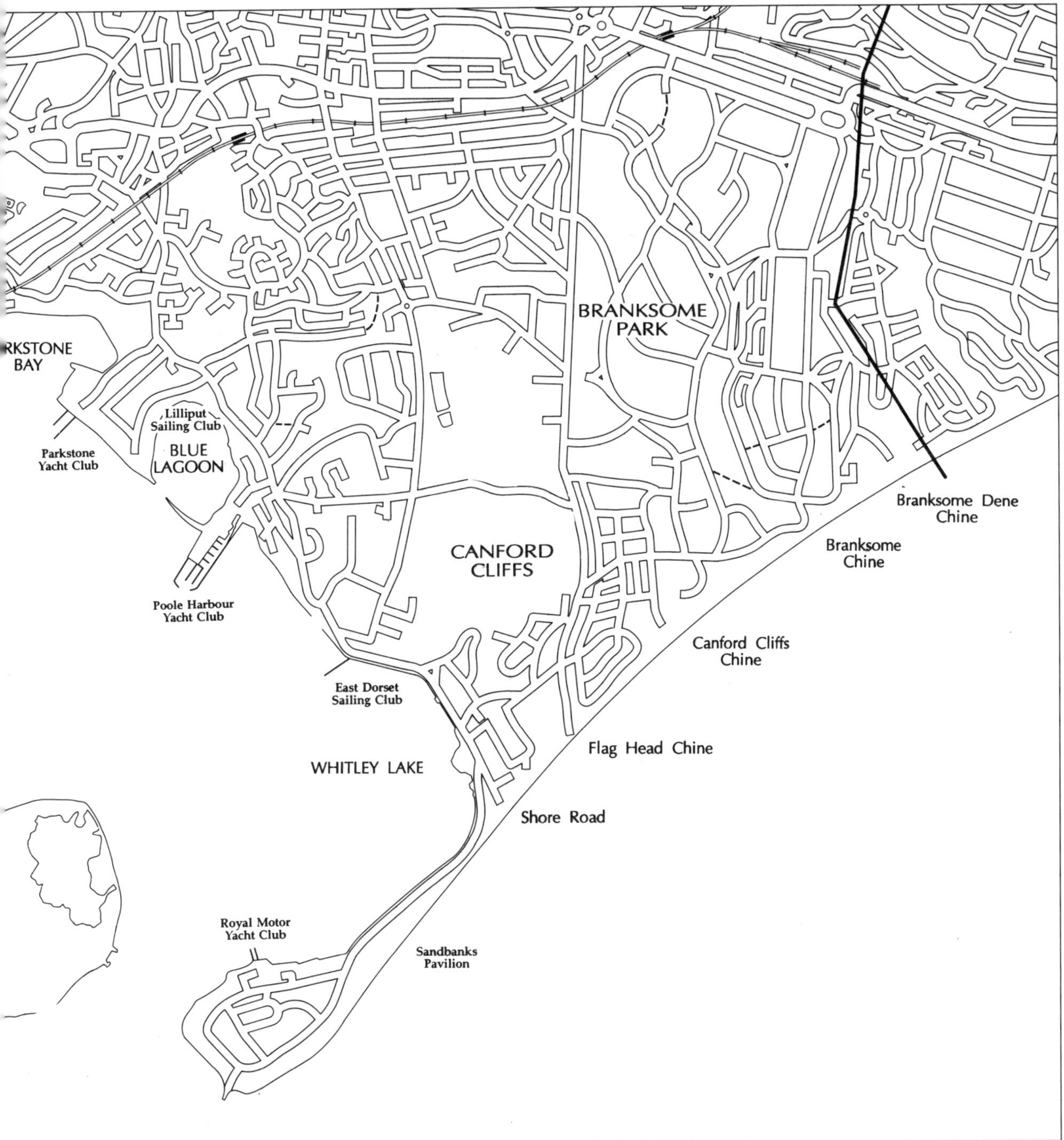
RKSTONE
BAY
Parkstone
Yacht Club
Lilliput
Sailing Club
BLUE
LAGOON
Poole Harbour
Yacht Club
BRANKSOME
PARK
CANFORD
CLIFFS
Branksome Dene
Chine
Branksome
Chine
Canford Cliffs
Chine
East Dorset
Sailing Club
Flag Head Chine
WHITLEY LAKE
Shore Road
Royal Motor
Yacht Club
Sandbanks
Pavilion

WEYMOUTH ☆☆☆☆☆

Standard Port
PORTSMOUTH

Harbour Entry
At all times, Berthing Master will advise

HM 760620

Lat: 50° 36' N **Long:** 02° 27' W

Admiralty charts 2172/2256/2268

Approach visual navigation aids:
Ldg Lts Ballast Quay Front F R 4M ◊ on W post
237° Rear F R 4M R ◊ on W mast

R/T: VHF Ch 16 calling Weymouth Harbour Radio. Ch 12 working

Yachting facilities: Toilets/showers Berth No. 7 within the building at No. 13 Customs House Quay. All repairs available

Visitors moorings available: On Berths 4, 5, 6 and 7 or "Cove" area subject to availability. May be rafted out twelve deep at peak periods

Distances: Lymington 39, Le Havre 116, Cherbourg 65

DESCRIPTION: A pleasant seaside town with shops, pubs and restaurants near to the yacht moorings. The harbour is long and narrow and lies at the mouth of the River Wey. There is sometimes a swell in the harbour if the wind is from the East. Town can get very crowded during summer months. Convenient rail connections to London etc.

Moorings charges:

Up to 20'	£4.50 per day
20'-30'	£6.00 per day
30'-40'	£8.00 per day
40'-50'	£10.50 per day
50'-60'	£12.00 per day
Over 60'	£12.00 + 20p per extra foot for 21 days
	After 21 days rate doubles
Catamarans	1½ times
Trimarans	Double

Available:
Water✓ Electric
Showers Custom House Quay
Petrol Diesel✓
Chandler 785663/786710

Repairs: Yacht 779550/785663
Engine 779550
Electrical 779550
Sail✓

☆☆☆☆☆ WEYMOUTH

Telephone Code	0305	**Post Office**	St. Thomas Street	**Pubs/restaurants** Sea Cow Bistro, 7 Custom House Quay. Large selection nearby
Customs	Ferry Terminal Building 771189/774747	**Bank**	Nearby	**Tourist attractions:** Berths 5, 6 and 7 – Pavilion Theatre, Diving Museum, "Cove" area Timewalk Museum, Nothe Fort Sealife Centre
Tourist Office	☎ 772444	**Yacht Clubs**	Royal Dorset 786258	
Hire Cars	☎ 773848	**Police**	☎ 763011	
Doctor	☎ 782226	**Laundrette**	Abbotsbury Road	
Hospital	☎ 772211	**Shops/supermarkets**	Asda and Tesco near	
Chemist	St. Marys Street			

Looking across to the town from the Cove moorings, Weymouth

TORQUAY ☆☆☆☆☆

Standard Port
DEVONPORT

Harbour Entry
At all times

HM 292429

Lat: 50° 27' N **Long:** 3° 29' E

Admiralty charts 26/1613

Approach visual navigation aids: Princess Pier Head Q R 6m metal col

R/T: VHF Ch 14/16 (0900-2000 Apr-Sept) Marina Ch 80/37

Yachting facilities: See below

Visitors moorings available: Marina Ch 80 37 (H24) ☎ 214624

Distances: Treguier 100, Guernsey 70, Yarmouth 75

DESCRIPTION: Torquay is a beautiful town and the marina is part of it. You step ashore at Princess Parade and the main shopping streets are adjoining, North Quay, The Strand and Victoria Parade surrounding the Inner Harbour. There are pubs and restaurants all around, large stores and various shops on the streets leading back into the town. Smart hotels are around and above, white buildings atop the seven green hills giving Torquay a continental atmosphere. As you enter the harbour the sign showing visitors pontoon is ahead of you. There is room for 70 visiting yachts. The berths suffer from an uncomfortable surge in strong south westerlies. Good day sailing in Torbay.

Available:
Water✓ Electric✓ Showers✓
Laundrette Petrol✓ Diesel✓
Chandler

Repairs:
Yacht✓ Engine✓ Electrical✓
Sail✓

Visitors' pontoon shown on entry

☆☆☆☆☆ TORQUAY

Telephone Code	0803
Customs	Kings Quay, Brixham 882130
Weather	Daily Harbour Master Office
Tourist Office	☎ 297428
Taxi	☎ 294404/213521
Hire Cars	☎ 292300
Doctor	☎ 605359
Dentist	☎ 211646
Hospital	☎ 614567
Chemist	Boots, Strand
Post Office	Fleet Street
Bank	Strand
Yacht Clubs	Royal Torbay 29006
Police	☎ 292293/214491
Laundrette	7 Old Mill Road & Marina
Shops/supermarkets	Haldon Centre, Market Street, Union Street. Shops adjacent to harbour

Pubs/restaurants
Burridges, 8 Victoria Parade 293734; Carnevaal, Rafters, 172 Union Street 297557, Rafteal, 22 Victoria Parade 296416; Carvery Restaurant, Victoria Parade

Tourist attractions:
Winner of awards for some of the best beaches in Europe. World famous Model Village, nearby Paignton Zoo, Steam Train, Theatres

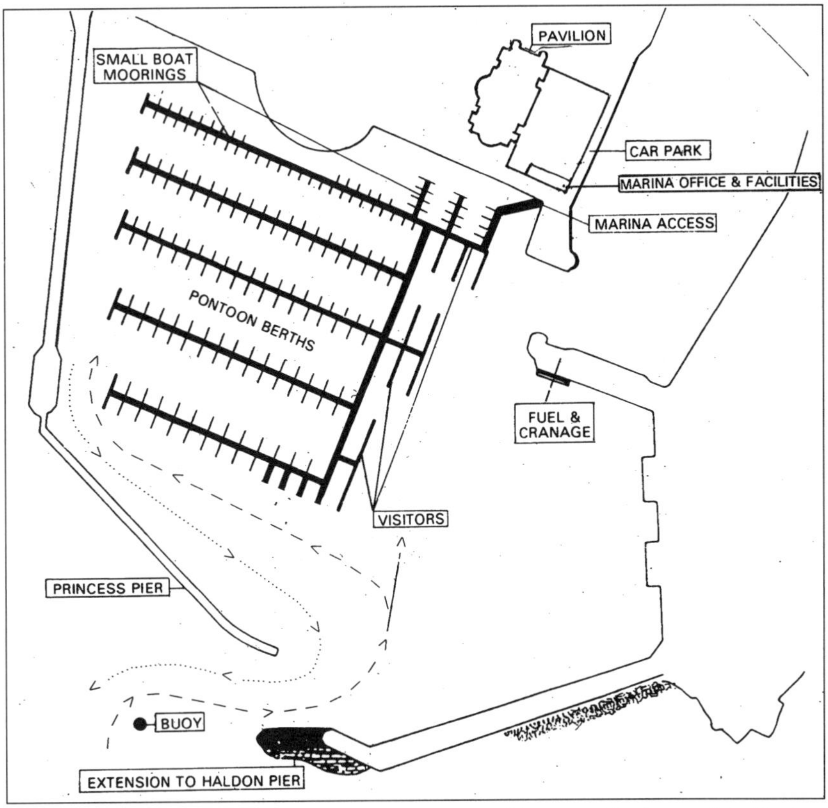

Torquay Marina within Torbay

BRIXHAM ☆☆☆

Standard Port
DEVONPORT

Harbour Entry
Inner harbour mostly dries, access to marinas

HM 883321

Lat: 50° 24'22 N **Long:** 3° 30'51 W

Admiralty charts 26/1613

Approach visual navigation aids: Victoria Breakwater Head Oc R 15s 6m W tower

R/T: VHF Ch 14/16 Marina Ch 37/80 Tel: 882711

Yachting facilities: See next page

Visitors moorings available: At Marina. Brixham YC maintains two moored pontoons in front of its premises capable of berthing 25-30ft. LOA ☎ 883332

Distances: Cherbourg 81, Guernsey 63, Lymington 75

DESCRIPTION: Busy fishing harbour with one of the country's largest trawler fleets, but the trawlers are on the other side of the harbour. Stalls and kiosks offer a fine display of fish. It was at Brixham that William, Prince of Orange arrived in 1688, thus the original name of the marina. This has now been changed to Brixham Marina, on being taken over by MDL. Good shelter, easy entrance but rough in strong north-westerlies.

Mooring charges:

Up to 3 hours no charge	
Daily 20'-30'	£5-£10
30'-40'	£11-£14
40'-50'	£15-£18
Weekly 6 x daily	

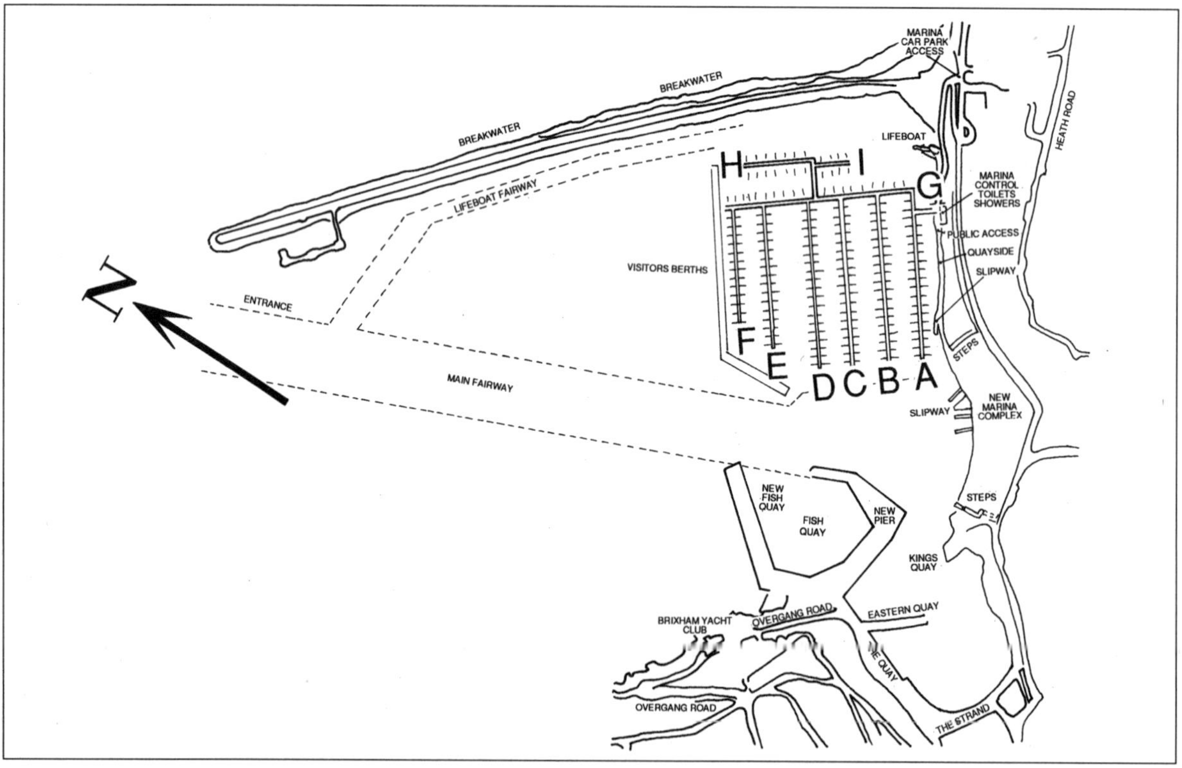

☆☆☆ BRIXHAM

Telephone Code	☎ 0803
Customs	Kings Quay
Weather	☎ 882704
Taxi	☎ 883883/3000
Hire Cars	Prouts Garage
Doctor	☎ 882731
Hospital	☎ 882153
Chemist	Bolton Street

Post Office	Bolton Cross
Bank	Fore Street
Yacht Clubs	Brixham
Police	☎ 882231
Laundrette	Marina
Shops/supermarkets	Nearby

Pubs/restaurants
Bullers; Captains Table; Crown & Anchor; Chandlers all near to harbour

Tourist attractions:
National Maritime Museum, Fisheries Museum, Full size replica of Sir Francis Drake's Golden Hind, colony of local artists, quaint houses

Available:
Water✓ Electric✓ Showers
Petrol Victoria Jetty Diesel 3332 Victoria Jetty
Chandler 882290/51888/6115

Repairs:
Yacht 845455 Engine 6115 Electrical 58158/3030 Sail

Yacht marina and fishing harbour beyond

DARTMOUTH *****

Standard Port
DARTMOUTH

Harbour Entry
At all times, at mouth of River Dart

HM 832337

Lat: 50° 19'5 N **Long:** 3°34' W

Admiralty charts 2253/1613/1634

Approach visual navigation aids: 1S0 WRG 3s 8m W round GRP tower

R/T: HM Ch 11; Marinas Ch 80/37; Fuel barge Ch 16; Water taxi 16/80

Yachting facilities: See below

Visitors moorings available: Darthaven Marina (Ancasta) Kingswear 080425/545. Dart Marina 833351

Distances: Cherbourg 85, Falmouth 65, Plymouth 36, Braye 64, St. Malo 120

DESCRIPTION: With its narrow streets, long flights of steps, overhanging medieval houses, old quays, speciality shops, restaurants and inns, Dartmouth has a special charm. During the summer months there are flowers everywhere and Dartmouth has won the Britain in Bloom competition for small towns for three successive years. The River Dart is navigable above Dartmouth, with a draught limit of 3m5 at MHWS and 2m5 at MHWN, as far as Totnes, a distance of about 10 miles.

Dartmouth Available:
Water✓ Electric✓ Showers
Petrol Diesel✓ Chandler

Repairs:
Yacht 2649/833351
Engine
Electrical 833351
Sail

Darthaven Marina (Kingswear 545) Available:
Water✓ Electric Showers✓
Laundrette Petrol Diesel
Chandler✓

Repairs:
Yacht✓ Engine Electrical✓
Sail

Dartside Quay, Galmpton Available:
Water✓ Electric✓ Showers
Petrol✓ Diesel✓ Chandler

Repairs:
Yacht Engine Electrical
Sail

Mooring charges:

	Day	Week
Dartside Quay	40p per foot	60p per foot

The River Dart

☆☆☆☆☆ DARTMOUTH

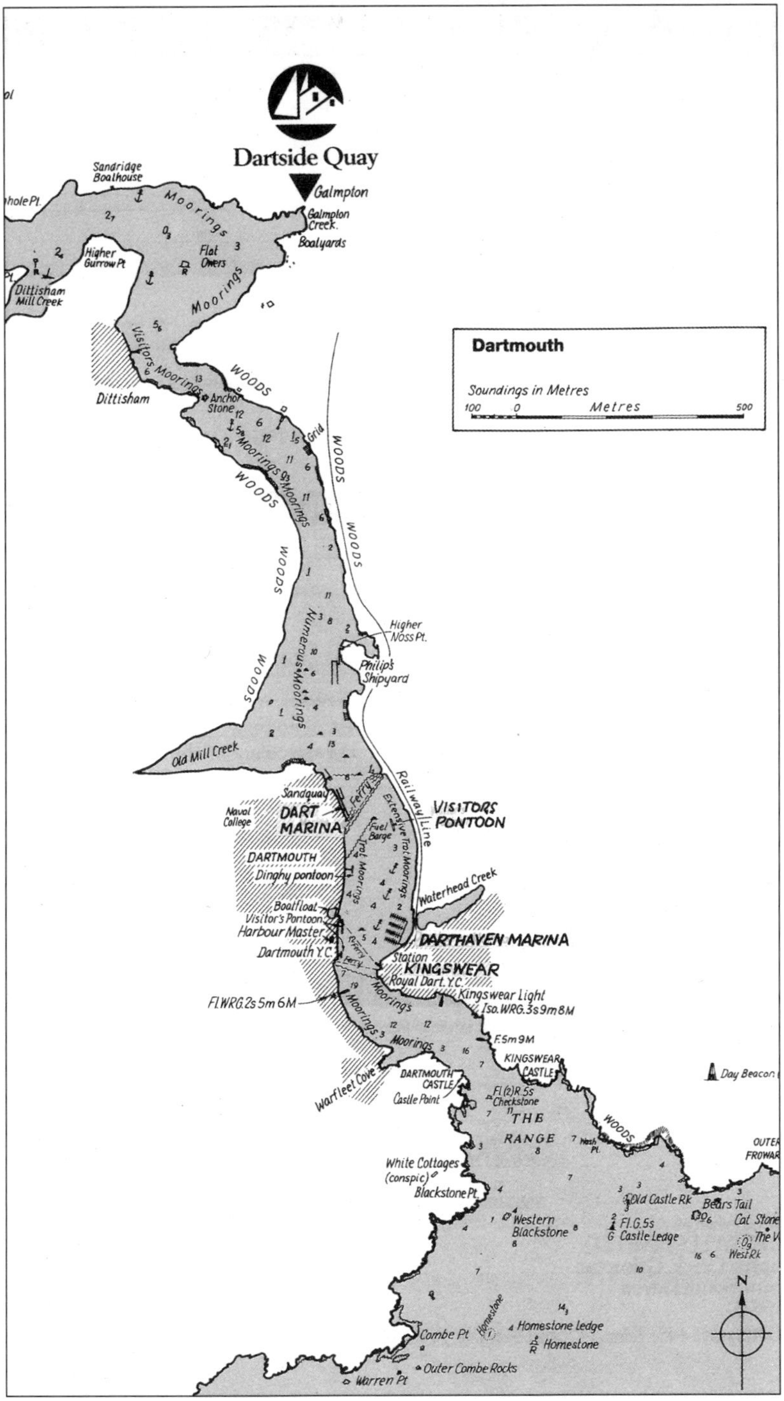

Telephone Code	08043
Customs	☎ 832609
Weather	☎ 842156
Tourist Office	☎ 834224
Taxi	☎ 294404
Doctor	☎ 834914
Dentist	☎ 833456
Hospital	☎ 832255
Chemist	The Quay
Post Office	Victoria Road
Bank	Duke Street
Yacht Clubs	Dartmouth 832305 Royal Dart Kingswear 83272
Police	☎ 832288
Laundrette	Dart Marina

Shops/supermarkets
Fairfax Place

Pubs/restaurants
Taylors, 8 The Quay 2748; Cranfords, 29 Fairfax Place 2328; Cherub Inn, Higher Street 2571; Carved Angel, 2 South Embankment 2465

Tourist attractions:
Steam Railway, Dartmouth Castle. You might even fancy a trip on a boat (let someone else drive!) up the River Dart to Totnes with many items of interest pointed out to you, such as the Royal Naval College, the Estate of the late Dame Agatha Christie and picturesque Greenaway Quay

SALCOMBE ☆☆☆☆

Standard Port
DEVONPORT

Harbour Entry
Sand bar with least depth of 0.9m visitors deep water moorings

HM 054 884 3791

Lat: 50° 13' N **Long:** 3° 46' W

Admiralty charts 28/1613/1634

Approach visual navigation aids:
Ldg Lts Front QW 8m Mast
042° Rear Oc W 4-5s 8m stone col

R/T: VHF Ch 14 (0830-2030) May-Sept

Yachting facilities: See next page

Visitors moorings available: Harbour Office

Distances: Paimpol 89, Treguier 86

DESCRIPTION: Some boat owners regard this as a yachting paradise and the sheltered moorings in beautiful surroundings certainly have wide appeal – as the summer crowds prove. The narrow streets are packed in summer time, mostly with yachting types. The estuary provides 4 miles of sheltered moorings in really delightful creeks and surroundings. Entrance should not be attempted in strong south winds. Visitors moorings, pontoons and anchorages in the Bag offer shelter from South swell.

Mooring charges:
70p-£1.00 per head

Telephone Code	054 884
Tourist Office	Kingsbridge 3195
Taxi	☎ 2739/Water Taxi VHF Ch 14
Hospital	☎ 2284
Chemist	Fore Street
Post Office	Market Street
Bank	Fore Street

Yacht Clubs
Salcombe

Police Kingsbridge 2326

Shops/supermarkets
Local shops

Pubs/restaurants
Wellingtons, 84 Fore Street; Dusters, 50 Fore Street; The Galley, 5 Fore Street; The Marina

Sheltered creeks in delightful surroundings

Available:
Water 0242-512568
Electric Showers
Petrol 3791 Diesel 3791
or fuel barge 0836-775644
or Ch 6 call sign "Fuel Barge"
Chandler 3655-3791

Repairs:
Yacht 3838
Engine 3838/Chivelstone 242/
Salcombe 2094
Electrical 3321/3791
Sail 3702/2343

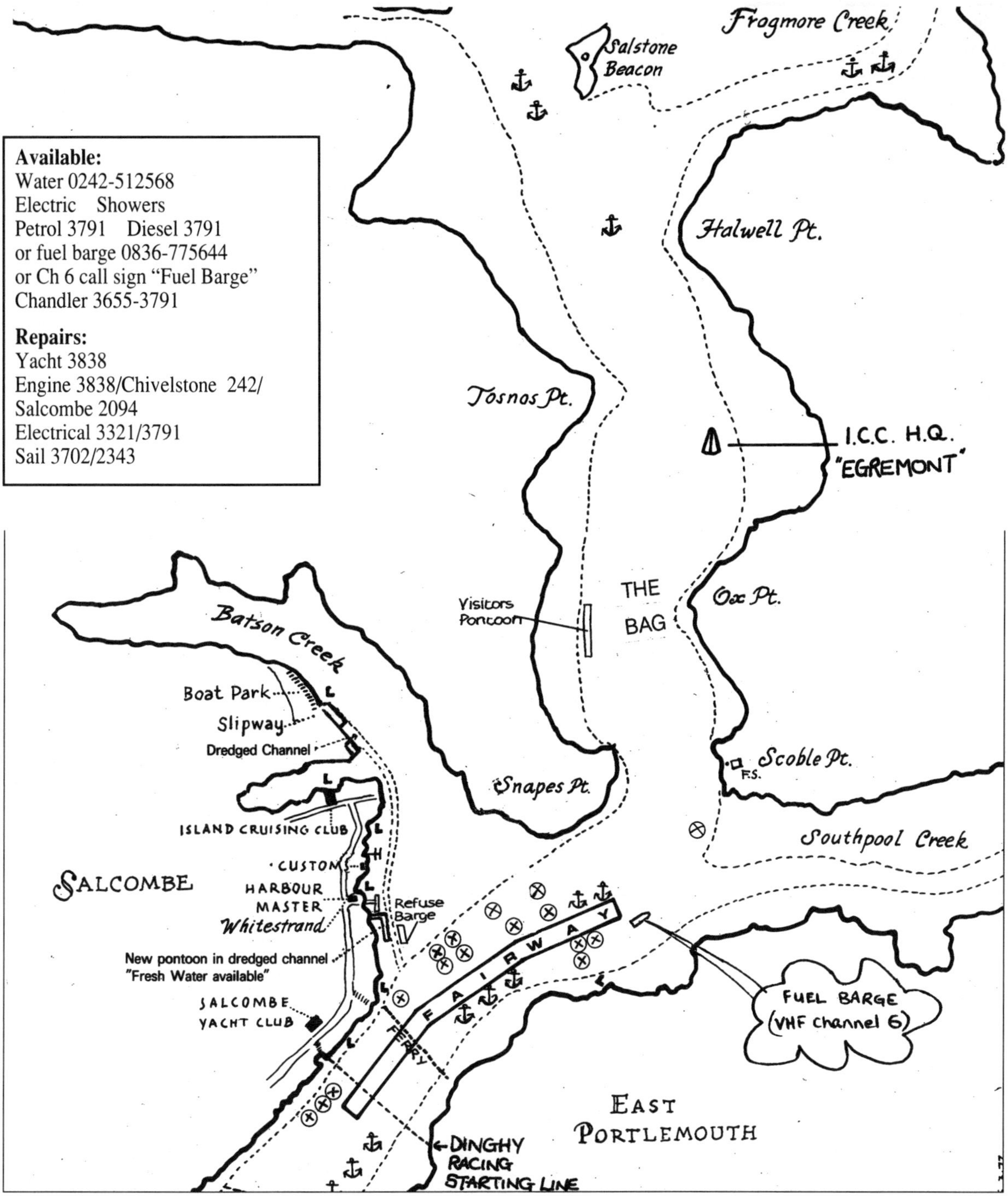

PLYMOUTH ☆☆☆☆☆

Standard Port
DEVONPORT

Harbour Entry
At any time through E or W channel

QHM Queens Harbour Master 663225

Lat: 50° 19' N **Long:** 4° 11' W
Penlee Point

Admiralty charts 1967/1900/1901/1902/30/871

Approach visual navigation aids: Wembury Point. Detached Breakwater W head Fl WR 10s 15m W round granite tower

R/T: Long Room Port Control VHF Ch 16; 08 12 14 (H24)

Yachting facilities: All available at marinas

Visitors moorings available: Preferred are Mayflower Marina, VHF Ch 80 37 556633, Queen Anne's Battery Marina 671142 or Sutton Harbour 664186 VHF Ch 16 80 37

Distances: Fowey 20, Falmouth 36

DESCRIPTION: The Dockyard Port of Plymouth includes the commercial harbours of Cattewater, Sutton Harbour, Millbay Docks and Stonehouse Pool. Plymouth is a large and interesting city. Wherever you decide to seek moorings you do not have far to walk for transport. There is a large shopping area, plenty of restaurants and pubs and splendid beer. Plymouth is host to many major yachting events when a festival atmosphere prevails. The Tall Race provides a splendid spectacle into the bargain. Plymouth Sound has witnessed many historic comings and goings and you can experience the full story at Plymouth Dome, built into the cliffs of The Hoe. At the south end of the Barbican you can see the Mayflower Steps where in 1620 the Pilgrim Fathers set sail for a better life in America. Excellent shelter, use either west or east channel in deep water with no hazards.

Plymouth Harbour

Telephone Code	0752
Customs	Millbay Docks
Tourist Office	☎ 264849
Taxi	☎ 669999/670022
Hire Cars	☎ 669859/705856
Doctor	☎ 667623
Hospital	☎ 668080
Post Office	St. Andrews Cross
Bank	Old Town Street
Police	☎ 701188
Laundrette	Marina

Yacht Clubs
Royal Western 660077
Mayflower Sc 662526
Royal Plymouth Corinthian 664327

Shops/supermarkets
Large selection

Pubs/restaurants
Baileys House that Jack Built, 11 Southside St., Barbican 266149; Barbican Revivial 664270; El Greco, 8 The Parade, Barbican 266067; Quo Vadis, 111 Vauxhall Street, Barbican 262444

Tourist attractions:
Aquarium, The Hoe, Plymouth Dome The Hoe, Plymouth Gin Distillery 665292, Smeateus Tower, The Hoe Theatre

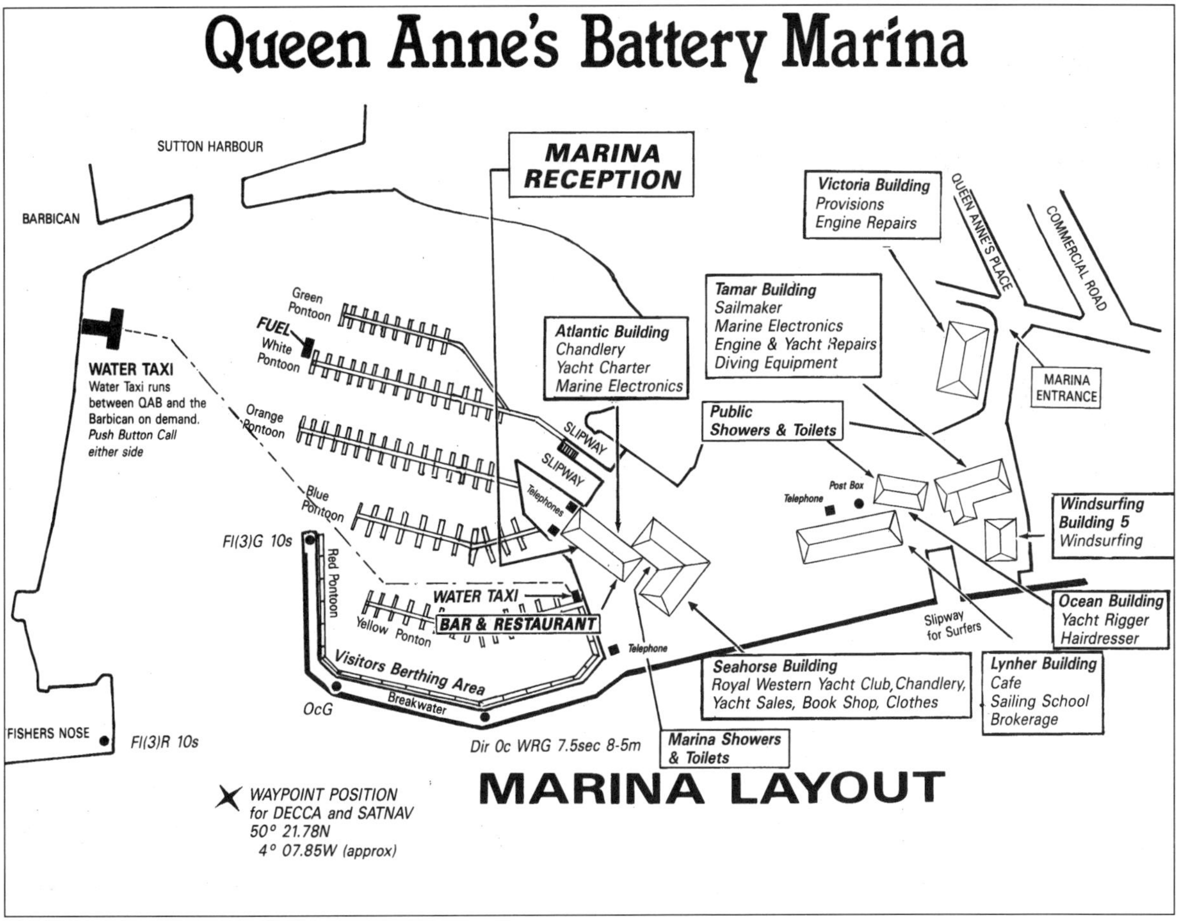

PLYMOUTH *****

ANCASTA

Mooring fees	per day	per week	per monthly
up to 20ft. to 30ft.	£7 to £11	£35 to £55	£119 to £187
31ft. to 60ft.	£14 to £22	£70 to £110	£238 to £374
61ft. to 80ft.	£25 to £28	£125 to £140	£425 to £476

QUEEN ANNE'S BATTERY

daily	40p per ft.	inc. electricity
weekly	£2 per ft.	inc. electricity
monthly	£6 per ft.	inc. electricity

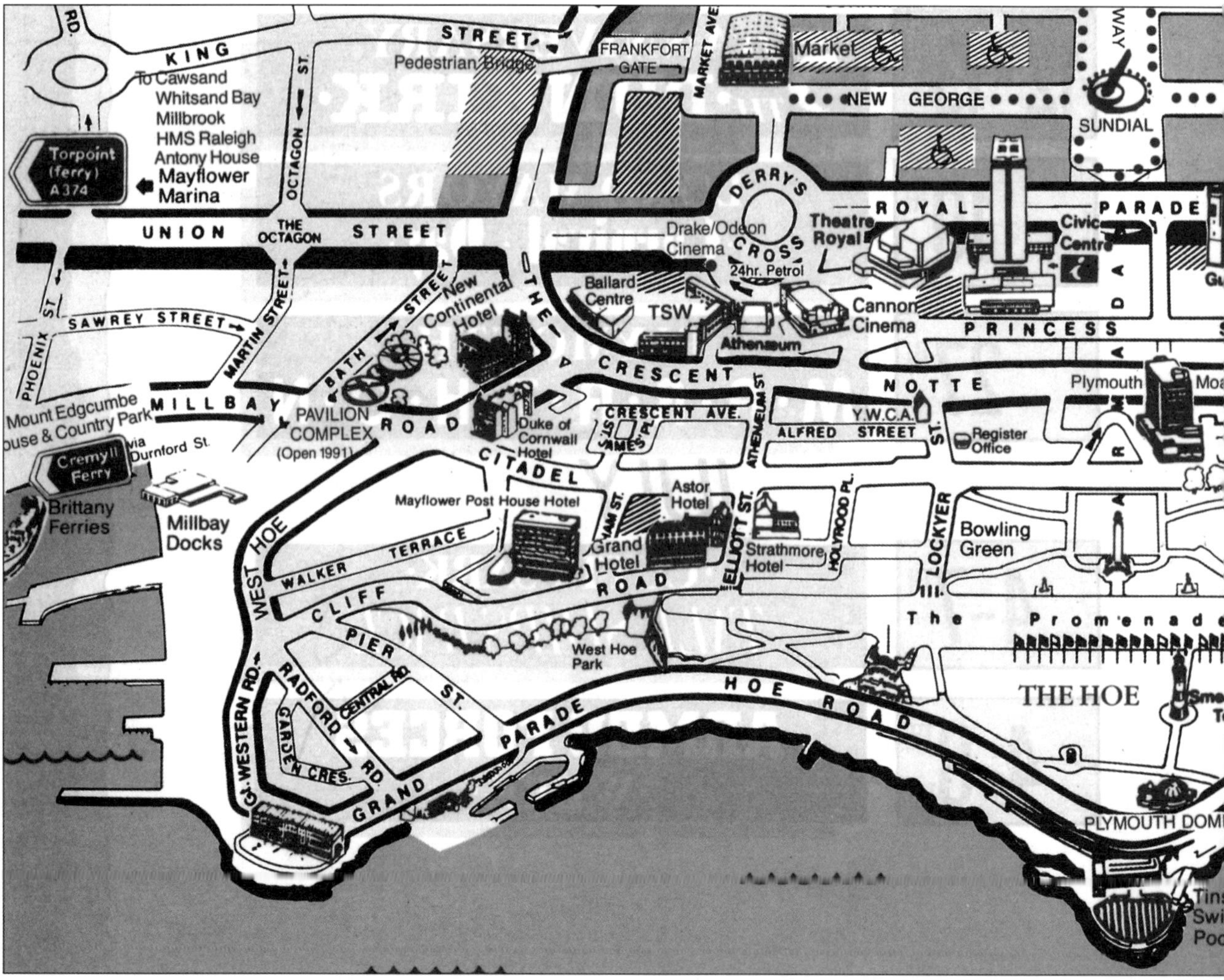

Queen Anne's Battery Marina
(240 + 60 visitors)

Available:
Water✓ Electric✓ Showers
Laundrette✓ Petrol✓ Diesel✓
Chandler✓

Repairs: Yacht✓ Engine✓
Electrical✓ Sail✓

Mayflower Marina
(220 + 60 visitors)

Available:
Water✓ Electric✓ Laundrette
Petrol✓ Diesel✓ Chandler✓

Repairs: Yacht✓ Engine✓
Electrical✓ Sail✓

Sutton Harbour
(310)

Available:
Water✓ Electric✓ Showers
Laundrette✓ Petrol✓ Diesel✓
Chandler

Repairs: Yacht✓ Engine✓
Electrical Sail✓

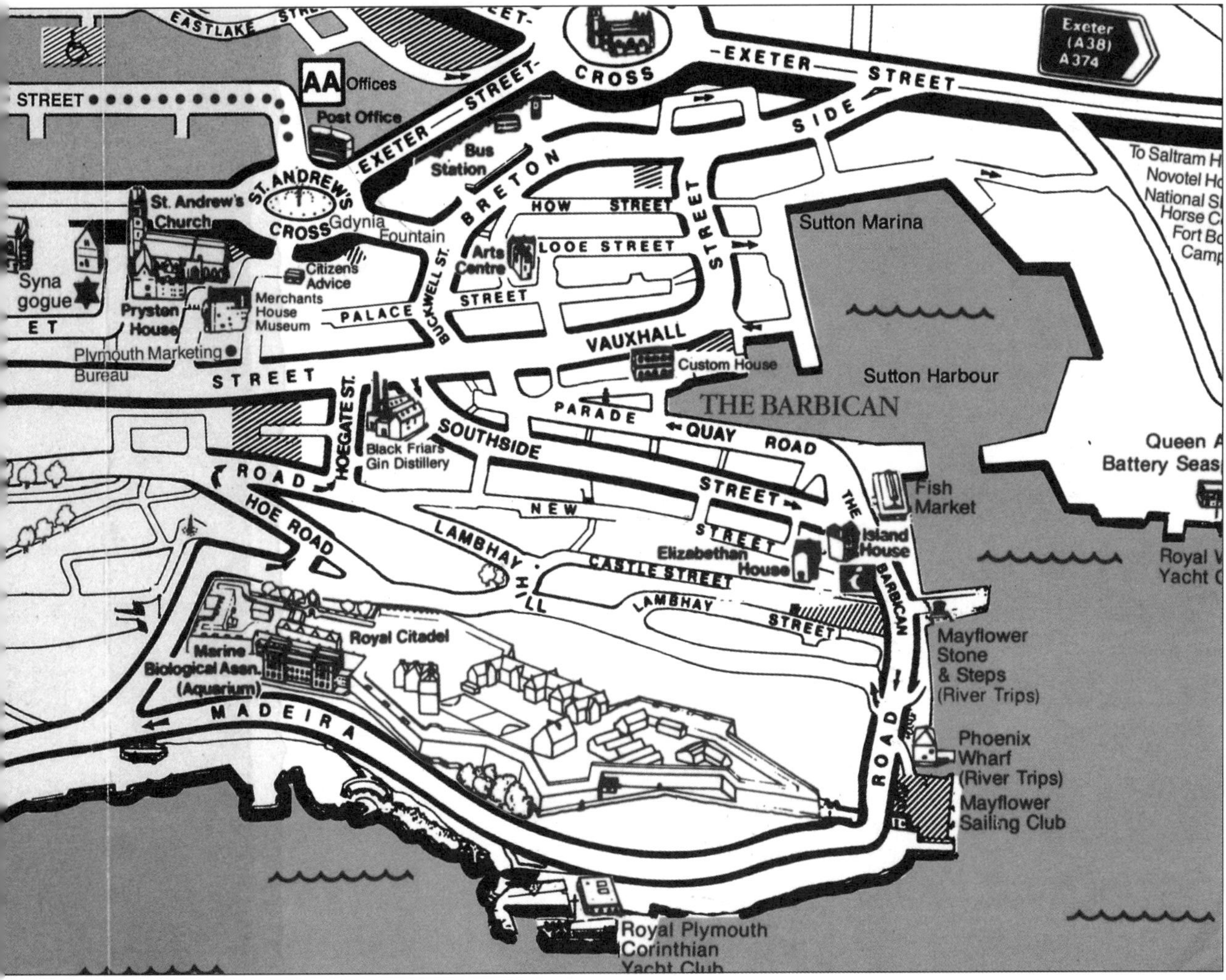

FOWEY ☆☆☆☆☆

Standard Port
DEVONPORT

Harbour Entry
At all times

HM 832471

Lat: 50° 20' N **Long:** 4° 38' W

Admiralty charts 31/1267/148

Approach visual navigation aids: Gribben Head Land Beacon, Cannis Rock S Cardinal Mark, St. Catherines Point L H West side of river entrance. Punches Cross Rock on E side. Whitehouse Point LH West side of river

R/T: Fowey Harbour Radio listening watch Ch 16; 12 (office hours)

Yachting facilities: See below

Visitors moorings available: There are no marinas and all visiting yacht facilities are owned by Fowey Harbour Commissioners under the direction of the Harbour Master (0726) 832471 Report H.M. at Albert Quay

Distances: Plymouth 20, Falmouth 21

DESCRIPTION: An ancient Cornish seaport of charm and tranquility, with narrow winding streets of flower-decked cottages and houses, quaint shops and pubs. From the days of pirates and smugglers this most beautiful of harbours has changed little. Today the Harbour Master makes welcome over five thousand visiting yachts a year, a tribute to his efficiency and the charm of Fowey. Quite large ships use the harbour exporting china clay and they tie up at the commercial jetties to the north of the town. Lower harbour can get rough in strong S-SW winds. Visitors' moorings in Pont Pill and Mixtow Pill, trots and pontoons, May to October

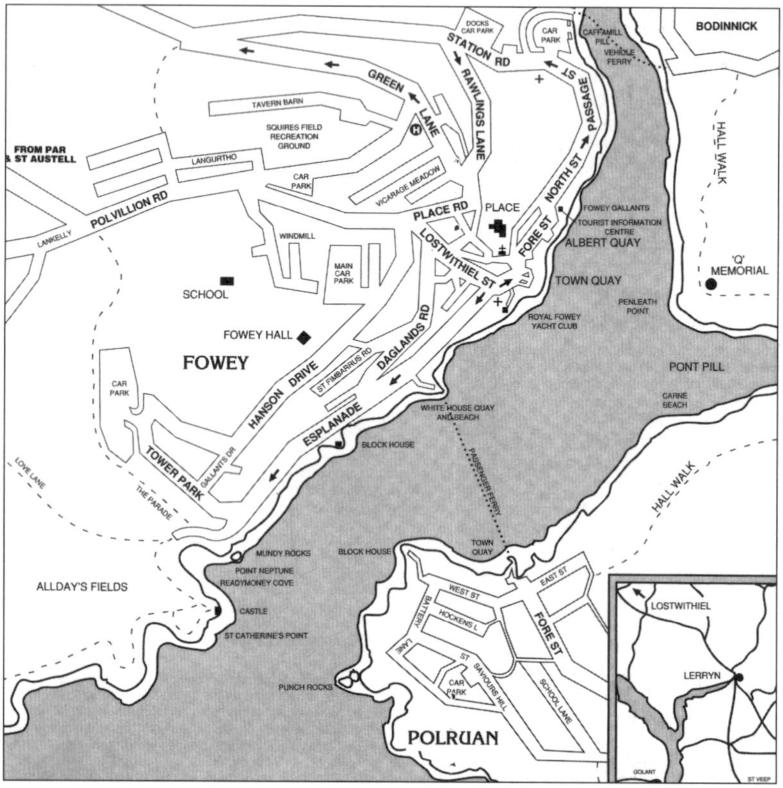

Available:
Water✓ Electric Showers
Laundrette Petrol Polruan
Diesel Polruan
Chandler 2287-3265

Repairs: Yacht Polruan 232
Engine Polruan 232
Electrical Polruan 232
Sail

Mooring fees	to 7m	7m-11m	11m-14m	14m-17m	17m-20m
1 night	£3	£5	£7	£10	£14.50
3 nights	£6	£10	£14	£20	£29.00
1 week	£15	£25	£35	£50	£72.50

Over 20m by arrangement

☆☆☆☆☆ FOWEY

Telephone Code 0726

Customs ☎ 833777

Weather Plymouth 8092

Tourist Office ☎ 833616

Taxi ☎ 833385/832676/832429
Water Taxi 832450

Hire Cars ☎ 833468

Doctor ☎ 832541

Dentist ☎ 833309

Hospital ☎ 832241

Chemist 833332

Post Office Custom House Hill

Bank Fore Street

Yacht Clubs
Royal Fowey 832245
Fowey Gallants SC 832335

Police ☎ 833438

Shops/supermarkets
Spar 39 Fore Street

Pubs/restaurants
King of Prussia 832450; The Ship Inn 832230; The Lugger Inn, 833435; The Galleon Inn 832323; The Safe Harbour Hotel 833379; The Commodore, Fore Street; Cordon Bleu, Esplanade; Stantons Restaurant, Esplanade; Food for Thought, Town Quay; Drifters, Fore Street

Tourist attractions:
St. Catherine's Castle,
The Museum, Trafalgar Square,
Aquarium, Town Quay

A deep water harbour

FALMOUTH ☆☆☆☆☆

Standard Port
DEVONPORT

Harbour Entry
At all times

HM 312285/314379

Lat: 50° 09' N **Long:** 5° 03' W

Admiralty charts 18/32/154

Approach visual navigation aids: Eastern Breakwater Fl R 2s 3m Grey mast

R/T: Falmouth Harbour Radio Ch 16; 12. Marinas and yacht harbours Ch 37/80

Yachting facilities: Available

Visitors moorings available: Visitors Yacht Haven situated at North Quay, apply Harbour Master Office 312285, Falmouth Marina 316620, Mylor 72121

Distances: Plymouth 36, Fowey 21, Dartmouth 65

DESCRIPTION: Said to be one of the finest natural harbours in the world, Falmouth has a lot to offer the visiting yachtsman, with miles of sheltered water and many attractions. The town is fortunate to overlook this beautiful harbour opening off Carrick roads. As well as being a well equipped harbour, Falmouth has a reputation as a sunny and popular seaside resort.

The Port of Falmouth visitors yacht haven is right in the town. How often can you berth with a supermarket and a Barclays Bank cashpoint not a cable's length away?

The yacht marina, at North Parade, is further from the town but there is a bus service.

Mylor Yacht Harbour, further upstream, has all facilities, including a clubhouse and a restaurant. On the east side St. Mawes provides shelter.

Falmouth – "one of the finest natural harbours"

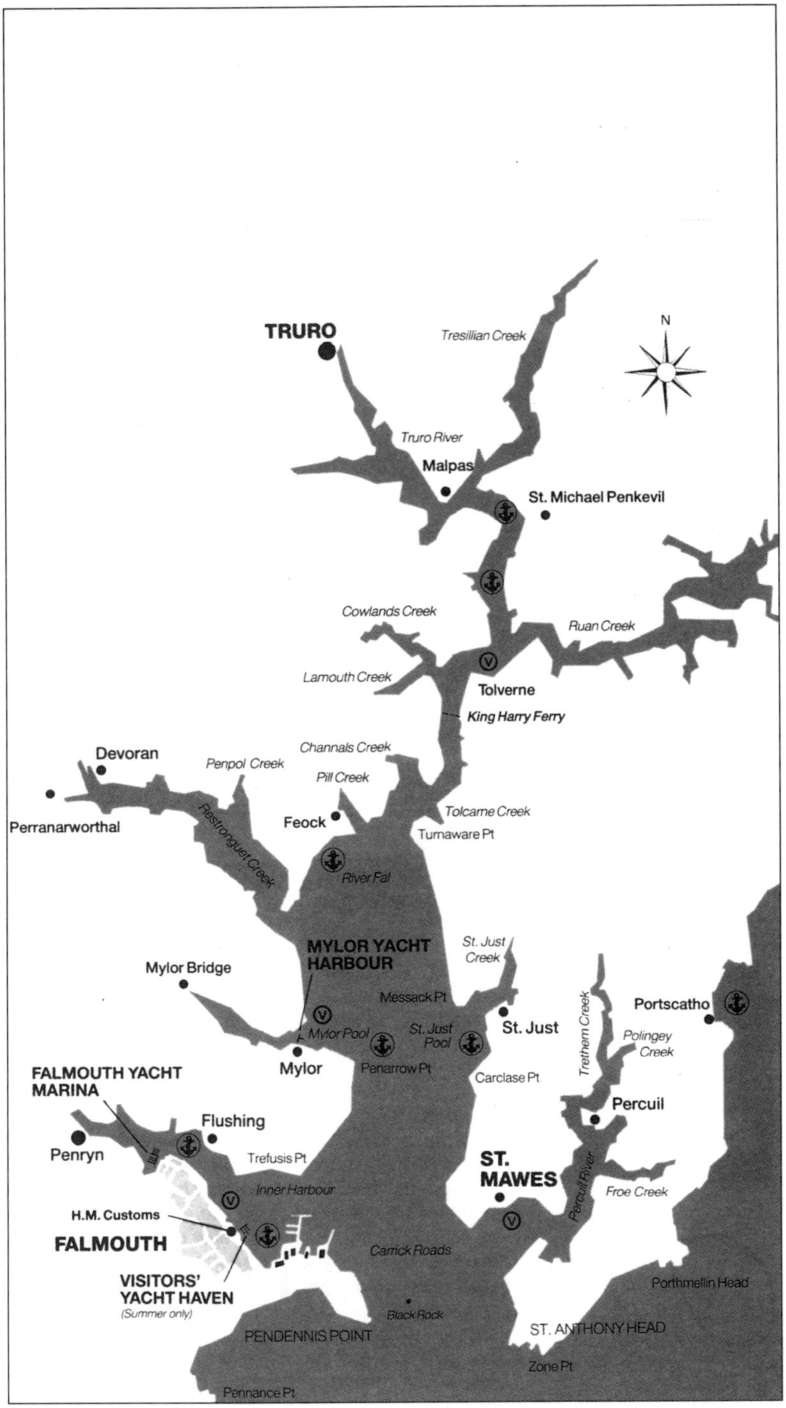

Telephone Code 0326

Customs ☎ 314156
Customs Launch Ch 16 14 12

Weather Posted Yacht Haven

Tourist Office ☎ 312300

Taxi ☎ 312181

Hire Cars ☎ 312192

Doctor ☎ 312143

Dentist ☎ 313310

Hospital ☎ 311841

Chemist Market Street

Post Office
By Town Hall, The Moor

Bank Church Street

Yacht Clubs
Royal Cornwall 312126
Mylor 74391
St. Mawes S, St. Mawes 270686
Flushing SC 74043
Restronguet SC 74536

Police ☎ 833438

Laundrette Marina

Shops/supermarkets
Market Street, Church Street, Gateway and good shopping area

Pubs/restaurants
Kings Head; Grape Inn, Restaurant 21, 21 Church St.; Secrets, 6 Arwenack St.; Amalfi, La Lucina, 25 Arwenack St.; Arwenack Street, Seafood Bar, Hornblowers, 2 Bank Place

Tourist attractions:
Pendennis Castle, Maritime Museum

FALMOUTH *****

Mooring fees:		Daily	Weekly
	Up to 6m LOA	£6	£30
At Yacht Haven over	60m up to 8.5m	£7	£35
	Over 8.5m up to 12m	£8	£40

Charge at moorings is less

YACHT HAVEN		
up to 8m	£3.50 daily	£17.50 weekly
8m to 12m	£5.50 daily	£27.50 weekly
over 12m	£8.50 daily	£42.50 weekly

surcharge 50% for multi-hulls

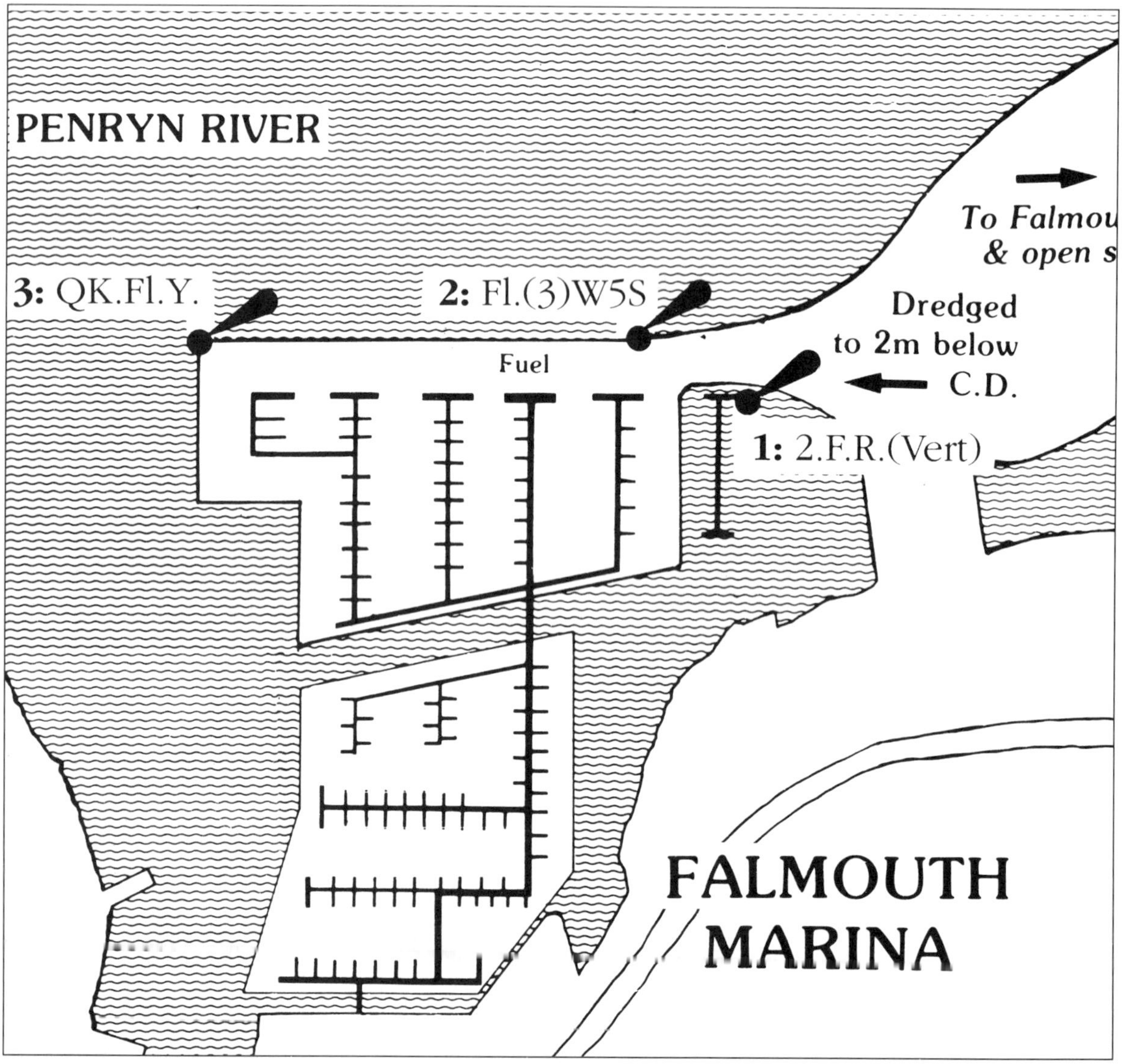

FALMOUTH YACHT MARINA

Mooring fees:

26ft. to 30ft.	£11 per day
31ft. to 35ft.	£12.50
36ft. to 40ft.	£13.50
41ft. to 43ft.	£14.50
Over 43ft.	40p per foot

MYLOR YACHT HARBOUR

up to 30ft.	£6 per night	£30 per week
over 30ft.	£7 per night	£35 per week

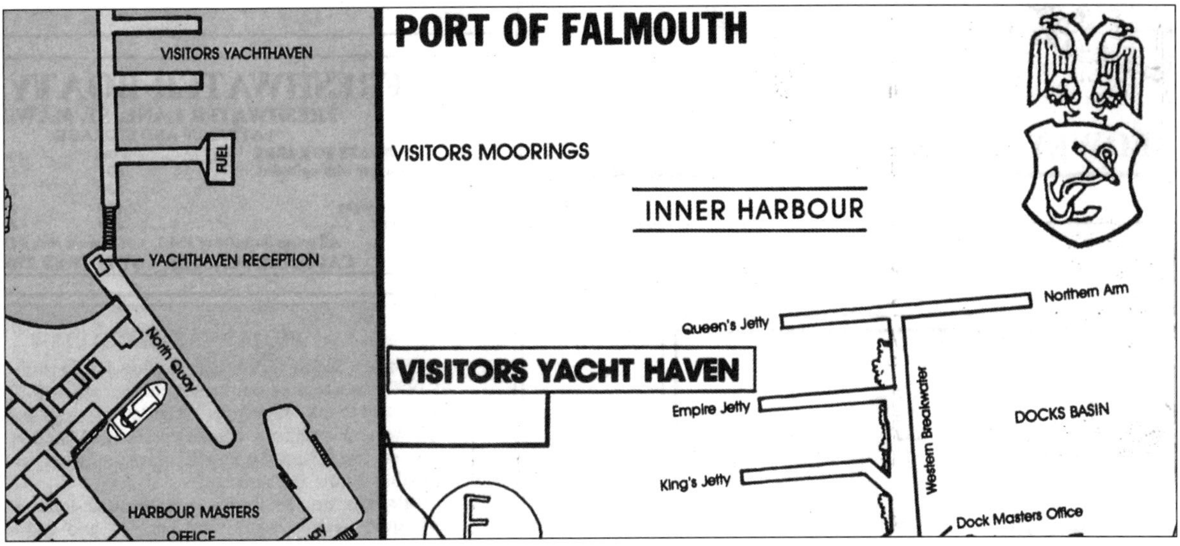

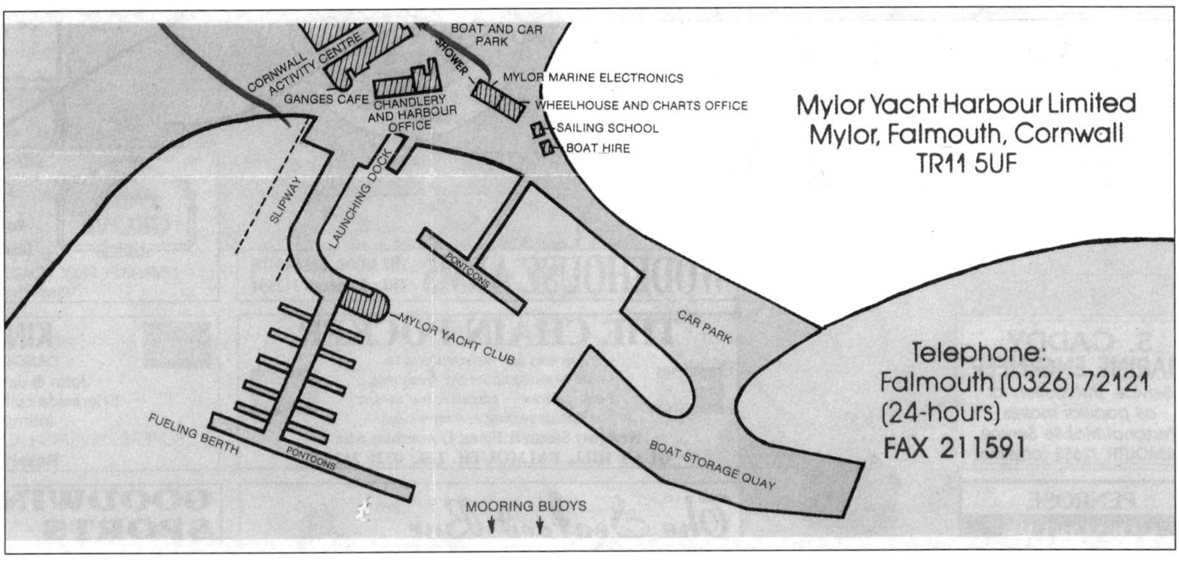

PENZANCE ☆☆☆☆☆

Standard Port
DEVONPORT

Harbour Entry
Lock in to wet dock entry 2h-HW-1h

HM 07415-66113

Lat: 50° 7' N **Long:** 5° 32' W

Admiralty charts 2345/777

Approach visual navigation aids: South Pier Head Iso W R 2s 9m. W round tower black base

R/T: VHF Ch 16; 09 12 (office hours and when lock operates) ☎ 66113

Yachting facilities: See below

Visitors moorings available: Normally lie alongside in the wet dock where 50 berths are made available. Outer harbour normally used by local craft

Distances: L'Aber-Wrac'h 98, Plymouth 70

DESCRIPTION: Penzance is a leisure harbour and from May to September is busy and interesting. The town is a holiday centre and as much a market town as a port so that it has a wide range of shops. The South Pier is the normal berth for the Scillonian, the Isles of Scilly ferry, although this berth is normally occupied only between 1830 and 0930 the following morning on Mondays to Friday, and additionally between 1130 and 1400 on summer Saturdays and all day Sundays. At other times this pier may be used by vessels waiting to enter the wet dock. There are no particular leading marks but the entrance between the pierheads is wide and you can land at any state of the tide at steps on the outer end of South Pier. Dangerous entrance in strong S-SE winds.

Mooring charges:
Daily 20p per foot, 3rd night free

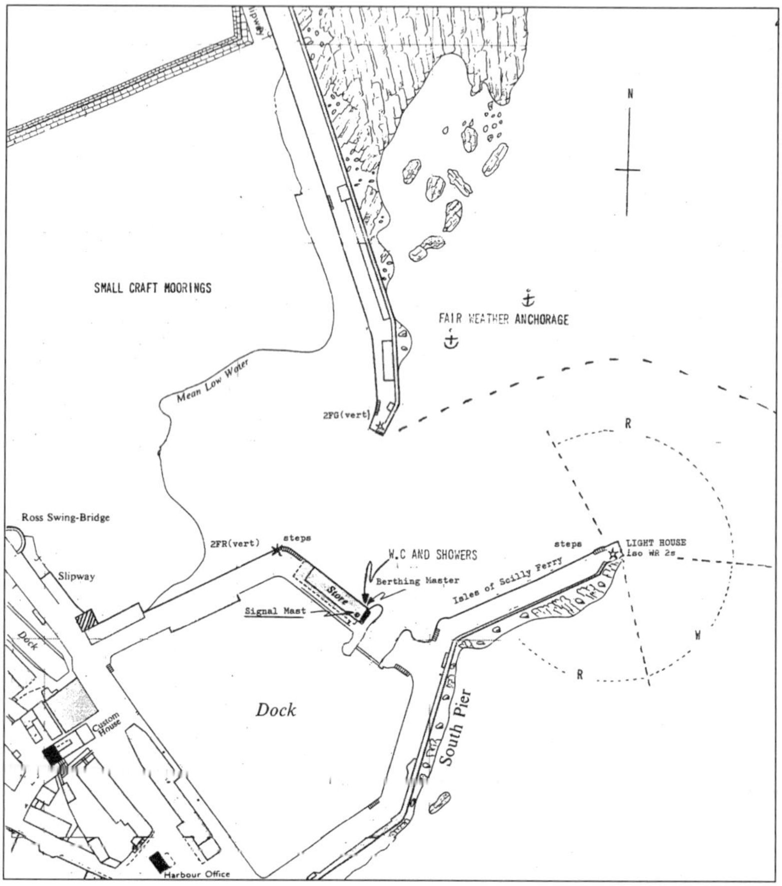

Available:
Water✓ Electric✓
Petrol Diesel 66113
Chandler 63838-64004

Repairs: Yacht
Engine 63838
Electrical 63838
Sail 64004

☆☆☆☆☆ PENZANCE

Telephone Code	0736
Customs	Quay Street
Weather	Harbour Office
Taxi	Albert Pier
Hire Cars	☎ 62980
Doctor	☎ 64946
Dentist	☎ 63866
Hospital	☎ 62382
Chemist	Market Jew Street
Post Office	Market Jew Street
Bank	Market Jew Street
Yacht Clubs	Penzance Sailing Club Mounts Bay SC
Police	☎ 62395
Laundrette	Near Railway Station

Shops/supermarkets
Nearby Market Jew Street, Causeway Head, Long Rock Supermarket

Pubs/restaurants
Viceroy 68413, Bosun's Locker, Dock Lane 66746; Harris's, 46 New Street; Lally's, Old Bakehouse Lane 63446; Dolphin Tavern, The Quay

Tourist attractions:
A trip to Land's End, St. Michael's Mount, Trinity House National Lighthouse Centre, Bird Hospital, Mousehole, Morrah Gardens, Barbara Hepworth Museum, Nautical Museum and Man O' War Display, Egyptian House in Chapel Street

Penzance Harbour

L'ABER-WRAC'H ☆☆☆☆☆

Standard Port
BREST

Harbour Entry
At all times

Cap 98.04.91.62

Lat: 48° 35' N **Long:** 04° 33'7 W

Admiralty charts 1432
SHOM 964/5772

Approach visual navigation aids:
Ldg Lts Ile Vrac'h Front Q R 7m W square tower O top.
100° Lanavon Rear Dir QW 12m W square tower O top

R/T: VHF Ch 9 16 (0700-2100)

Visitors moorings available: Some available out of the 80 pontoon berths. Pick up buoys at stern, moor bows to pontoon. Plus mooring buoys in river – water taxi included

Distances: St. Peter Port 100, Morlaix 45, Roscoff 34, St. Malo 114, Perros-Guirec 57

DESCRIPTION: Easily identified by reference to the 252ft. Vierge lighthouse, L'Aber-Wrac'h offers a sheltered anchorage available at all states of the tide. Regarded by many as no more than a temporary stop on passage between Ushant and the mainland. The coast west of Roscoff has a number of deep Abers, or estuaries and the yachting port of L'Aber-Wrac'h is the most attractive, a medium size resort with sandy beaches nearby. There are three approach channels, the principal approach being Grand Chenal which is navigable by day or night. Up river, Paluden offers a cheaper more sheltered berth.

Available:
Water✓ Electric✓ Showers
Laundrette Petrol Diesel✓
Chandler✓

Repairs:
Yacht✓ Engine✓
Electrical Sail

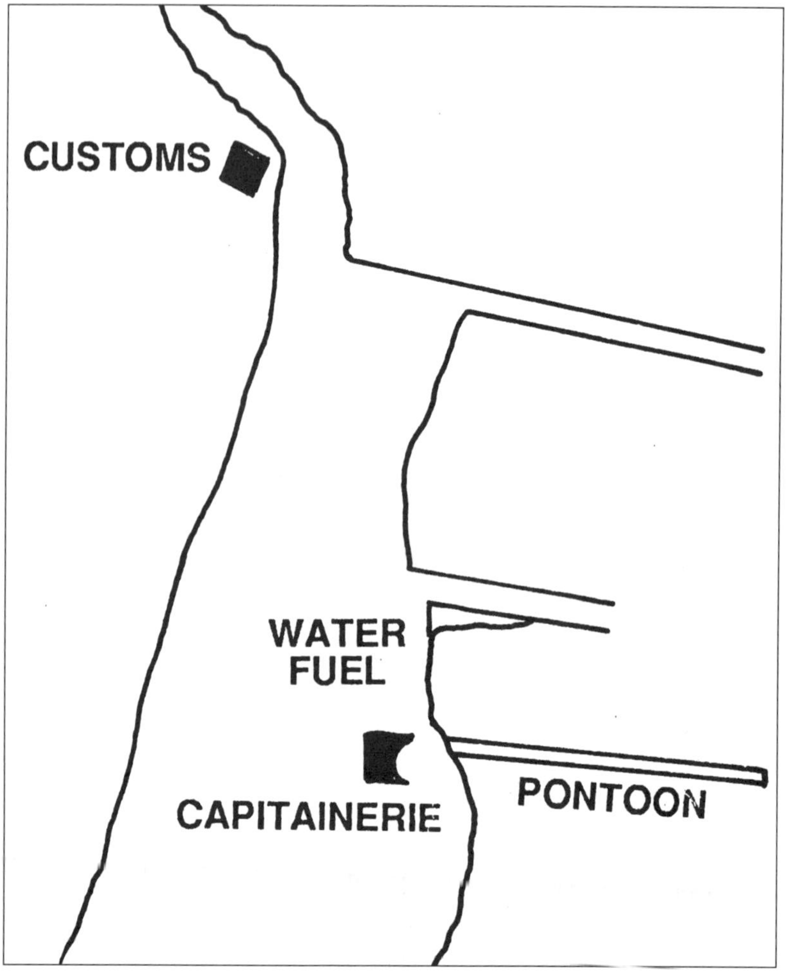

☆☆☆☆☆ L'ABER-WRAC'H

Telephone Code	98
Customs	☎ 98.04.90.27
Weather	☎ 98.84.60.64
Hospital	☎ 98.46.11.33
Yacht Clubs	des Aber

Police	☎ 96.04.00.18

Shops/supermarkets
Few nearby, but mostly at Landeda, 2kms away. There are no shore-side attractions but the yacht club makes visiting yachts welcome.

Pubs/Restaurants
Le Relais de l'Aber (7 menus 48-100F weekdays, 5 menus 87-140F weekends); L'Escale (2 menus 60 and 120F)

L'Aber-Wrac'h Harbour

ROSCOFF ☆☆☆

Standard Port
BREST

Harbour Entry
Harbour dries. Inner and outer harbour. Access 2h-HW-2h

Cap 98.69.76.37

Lat: 48° 43' N **Long:** 3° 59' W

Admiralty charts 2745
SHOM 5827, 5828

Approach visual navigation aids:
Ldg Lts Mole Nord Front Oc (2 + 1) G 12s 7m W col G top 209° rear Oc (2 + 1) W 12s 15m G Sq tower W NE side

R/T: VHF Ch 9 16 (0700-1100/1300-2200)

Yachting facilities: See below

Visitors moorings available: 40 berths out of 350 in harbour. The ferry terminal is at Bloscon

Distances: Morlaix 12, Perros-Guirec 25, St. Malo 82, Lezardrieux 46

DESCRIPTION: Roscoff is a small resort, a town of flowers and gardens yet with a trading reputation that was flourishing in the 16th century. Roscoff enjoys a mild climate. You are not allowed to enter the ferry harbour at Bloscon without permission. Berthing is not allowed at the Jetée de Pen-Ar-Vil which is used for landing purposes. Approach to Roscoff is well-marked but it is advisable to do so at high tide in view of the large rocks in the area. Local knowledge would be an advantage. Visitors' buoys, anchor, or find space alongside.

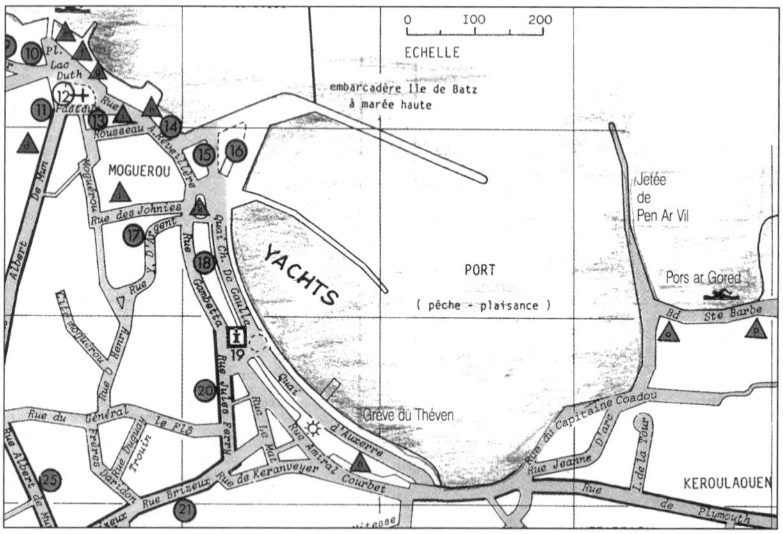

Vieux Port Available:
Water✓ Electric✓ Showers
Laundrette Petrol/Diesel available
Chandler

Repairs:
Yacht✓ Engine✓ Electrical
Sail

KEY

1, Rest Centre; 2, Institute Sea Water Therapy; 3, First Aid Station; 11, Library; 12, Church; 13, Town Hall; 18, Post Office; 23, Railway Station

Roscoff at low water

☆☆☆ ROSCOFF

Telephone Code	98
Customs	☎ 98.61.27.86
Weather	Meteo 98.84.60.64
Tourist Office	☎ 98.69.70.70
Taxi	☎ 98.69.70.69
Hire Cars	☎ 98.69.70.69
Doctor	☎ 98.69.78.04/98.69.71.18
Dentist	☎ 98.61.24.85/98.69.71.14
Hospital	☎ 98.88.40.22
Chemist	Rue Amiral Réveillère
Post Office	Rue Gambetta
Bank	Rue Louis Pásteur
Yacht Clubs	Club Nautique de Roscoff 98.69.72.79
Police	☎ 98.69.00.48

Shops/supermarkets
Nearby

Pubs/restaurants
Le Temps de Vivre, Place de l'Eglise (4 menus 98 and 140-210F); Le Bellevue, Rue Jeanne D'Arc; Le Regina, Rue Ropartz-Morvan; Le Brittany, Bd. Sainte Barbe; Le Gulf Stream, Rosko-Coz

Tourist attractions:
Le Musée Militaire, Aquarium

Roscoff Harbour and Bloscon ferry terminal, bottom right

MORLAIX ☆☆☆☆☆

Standard Port
BREST

Harbour Entry
6 miles up Morlaix River Lock opens hours of daylight 1½-HW-1h

Cap 98.62.13.14

Lat: 48° 35' N **Long:** 03° 50' W

Admiralty charts 2744/2644/2745
SHOM 5827/5950

Approach visual navigation aids:
Ldg Lts Ile Noire Front Oc (2) WRG 6s W 11m W Sq tower R top
190° La Laude Rear Fl W 5s 23m W Sq. tower B top

R/T: VHF Ch 09/16

Yachting facilities: See below

Visitors moorings available: 30 moorings, 200 berth marina

Distances: L'Aber-Wrac'h 45, Treguier 45, Roscoff 12, Perros-Guirec 30, St. Malo 88

DESCRIPTION: An old town and port, with old stone houses climbing up the hill and a pink viaduct above the town centre carrying trains to and from Paris. There are medieval houses in the old town. It is worth the fairly lengthy approach up to the harbour – daytime only – because Morlaix is an attractive place. There are good train connections to the ferry port of Roscoff. This is a safe marina berth to change crews or to leave the boat for any length of time.

Available: Water✓ Electric✓
Showers Laundrette
Petrol/Diesel Yacht Club 98.62.13.14
Chandler 98.72.32.76

Repairs:
Yacht 98.88.13.54
Engine 98.88.13.54
Electrical 98.88.13.54 Sail

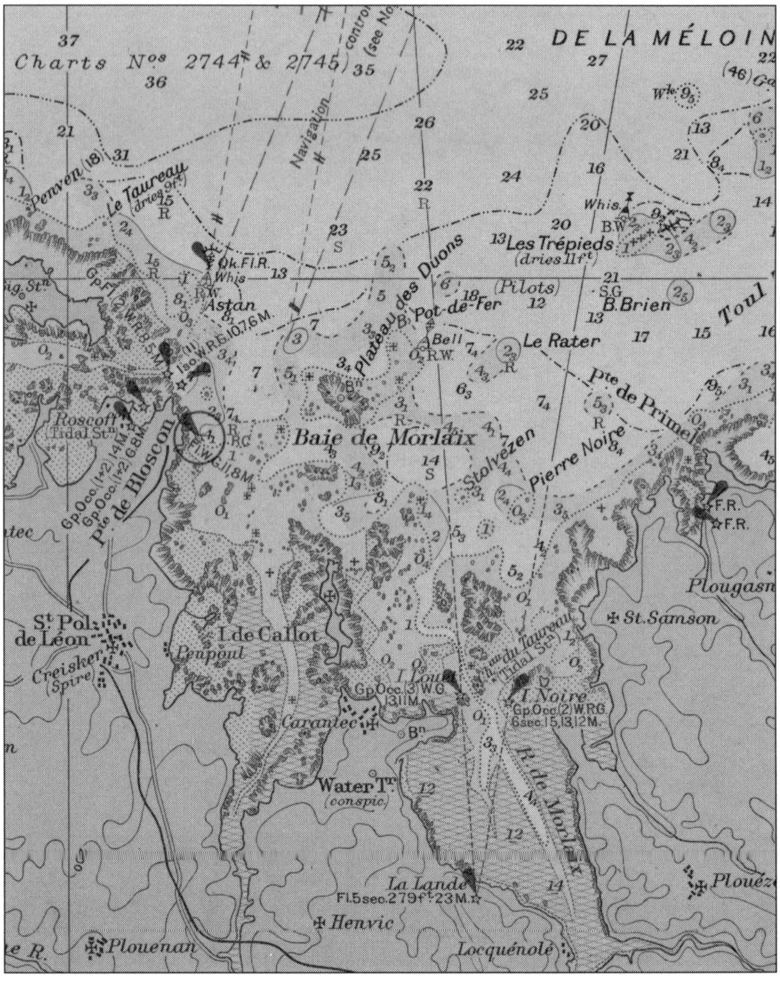

☆☆☆☆☆ MORLAIX

Telephone Code	98
Customs	Quai de Lion 98.62.10.22
Weather	Meteo 98.84.60.64
Tourist Office	☎ 98.88.17.61
Taxi	☎ 98.88.08.32
Hire Cars	Europcar 98.62.11.94
Doctor	☎ 96.72.58.33
Dentist	☎ 98.88.08.15/98.88.44.27
Hospital	☎ 98.62.61.60
Chemist	Place General de Gaulle
Post Office	Rue de Brest
Bank	Place General de Gaulle
Yacht Clubs	de Morlaix Morlaisien
Police	☎ 98.88.58.13
Laundrette	Marina

Shops/supermarkets
Town nearby

Pubs/restaurants
La Gavotte, Rte de Morlaix 98.78.63.65; La Marée Bleue, 3 Rampe St. Mélaine 98.63.24.21; El Marisco, 15 Rue Auge de Guernisac 98.88.70.99; La Table de Rabelais, 9 Rue Au Fil 98.88.83.73; La Cigale, Place de Viarmes 98.88.00.49

Tourist attractions:
Town Museum, Brewery, Royal Tobacco Factory

Looking up towards the Marina – the viaduct carries the railway

PERROS-GUIREC ****

Standard Port
ST. HELIER

Harbour Entry
Lock in 1h-HW-1h

Cap 96.23.37.82

Lat: 48° 48' N **Long:** 03° 26' W

Admiralty charts 3672/2668
SHOM 967, 974

Approach visual navigation aids:
Ldg Lts Le Colombier Front Dir Oc (4) W 12s 18m W house
224° Kerprigent Rear Dir QW 22m W tower

R/T: VHF Ch 9; 16

Yachting facilities: See below

Visitors moorings available: 60 places reserved in 800 berth harbour. Dries in offing. Other moorings available at Ploumanac'h

Distances: St. Peter Port 54, Lezardrieux 27, L'Aber-Wrac'h 57, Morlaix 30, St. Malo 63

DESCRIPTION: It is quite an uphill climb to the old town, but all the buses seem to congregate around the harbour. Perros is a popular holiday resort, probably the most popular along the coast, with fine beaches and a selection of holiday attractions, although families with children seem to prefer Ploumanac'h. They pour from the forty hotels to the Trestriguel and Trestraou beaches, the latter being the best and on the opposite side of the town to the port. Perros-Guirec lies in the south-east corner of the Anse de Perros, to which there are two approaches, passing either east or west of Ile Tomé.

Available:
Water✓ Electric✓ Showers
Laundrette✓ Petrol✓ Diesel✓
Chandler 96.91.11.88

Repairs:
Yacht✓ Engine✓ Electrical✓
Sail✓

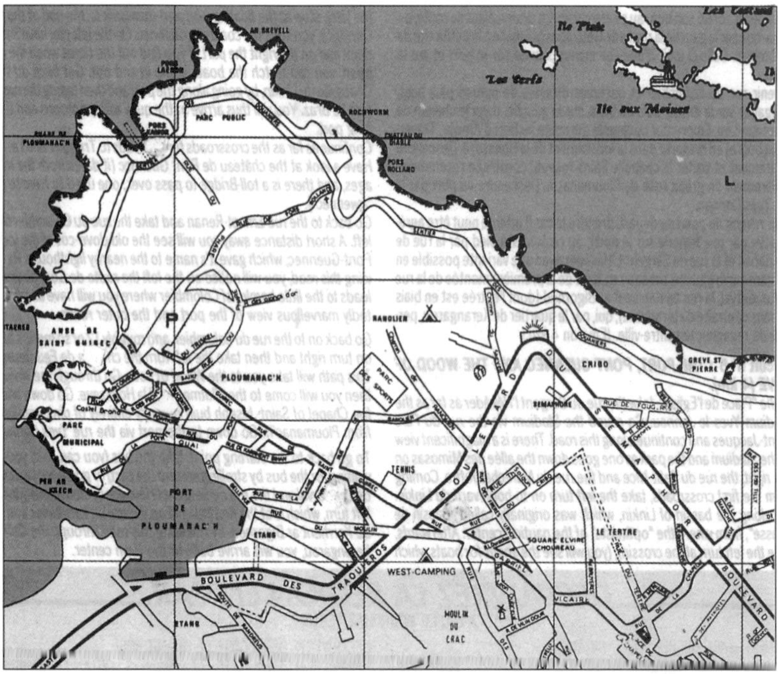

Mooring fees	per day	per week	per month
5m to 8m	54F to 64F	280F to 320F	1120F to 1280F
8m50 to 11m50	64F to 88F	320F to 440F	1280F to 1760F
12m to 15m	96F to 120F	480F to 600F	1920F to 2400F

☆☆☆☆ PERROS-GUIREC

Telephone Code	96
Customs	☎ 96.23.18.12
Weather	Meteo
Tourist Office	☎ 96.23.21.15 21 Place de l'Hotel de Ville
Taxi	☎ 96.26.20.35
Hire Cars	Europcar 96.23.20.35 Henry 96.91.03.33
Doctor	☎ 96.23.20.01
Dentist	☎ 96.23.23.94
Hospital	☎ 96.37.06.03
Chemist	96.37.43.05
Post Office	Rue Anatole le Braz
Bank	Rue de Landerval
Yacht Clubs	Societé Nautique de Perros-Guirec
Police	☎ 96.23.22.64
Laundrette	Rue Anatole le Braz

Shops/supermarkets
Some nearby, also at Perros, a 20 minute uphill walk away

Pubs/restaurants
Au Bon Accueil, Rue de Landerval 96.23.24.11; Le Levant, Rue Ernest Renau 96.23.20.15 (8 menus 65-190F); Le Suroit, Rue Ernest Renau 96.23.23.83 (2 menus 89-140F); Les Huniers, Rue Anatole Le Braz 96.23.34.13; Les Sept-Iles, Plage de Trestraou

Tourist attractions:
Casino, the island bird sanctuary of Sept-Iles, fine beaches

Perros-Guirec Harbour

TREGUIER ☆☆☆☆

Standard Port
ST. HELIER

Harbour Entry
6 miles up Treguier River, access at all times

Cap 96.92.42.37

Lat: 48° 47' N **Long:** 3° 14' W

Admiralty charts 2668/3672/972/967
SHOM 972/973

Approach visual navigation aids:
Ldg Lts (Grand) Port de la Chaine Front Oc W 4s 12m W house
137° (Passe) Sainte-Antoine Rear Dir Oc R 4s 15m R & W house

R/T: Ch 9

Yachting facilities: See below

Visitors moorings available: Over 100 berths in this 350-berth marina (take care to approach berth against the stream unless at slack water. Leave with care!)

Distances: L'Aber-Wrac'h 92, St. Malo 53

DESCRIPTION: A charming town, with cathedral square and half-timbered houses. The Riviére de Treguier is well marked on each side by buoys, leading up to Treguier. Anchoring in the river is allowed. The marina of Treguier is situated at the confluence of the rivers Jeudy and Guindy. Treguier is one of the few hill towns in Brittany and its most important feature is the Cathédrale de St. Tugdual, containing the tomb of St. Yves, patron saint of lawyers.

Available:
Water✓ Electric✓ Showers
Laundrette Petrol 96.92.30.52
Diesel Chandler✓

Repairs:
Yacht Engine✓ Electrical
Sail

Mooring charges (including showers)
Daily

7m 50 to 8m 49	60F
8m 50 to 9m 49	65F
9m 50 to 11m 99	70F
11m to 11m 99	75F

Yacht harbour and cathedral

☆☆☆☆ TREGUIER

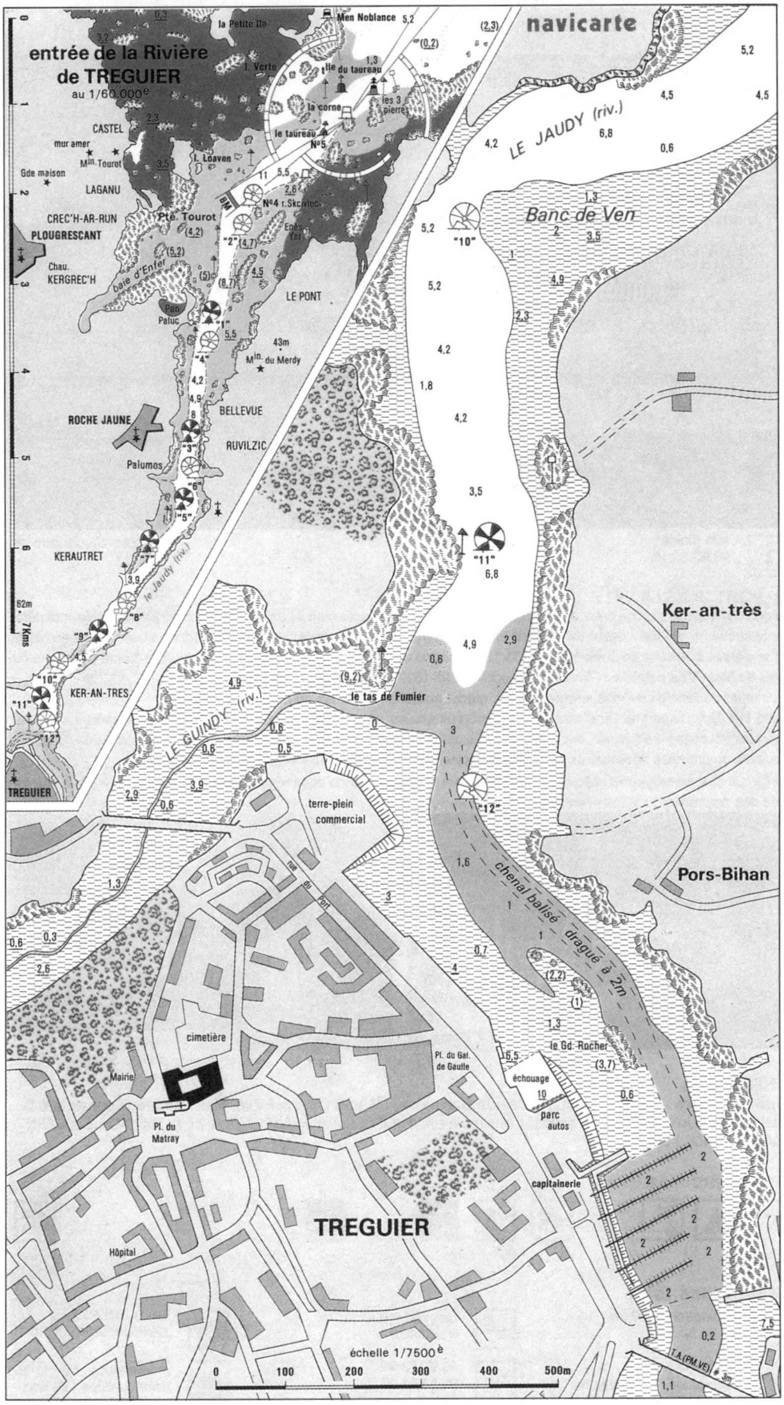

Telephone Code	96
Tourist Office Hotel de Ville 96.92.30.19	
Taxi	☎ 96.92.23.95
Doctor	☎ 96.92.31.35
Hospital	☎ 96.92.30.72
Chemist	☎ 96.92.30.17
Post Office	Rue St. André
Yacht Clubs Club Nautique du Tregor 96.92.42.37	
Police	☎ 96.92.30.38

Shops/supermarkets

Fifteen minutes uphill walk to the town where plenty of shops are of interest

Pubs/restaurants

Hotel de l'Estuaire on the quay 96.92.30.25 (3 menus 59-100F weekdays; Sunday 170F); Le Saint-Bernard opp. the port 96.92.20.77 (41F lunch, 4 menus 75-140F); Au petit Savoyard, 12 Rue le Peltier

Tourist attractions:

Cathédrale de St. Tugdual, Wednesday market

LEZARDRIEUX and PONTRIEUX ☆☆☆☆

Standard Port
ST. HELIER

Harbour Entry
On the W bank of River Trieux access at all times

Cap 96.20.14.22

Lat: 48° 47' N **Long:** 03° 05' W

Admiralty charts 3673/2668
SHOM 832/2845

Approach visual navigation aids:
Ldg Lts La Creix Front Oc W 4s 19m 2 G round tower
225° Bodic Rear Dir QW 22m W house G gable

R/T: Ch 09 (0800-2000 July/Aug)

Yachting facilities: See below

Visitors moorings available: In Marina (96.20.14.22) preferred to visitors' buoys in river, also 11km up the Trieux River to Pontrieux. 50 places for visitors in 400-berth harbour

Distances: St. Peter Port 48, Treguier 23, Perros 27, St. Helier 46, St. Malo 46, Morlaix 54

DESCRIPTION: The town is about ten minutes away up the hill. There are not many shops but there is a supermarket.
Up river from Lezardrieux is an interesting experience, but to what extent you will be able to notice the beauty of the scenery, the chateau, etc. will depend upon the draft of your vessel and your judgement of the state of the tide. However you get there it is worth visiting Pontrieux.
Lezardrieux is a popular port of call and you find many other visitors in its yacht club and in the modest grocery stores. Not all venture up the river.

Pontrieux: Capitainerie 96.95.60.72. Lock (Ecluse de Pontrieux) 96.95.60.70. Access 1½h-HW-1h. 40 alongside places for visitors in 200-berth harbour. HW Pontrieux is approximately the same as for St. Malo.

Available:

Water✓	Electric✓	Showers
Laundrette	Petrol✓	Diesel✓
Chandler✓		

Repairs:

Yacht✓	Engine✓
Electrical✓	Sail✓

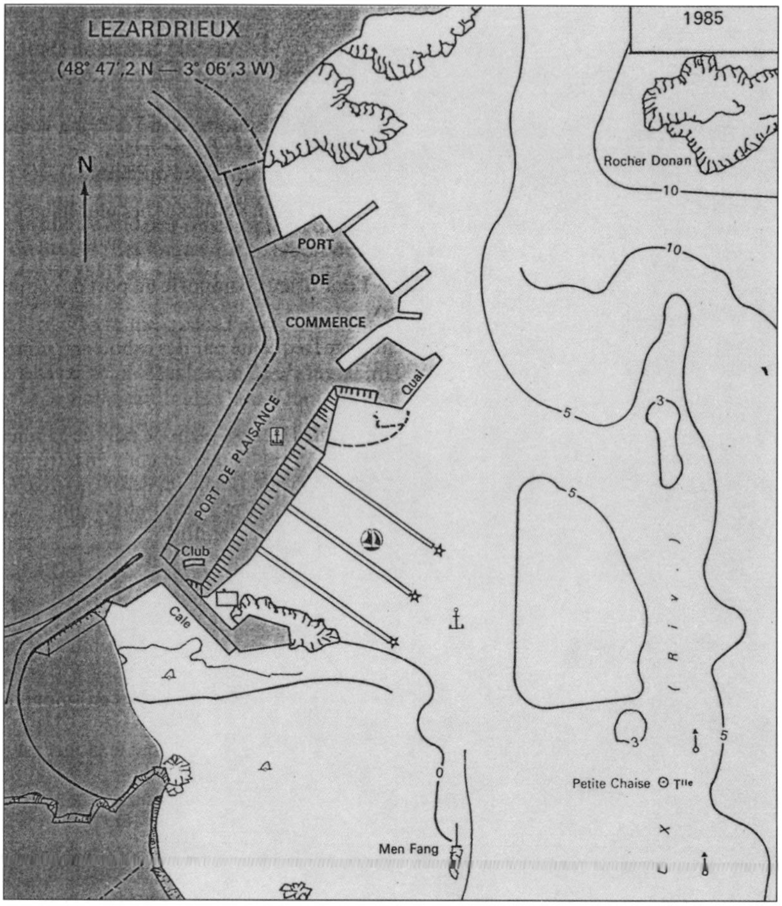

"Extrait des I.N. C. 21 (ou C. 22) du SHOM, reproduit avec son aimable autorisation"

☆☆☆☆ LEZARDRIEUX and PONTRIEUX

Telephone Code	96	**Hospital**	Paimpol	**Pubs/restaurants** Restaurant de Trieux, Relais Brenner, Pont de Lezardrieux **Pontrieux:** Moulin le Richel; Restaurant Jaqueline; le Bail Marcel
Weather	Bureau du Port	**Yacht Clubs**	de Trieux	
Tourist Office	☎ 96.20.10.20	**Laundrette**	Paimpol	**Tourist attractions:** Casino, the island bird santuary of Sept-Iles, fine beaches
Taxi	☎ 96.20.19.50	**Shops/supermarkets** Few stores		
Hire Cars	☎ 96.20.19.50			

Pontrieux

The "Pink Bridge" Pontrieux showing un-navigable river Trieux

PAIMPOL ☆☆☆

Standard Port
ST. HELIER

Harbour Entry
Through the lock (opens 1½h-HW Springs; 1h-HW Neaps) straight ahead to No. 2 Basin (outer harbour dries)

Cap 96.20.80.77

Lat: 48° 47' N **Long:** 3° 03' W

Admiralty charts 2557/2668/3673 SHOM 832, 3670

Approach visual navigation aids:
Ldg Lts Jetée de Kernoa Front F R 7m W & R hut
264° Rear Dir F R 14m W pylon R top

R/T: VHF Ch 09 (0800-1200 and when lock operates)

Yachting facilities: See below

Visitors moorings available: Visiting yachts are met and directed to berth 96.20.47.65. About 10 in 260 berth marina

Distances: St. Malo 42, Perros-Guirec 37

DESCRIPTION: A pleasant holiday town with shops and restaurants around an attractive square. Once an important fishing centre but now given over to tourism. You will see from your chart that the Anse de Paimpol largely dries and it is possible to be aground on the mud banks. Also, there are numerous rocks at the approach to the Anse de Paimpol. Paimpol Harbour is situated at the west end of the bay. Quays and houses surround you as you lie at your berth and you step ashore into a lively little town with everything you need.

Mooring fees	per day	per week	per month
up to 10m99	40F to 70F	200F to 350F	450F to 787F
11m to 15m99	75F to 95F	375 to 475F	844F to 1069F
16m to 20m	100F to 150F	500F to 750F	1125F to 1687F

Available:
Water✓ Electric Showers Laundrette Petrol✓ Diesel✓ Chandler✓

Repairs: Yacht 96.20.82.00/96.20.85.18 Engine 96.20.82.00/96.20.85.18 Electrical✓ Sail

Paimpol Yacht Marina

☆☆☆ PAIMPOL

Telephone Code	96
Customs	☎ 96.20.81.87
Weather	☎ 96.20.01.92
Tourist Office	☎ 96.20.83.16 Rond Point du Goelo
Taxi	☎ 96.20.83.87
Hire Cars	Europcar 96.20.73.15 Hertz 96.20.80.55
Doctor	☎ 96.20.80.32
Dentist	☎ 96.20.81.98
Hospital	☎ 96.20.80.02
Chemist	Place du Martray
Post Office	Av. General de Gaulle
Bank	Place du Martray
Yacht Clubs	Centre Nautique des Glenans
Police	☎ 96.20.80.17

Shops/supermarkets
Intermarche, shops and facilities nearby. Mammouth hypermarche, Route de Saint-Brieuc

Pubs/restaurants
L'Escale, Quai Morand; La Cotriade, Vielle Tour; de Kerroc'h, Quai Morand; La Vieille Tour, 13 Rue d l'Eglise 96.20.83.18

Tourist attractions:
Maritime museum

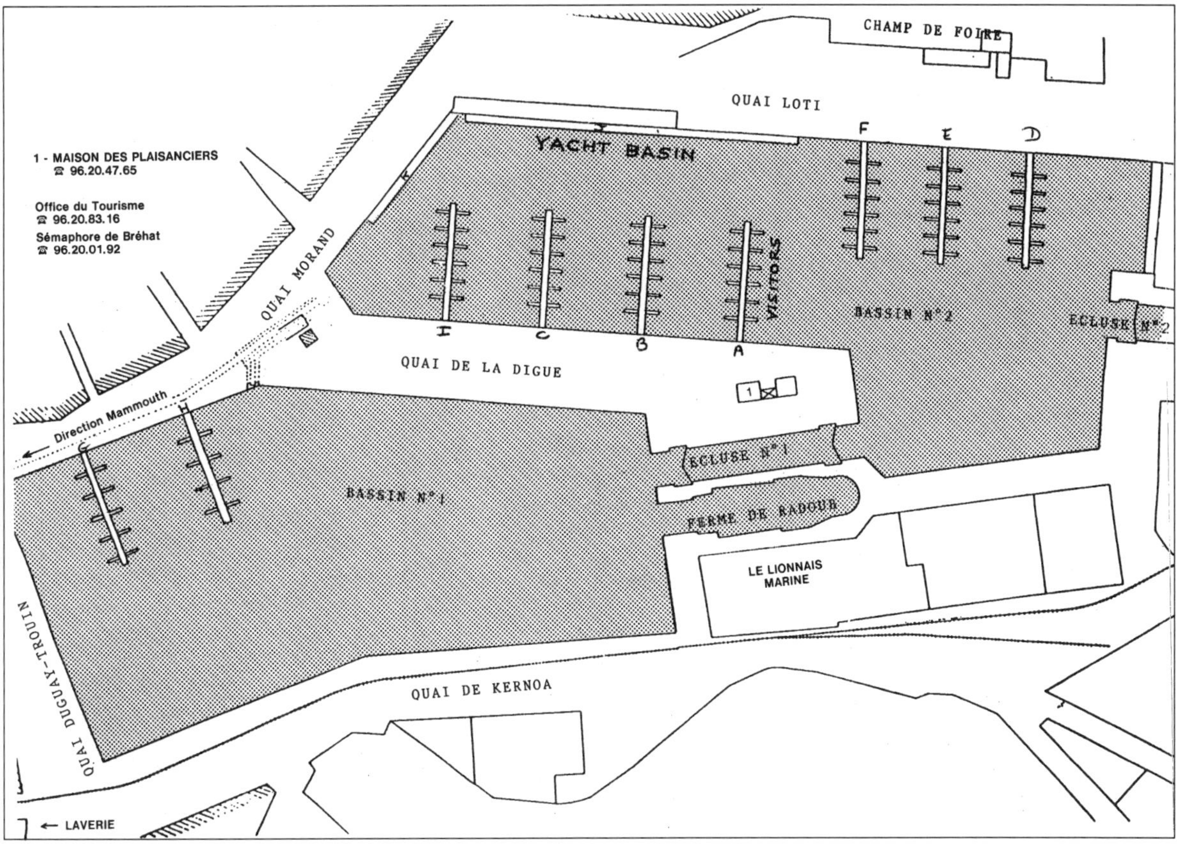

ST. QUAY PORTRIEUX ☆☆☆☆☆

Standard Port
ST. HELIER

Harbour Entry
Access to new marina at all times, old harbour dries

Cap 96.70.95.31

Lat: 48° 39' N **Long:** 2° 50' W

Admiralty charts 3672/3674/2668/2669
SHOM 833/5725

Approach visual navigation aids: Ile Harbour, Roches de Saint-Quay Oc (2) W R G 6s 16m W tower R top

R/T: VHF Ch 9

Yachting facilities: See below

Visitors moorings available: 10 berths in this 450-berth port

Distances: St. Malo 35, Paimpol 16, Dahouet 11, Granville 54, Needles 132, St. Brieuc 20

DESCRIPTION: St. Quay a little to the north always seemed to be slightly superior to its sister Portrieux but now there is the fine new harbour of Saint-Quay Portrieux and the place is known by that name. What was a fishing port has given way to tourism. Facilities are being installed in this new harbour. Berths subject to swell SE-N.

Available:
Water✓ Electric✓ Showers
Laundrette Petrol✓ Diesel✓
Chandler✓

Repairs:
Yacht✓ Engine✓
Electrical 96.70.57.83 Sail

Berthing charges

	7m	8m	10m	12m
per day	85	115	150	190
per week	510	690	900	1140

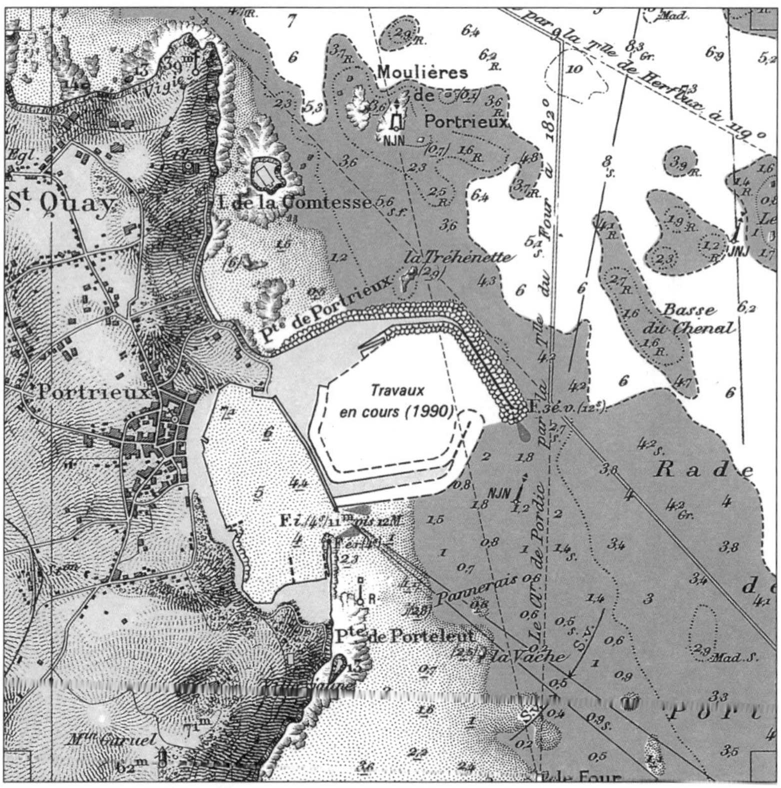

(Before completion of marina)

"Extrait des I.N. C. 21 (ou C. 22) du SHOM, reproduit avec son aimable autorisation"

☆☆☆☆☆ ST. QUAY PORTRIEUX

Telephone Code	96
Customs	☎ 96.33.13.83
Weather	Meteo 99.46.10.46
Tourist Office	☎ 96.70.40.64 rue Jeanne d'Arc
Taxi	☎ 96.70.59.46/96.70.55.37
Hire Cars	☎ 96.70.40.64
Doctor	☎ 96.70.57.89/96/70.41.31
Chemist	Boulevard Foch
Bank	Quai de la Replublique
Yacht Clubs	du Nouveau Port de Saint-Quay Portrieux
Laundrette	Rue Clemenceau

Shops/supermarkets
Nearby

Pubs/restaurants
Hotel le Ker Moor, 13 Rue Président le Sénécal; La Bieuvenue, 2 Place du Centre; Hotel le Gerbot d'Avoine, 2 Bd. du Littoral; Le Mouton Blanc, 52 Quai de la Republique (2 menus 98 and 140F); Bellec-Le Rigoleur, 58 Bd Foch

Tourist attractions:
Casino

Saint Quay Nouveau Port

BINIC ☆☆☆☆

Standard Port
ST. HELIER

Harbour Entry
Lock in to Bassin a flot when tide reaches 9.5m above datum. Entry to Port de Penthievre at 3h-HW-3h (but not near Neaps). Dries in the offing

Capitainerie 96.73.61.86

Lat: 48° 36' N **Long:** 02° 49' W

Admiralty charts 2668/2669/3674
SHOM 833/5725

Approach visual navigation aids: Môle de Penthievre Head Oc (3) W 12s 12m W tower G gallery

R/T: VHF Ch 9

Yachting facilities: See below

Visitors moorings available: 60 berths reserved for visitors in this 600-berth marina

Distances: Paimpol 21, St. Brieuc 9, St. Malo 33, St. Peter Port 54, St. Helier 45

DESCRIPTION: Quite a small town with a narrow port, one time an important fishing harbour, but now, with a large marina, of greatest interest to yachtsmen. Around the town is a mini-promenade and tourists are attracted to the sandy beach. There is not a great deal to Binic itself apart from a few streets around the quayside. The Avant Port, or Port de Penthievre, dries but there are good berths. The Bassin á Flot is entered over a sill. It is a large marina for a small holiday resort.

Available:
Water✓ Electric Showers
Laundrette Petrol Diesel
Chandler 96.73.75.28/96.73.60.55

Repairs:
Yacht 96.73.75.28
Engine 96.73.75.28
Electrical 96.73.75.28 Sail

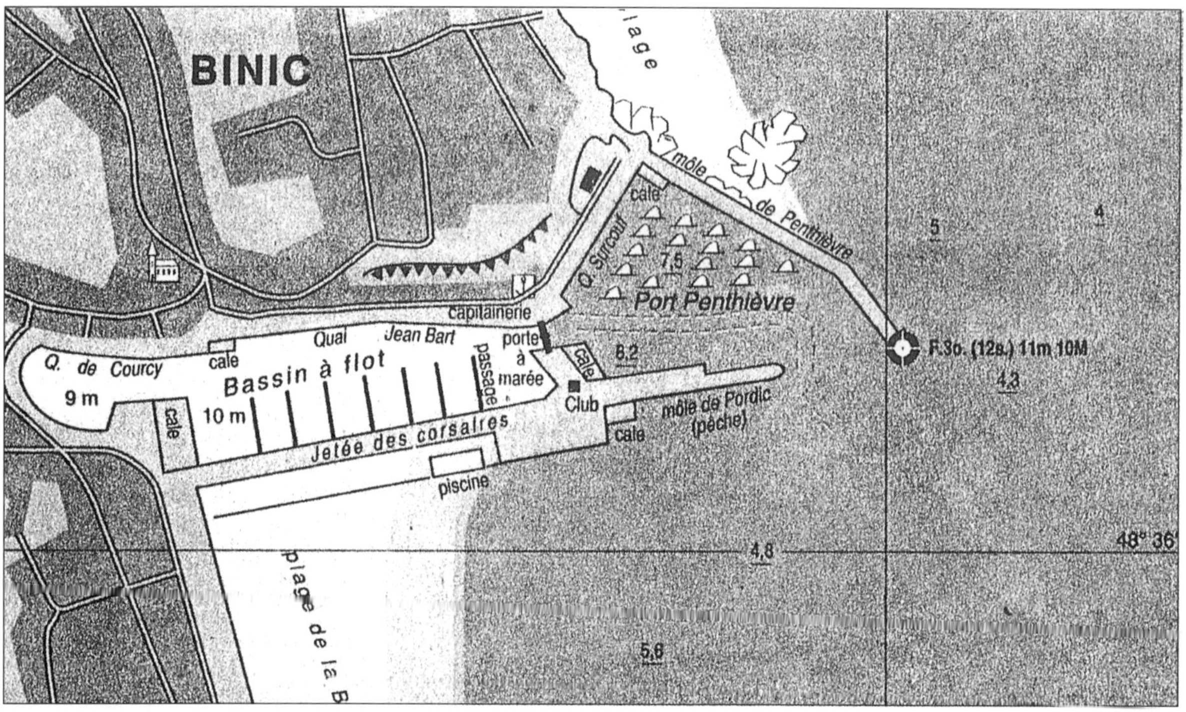

☆☆☆☆ BINIC

Telephone Code	96
Customs	Le Legue 22190
Weather	Bureau du Port
Tourist Office	☎ 96.73.60.12
Taxi	☎ 96.73.66.91
Hire Cars	☎ 96.33.37.71
Doctor	☎ 96.23.20.01
Dentist	☎ 96.70.68.09
Yacht Clubs	Club Nautique de Binic 96.61.93.55
Police	☎ 96.61.22.61

Shops/supermarkets
In quayside street

Pubs/restaurants
L'Auberge des Prés-Calans (4 menus 100-175F, 78F during week); Printania; La Mascotte, Quai de Courcy 96.73.30.77; Le Galion, 4 Ave Foch; Le Neptune, Place de l'Eglise

Tourist attractions:
Pleasant beach

Mooring charges:

	7m to 8m99	9m to 9m99	10m to 20m per metre
Day	48F	60F	6F
Week	245F	300F	30F

The harbour at Binic

DINARD ☆☆☆☆

Standard Port
ST. HELIER

Harbour Entry
Yacht anchorage exposed
Port Public de Plaisance

Cap 99.46.65.55

Lat: 48° 36' N **Long:** 02° 03' W

Admiralty charts 2669/2700
SHOM 844, 5645

Approach visual navigation aids: Mole Oc G 4s 6 m W col G top

R/T: VHF Ch 9

Yachting facilities: See below

Visitors moorings available: Either Bassin a Flot where there are a total of 160 moorings or at anchorage where there are a total of 250

Distances: Portsmouth 150, Paimpol 42, Jersey 41

DESCRIPTION: Once one of the most fashionable resorts in Europe and still a fine seaside resort with splendid beaches and promenade along the seafront. The villas remain, of course, and the gardens with their Mediterranean atmosphere. The yachting rivalry that has existed between Dinard and its neighbour St. Malo, on the other side of the Rance seems to have been determined in favour of St. Malo but Dinard attracts the tourist; in summer its beautiful beaches have few spare inches available. An enjoyable walk is up from the estuary beach on the Promenade du Clais du Lune which takes you over the harbour. Ferries run to and from St. Malo.

Available:

Water✓	Electric	Showers
Laundrette	Petrol✓	Diesel✓

Chandler 99.46.22.49

Repairs:
Yacht Engine 99.46.22.49
Electrical 99.46.22.49 Sail

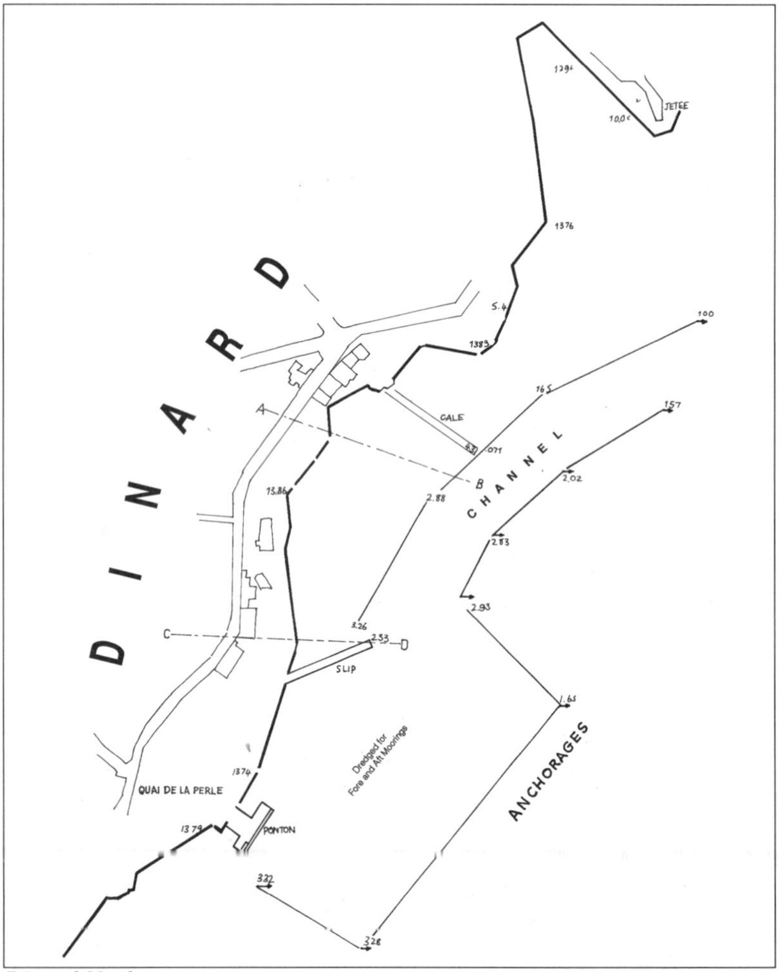

Dinard Harbour

☆☆☆☆ DINARD

Telephone Code	96
Customs	☎ 96.23.18.12
Weather	Meteo
Tourist Office	☎ 96.23.21.15 21 Place de l'Hotel de Ville
Taxi	☎ 96.26.20.35
Hire Cars	Europcar 96.23.20.35 Henry 96.91.03.33
Doctor	☎ 96.23.20.01
Dentist	☎ 96.23.23.94
Hospital	☎ 96.37.06.03
Chemist	96.37.43.05
Post Office	Rue Anatole le Braz
Bank	Rue de Landeaval
Yacht Clubs	Societé Nautique de Perros-Guirec
Police	☎ 96.23.22.64
Laundrette	Rue Anatole le Braz

Shops/supermarkets
Some nearby, also at Perros, a 20 minute uphill walk away

Pubs/restaurants
Les Bains, 38 Ave George V; La Coquille, 4 Rue Georges-Clemenceau; La Guais, La Basse-Guais; La Paix, 6 Place de la Republique

Tourist attractions:
Casino, the island bird santuary of Sept-Iles, fine beaches

Dinard Port

ST. MALO ☆☆☆☆☆

Standard Port
ST. HELIER

Harbour Entry
(See right)

Cap 99.81.62.86

Lat: 48° 39' N **Long:** 2° 01' W

Admiralty charts 2700/2669
SHOM 844, 5645

Approach visual navigation aids:
Ldg Lts Le Grand Jardin S Front Fl (2) R 10s 15m G tower R top 089° Rear Dir FR 24m G sq tower R top

R/T: Port Vauban Ch 09; St. Servan (Bas Sablons) Ch 09

Visitors moorings available: Bassin Vauban or Bassin Duguay-Trouin wait for tide and lock 2½h-HW-1½h. Light signals GWG: No entry without instructions. GGG: Enter lock. RRR: No entry. Port de Plaisance des Sablons entry over sill 2m above chart datum. Sill with digital depth recordings

Distances: Needles 130, St. Peter Port 55, Cherbourg 86, Le Havre 156, Granville 23, Binic 33, St. Quay Portrieux 35, Paimpol 42, Lezardrieux 46, St. Helier 41

DESCRIPTION: Bassin Vauban, directly below the city walls of grey granite, is a good viewpoint from which to get an impression of St. Malo, the view from the sea is best. Through the ramparts the attraction of so many open restaurants is bewildering and there always seem to be too many tourists for such an enclosed space. But there is freedom on the ramparts or, through them, to the beaches. Despite the crowds there is a charm about the covered passageways, flagged courtyards and cobbled squares. Souvenir shops and restaurants and crowds seem to make St. Malo a lively place but you can eat and drink in splendid fashion in keeping with the mood of the place.

From St. Malo it is possible to enter a minor section of the French canal system, if one's draft allows, across to St. Nazaire and an excursion up the River Rance to Dinan is possible.

Port Vauban Available:
Water✓ Electric✓ Showers
Laundrette Petrol 99.56.13.61
Diesel 99.56.13.61
Chandler 99.56.48.06

Repairs:
Yacht 99.56.48.06/99.56.31.72
Engine 99.56.48.06
Electrical 99.56.31.72/99.81.52.01
Sail

Marina Sablons Available:
Water✓ Electric✓ Showers
Laundrette Petrol✓ Diesel✓
Chandler

Repairs:
Yacht Engine Electrical
Sail

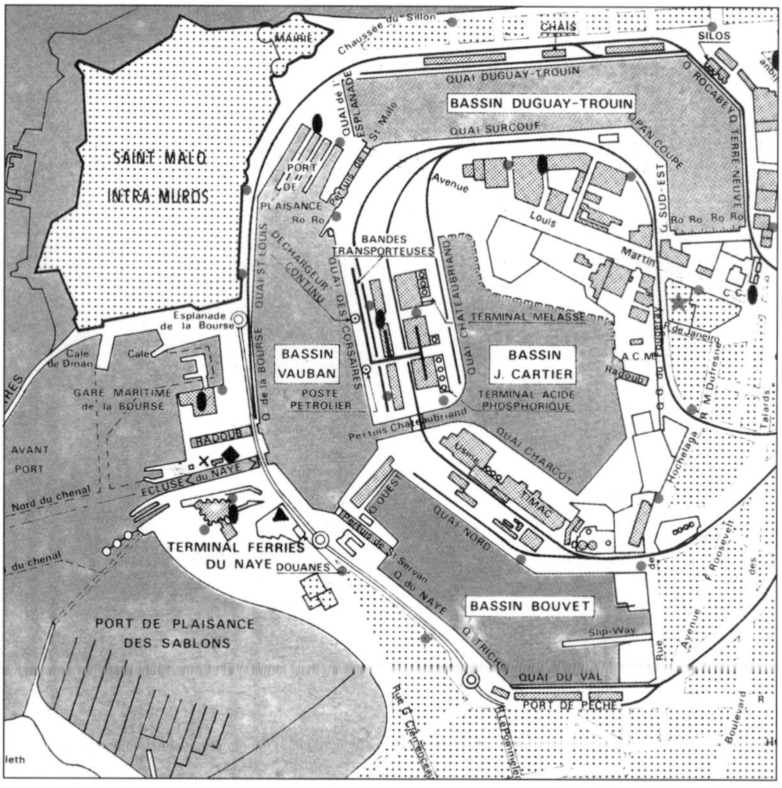

☆☆☆☆☆ ST. MALO

Telephone Code 99

Customs ☎ 99.56.65.90

Weather Meteo 99.46.10.46

Tourist Office ☎ 99.56.64.48
Esplanade St. Vincent

Taxi ☎ 99.81.48.05

Hire Cars
☎ 99.56.75.17/99.81.73.24

Doctor ☎ 99.40.85.06

Hospital ☎ 99.56.56.19

Chemist Rue Amiral Magon

Post Office Rue Ville Pepin

Bank Bd. de la République

Yacht Clubs
Societé Nautique Baie de Saint-Malo

Police ☎ 99.40.85.80

Shops/supermarkets
Nearby, all the food shops are within a few minutes walk from the harbour

Pubs/restaurants
Le Bar de l'Univers (2 menus 90 and 140F); La Duchesse Anne, 4 Place- Guy-La-Chambre; Le Récif, 11 Rue du Boyer; Les Ecuses, Glare Maritime de la Bourse

Tourist attractions:
Market Tuesday and Friday, Town Museum, Castle, Casino

St. Malo

GRANVILLE (Port de Hérel) ☆☆☆☆

Standard Port
ST. HELIER

Harbour Entry
Subject to digital depth 2½h-HW-3½h display on outer breakwater. Zero means no depth on sill

Le Hérel 33.50.20.06/33.50.12.45

Lat: 48° 50' N **Long:** 1° 36' W

Admiralty charts 240/2669
SHOM 824, 5897

Approach visual navigation aids: Le Loup Light Fl (2) W 6s 11m 8 on B tower R band

R/T: VHF Ch 9 (Marina)

Yachting facilities: See next page

Visitors moorings available: 150 available in this 1,000-berth marina

Distances: St. Malo 23, St. Helier 30, Cherbourg 74

DESCRIPTION: A popular seaside resort, popular because of the huge expanse of beach revealed at low tide; it is fascinating to watch it advance, hurrying across the sand. The strongest tides in Europe occur along this coast and the range at Springs exceeds 13m. Way above the harbour is the picturesque High Town or Haute-Ville of 16th to 18th century houses and the Church of Notre-Dame. Around the yacht harbours are shops and restaurants; adjoining is the Port de Commerce that handles quite a surprising tonnage every year in the old harbour. It is a pleasant and lively town. Guarding the Norman approach to the bay of Mont St. Michel, Granville looks across to Cancale in Brittany. The approach is rough in strong westerlies.

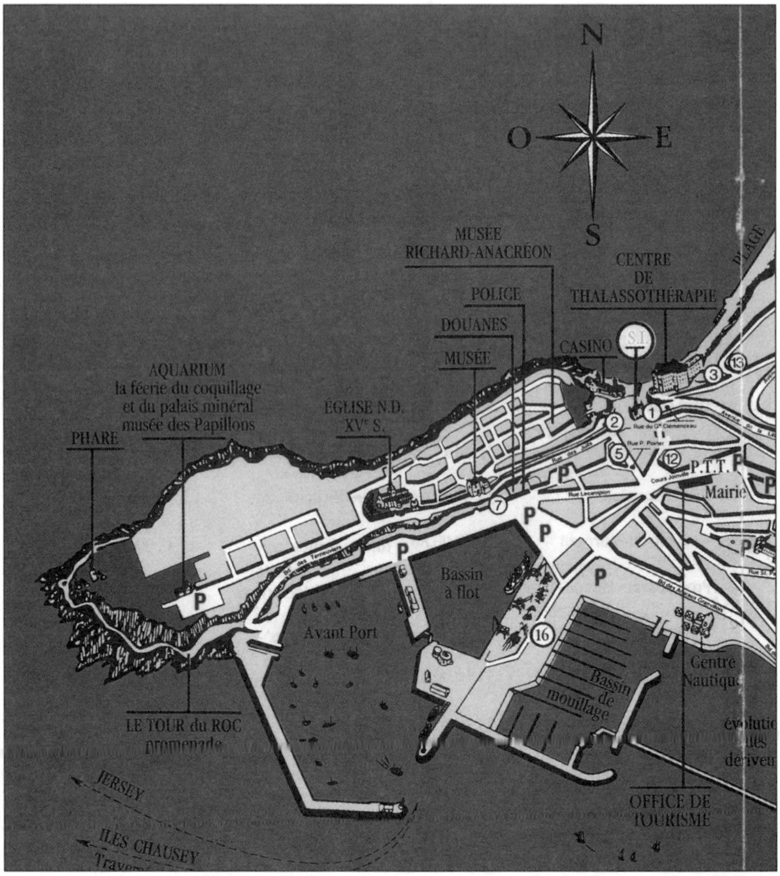

Mooring charges

	May, June, Sept	July/Aug
1st 20m	2.55F	3.50F
beyond 20m	1.75F	2.45F

☆☆☆☆ GRANVILLE (Port de Hérel)

Telephone Code	33
Customs	☎ 33.50.19.90
Weather	☎ 33.50.10.00
Tourist Office	☎ 33.50.02.67
Taxi	☎ 33.50.50.06
Hire Cars	Europcar 33.90.64.99 Avis 33.50.30.89
Doctor	☎ 33.50.00.07
Hospital	☎ 33.90.74.75
Chemist	Rue St. Saveur
Post Office	☎ 33.50.05.03
Bank	Rue Couraye
Yacht Clubs	de Granville
Police	☎ 33.50.11.16
Laundrette	Rue St. Saveur

Shops/supermarkets
Rue Clement, des Maisons near harbour

Pubs/restaurants
Le Jardin de Neptune 33.51.51.50; L'Echanguette, 24 Rue St.-Jean; Le Phare, 11 Rue de Port (4 menus 72-295F); La Potinerie, 19 Rue Georges-Clemenceau

Tourist attractions:
Casino, covered market on Saturdays, Aquarium with fairy-tale shells

Available:

Water✓	Electric✓	Showers✓	
Laundrette✓	Petrol✓	Diesel✓	Chandler 33.50.18.71

Repairs:

Yacht✓	Engine✓	Electrical	Sail✓

Port de Plaisance

CHERBOURG (Port Chantereyne) ☆☆☆☆☆

Standard Port
CHERBOURG

Harbour Entry
At all times

Port Chantereyne 33.53.75.16

Lat: 49° 40' N **Long:** 1° 39' W

Admiralty charts 1106/2602
SHOM 5627/5628

Approach visual navigation aids:
Passe de l'Ouest, Jetée du Homet Front Dir Q W (2 hor) 15m W Δ on parapet – jetty Lts in line 140° 30'
and 142° 30' Gare Maritime Rear Dir Q W 23m G pylon with W Δ

R/T: (Yacht Harbour) VHF Ch 09

Yachting facilities: See below

Visitors moorings available: At all states of the tide in this 614-berth marina, with over 100 visitors berths. 33.55.75.16/33.44.00.13

Distances: Needles 61, St. Malo 86, Le Havre 70, St. Peter Port 41, Granville 74, Poole 65, Brighton 90

DESCRIPTION: An important naval and commercial port. The marina is situated in the centre of a 3,700 acre roadstead. The town is, of course, a centre of business and commerce rather than a tourist resort but there is plenty of interest, particularly if this is your entry port into France, not least being the display and prices of the wine. From a tourist point of view it is not a place in which to linger but it is a yachtsman's favourite. Of the three entrance channels the Passe de l'Ouest is the deepest and the most frequently used. Once in the Port de Plaisance the first pontoons to starboard are for visiting yachts, of which Cherbourg entertains about 7,000 a year. A busy ferry port.

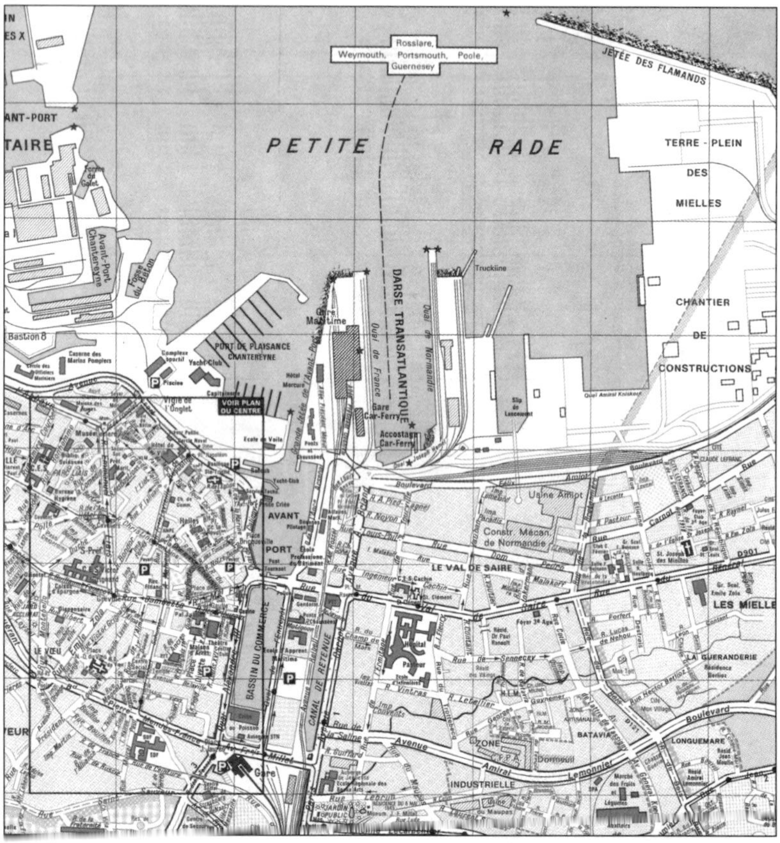

Available:
Water✓ Electric✓ Showers
Laundrette Petrol 33.93.11.36
Diesel 33.93.11.36
Chandler 33.93.11.36/33/53.27.34

Repairs:
Yacht 33.93.11.36
Engine 33.93.11.36
Electrical 33.93.11.36
Sail

Mooring fees	daily	weekly
7m to 9m49	51F to 78F	275F to 396F
9m50 to 11m99	86F to 120F	437F to 618F
12m to 18m plus	141F to 241F	722F to 1301F

☆☆☆☆☆ CHERBOURG (Port Chantereyne)

Telephone Code 33

Customs ☎ 33.53.75.16

Weather ☎ 33.22.91.77

Tourist Office ☎ 33.43.52.02
2 Quai Alexandre 111

Taxi ☎ 33.53.36.38/33.20.08.59/33.53.17.04

Hire Cars
☎ 33.20.34.57/33.44.31.11

Hospital ☎ 33.52.61.11

Chemist Place de la Revolution

Post Office Rue Francois 1

Bank Rue du Maréchal-Foch

Yacht Clubs
de Cherbourg

Police ☎ 33.44.20.22

Laundrette Marina

Shops/supermarkets
Continental and shops nearby

Pubs/restaurants
L'Ancre Dorée, 27 Rue de l'Abbaye (3 menus 88-172F); Le Cotentin, 30 Quai de Caligny; Le Briqueville, 16 Quai de Caligny; Le Rubens, 6 Quai Alexandre 111; Hôtel de France; Cafe de Paris, 40 Quai de Caligny; Le Plouc, 59 Rue au Blé; Le Grandgousiex, 21 Rue de l'Abbaye

Tourist attractions:
Casino, Liberation Museum, Thomas Henry Museum, Thursday market around Rue des Halles, Basilique de la Trinité. Tuesday and Saturday market at Place Général de Gaulle

Cherbourg Port de Plaisance Chantereyne

ST. VAAST-LE-HOUGUE ☆☆☆

Standard Port
CHERBOURG

Harbour Entry
Lock in 3h-HW-3h outer harbour dries

Cap 33.54.48.81

Lat: 49° 35' N **Long:** 1° 35' W

Admiralty charts 1349/2073/2613
SHOM 847, 5522

Approach visual navigation aids: St. Vaast Lt Ho Oc (2) W R 6s 11m W 8 sided tower R top

R/T: VHF Ch 9

Yachting facilities: See below

Visitors moorings available: 100 or more in this 650-berth harbour

Distances: Grandcamp-Maisy 16, Cherbourg 25, St. Valery-en-Caux 76

DESCRIPTION: A charming fishing and yachting harbour, noted for oysters, a resort with a considerable history. Although the yachting harbour has not been long established it has become a favourite with yachtsmen, and the entrance is impressive, between the forts on La Hougue and Ile de Tatihou. The marina has changed the character of the town, as so often happens. Fort de la Hougue is now a military installation, once a French fleet base from which its sailing ships made ready for attack. In this bay, too, Edward III landed on his way to Crecy, scene of his victory, you will recall, over Philip VI of France in 1346.

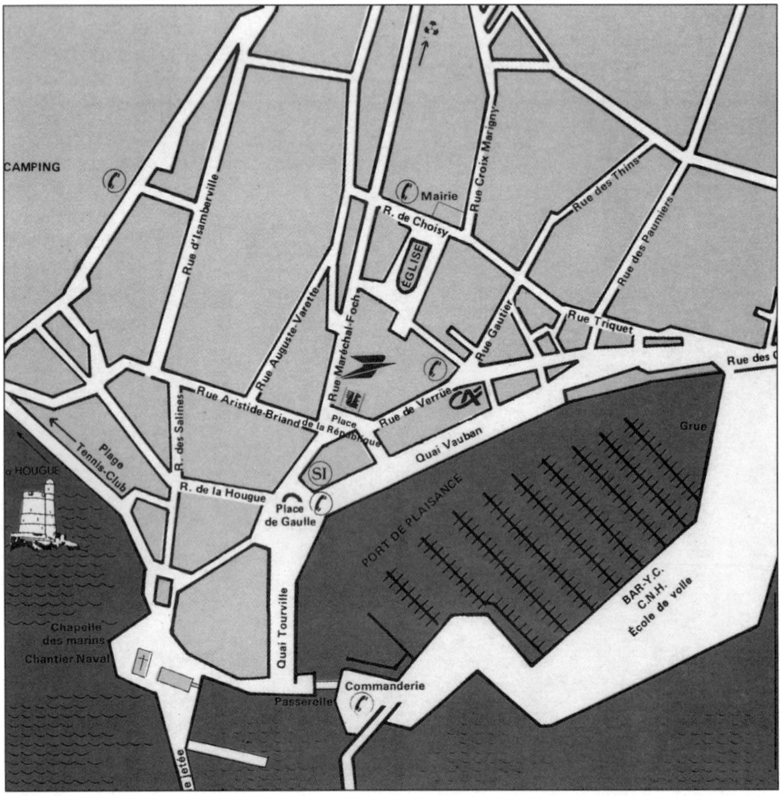

Available:
Water✓ Electric✓ Showers
Laundrette✓ Petrol✓ Diesel✓
Chandler 33.54.53.01

Repairs:
Yacht✓ Engine✓
Electrical Sail

Mooring fees	5m-6.49	6m50-7.99	8m-9.49	9m50-10.99	11m-12.99	13m 16
per day	30F-42F	47F-59F	67F-83F	90F-110F	117F-146F	167F-281F
per week	144F-245F	278F-353F	376-418F	437F-486F	515F-606F	670F-843F
per month	473F-797F	910F-1155F	1228F-1364F	1431F-1588F	1684F-1982F	2189F-2754F

☆☆☆ ST. VAAST-LE-HOUGUE

Telephone Code	33
Customs	☎ Bureau du Port
Weather	☎ 33.43.20.40
Tourist Office	☎ 33.54.41.37 Quai Vauban
Taxi	☎ 33.54.40.29/33.54.42.13
Doctor	☎ 33.54.43.42
Dentist	☎ 33.54.40.27
Hospital	☎ 33.97.00.11
Chemist	Rue de Choisy
Post Office	Rue Maréchal Foch
Bank	Rue de Verrue
Yacht Clubs	Port de Plaisance 33.54.55.38; Cercle Nautique de la Hougue 33.54.55.73
Police	☎ 33.54.12.11
Laundrette	Quai Vauban
Shops/supermarkets	Nearby

Pubs/restaurants
Les Fuchias, 16 Rue Maréchal Fock (4 menus 65-180F); L'Escale, 9 Quai Vauban (3 menus 75-140F)

Tourist attractions:
Saturday market, 11th Century Seaman's Chapel

"St. Va" Yacht Harbour

CARENTAN ☆☆☆

Standard Port
LE HAVRE

Harbour Entry
Up canal to Port de Plaisance
2h-HW-3h; lock signals

Cap 33.71.10.85

Lat: 49° 19' N **Long:** 01° 15' W

Admiralty charts 257/2073
SHOM 847, 6614

Approach visual navigation aids:
Ldg Lts Front Dir Oc (3) R 12s 17m W mast R top
209° 30' Rear Oct (3) W 12s 14m W gantry G top

R/T: VHF Ch 9 (0800-1800 and when lock operates)

Yachting facilities: See below

Visitors moorings available: 55 berths are reserved for visitors in this 550-berth marina 33.42.24.44

Distances: Grandcamp 13, Ouistreham 45

DESCRIPTION: A pleasant setting for the harbour, almost in the town, with all the shops you need available. The Contentin Peninsula, with its capes and inlets and headlands, equals the Brittany coast in this respect and to cruise up to Carentan is a charming refuge. By train it is only 2½ hours from Paris. Carentan is in the Baie du Grand Vey which dries almost completely at low water. The buoyed channel entry to the bay, between Pointe de la Madeleine and Pointe de Maisy, is between drying sandbanks where one does not want to touch bottom on a falling tide. There are waiting pontoons both sides of the lock.

Mooring fees

Up to 20m²	1.50FF per day per m²
Over 20m²	1.20FF per day per m²

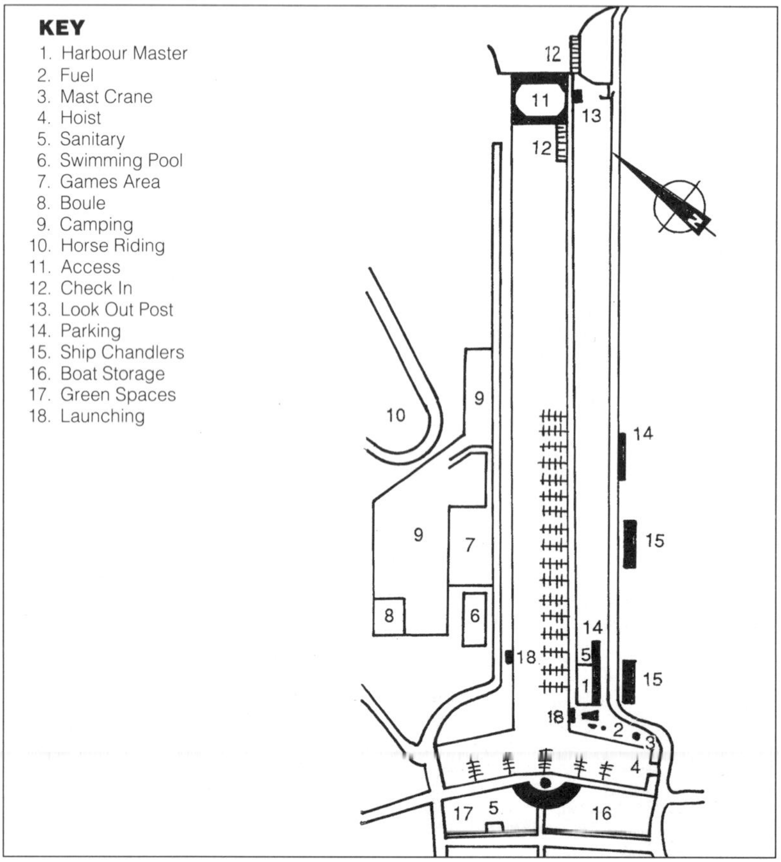

Available:
Water✓ Electric✓ Showers
Laundrette Petrol✓ Diesel✓
Chandler 31.22.10.67

Repairs:
Yacht 31.22.10.67
Engine 31.22.10.67
Electrical 33.42.23.02
Sail

☆☆☆ CARENTAN

Customs	☎ 33.44.16.00
Weather	Meteo 33.43.20.40
Tourist Office	☎ 33.42.33.54 Bd. de Verdun
Taxi	☎ 33.42.08.11
Hire Cars	☎ 33.42.04.55
Doctor	☎ 33.42.33.21
Dentist	☎ 33.42.00.23
Hospital	☎ 33.42.14.12
Chemist	Place de la Republique
Bank	Place Desplananques-Dumesnil
Yacht Clubs	Croiseurs Côtiers de Carentan
Police	☎ 17

Shops/supermarkets
All available nearby

Pubs/restaurants
Le Haut-Dyck, Port de Plaisance; Auberge Normande, 17 Bd. de Verdun; du Commerce et de la Gare 33.42.02.00

Tourist attractions:
Notre-Dame, Landing Beaches

Carentan Harbour

GRANDCAMP-MAISY ☆☆☆

Standard Port
LE HAVRE

Harbour Entry
Lock in 2h-HW-2h
access day or night

Cap 31.22.63.16

Lat: 49° 23' N **Long:** 1° 03' W

Admiralty charts 258/1821/2073/2613
SHOM 847

Approach visual navigation aids:
Ldg Lts Front QW 7m grey mast
146° Rear QW 7m grey (90m from Front)

R/T: VHF Ch 9

Yachting facilities: See below

Visitors moorings available: 25 berths for visitors in this 300-yacht marina

Distances: Port-en-Bassin 12, St. Vaast-la-Hougue 16, Courseulles 23, Carentan 13, Cherbourg 35

DESCRIPTION: A small fishing harbour that is developing a tourist trade. Calvados offers a variety of landscapes, vast sandy beaches and green countryside, a range of leisure activities and choice of food. The town is rather bleak but all facilities are here. It is a difficult entrance in strong north winds and approach is over flat rocks. The entrance channel is guarded by two diverging jetties, with a light on a white column at the end of the east jetty. You proceed through the lock in to the wet basin and the yacht moorings are to starboard.

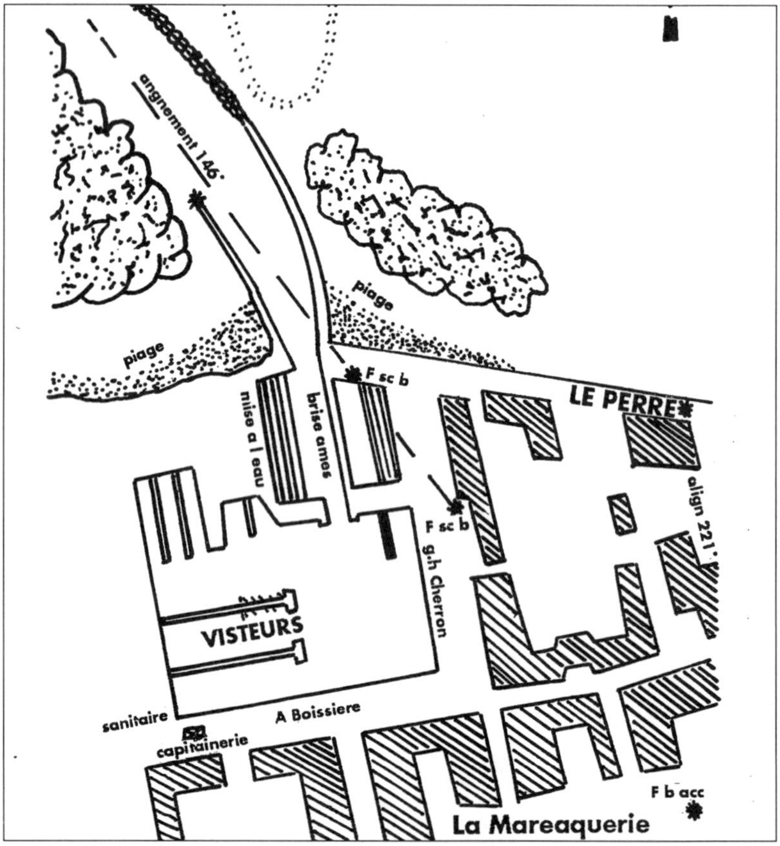

Available:
Water✓ Electric✓ Showers✓
Laundrette Petrol Diesel
Chandler 31.22.61.95

Repairs:

Yacht 31.22.61.95
Engine 31.22.62.79/31.22.61.95
Electrical 31.22.61.95
Sail

Mooring fees	LOA	5-5.99	7-7.99	9-9.99	11-11.99	13-13.99	16-17.99
	day	28FF	37	47	58	74	108
	week	168	222	276	350	459	652
	month	557	731	914	1095	1280	1685

☆☆☆ GRANDCAMP-MAISY

Telephone Code	31
Weather	Meteo Capitainerie
Tourist Office	☎ 31.22.62.44 Quai Crampon
Taxi	☎ 31.22.00.36
Doctor	☎ 31.22.60.44/31.22.71.10
Chemist	☎ 31.22.60.50
Post Office	Rue Aristide Briand
Bank	Quai Cheron
Yacht Clubs	Circle Nautique de Grandcamp-les-Bains
Police	☎ 31.22.00.18

Shops/supermarkets
Quai de Petit-Nice

Pubs/restaurants
La Marée, l'Hotel de la Mer, Quai Chéron

Tourist attractions:
Tuesday market, Saturday market

The marina pontoons

LESSER HARBOURS

SWANAGE

Between Poole and Weymouth

Admiralty chart 2172
Piermaster 423565

Visiting yachts secure by the pier, subject to any commercial traffic. At one time there were plans to build a marina here. A small holiday resort with all necessary shops ashore, but limited yacht facilities. Good shelter in winds from SW to N, otherwise open to E to S Easterlies, when uncomfortable in F4.

Swanage

BRIDPORT

Between Weymouth and Lyme Regis

50° 43' N, 2° 46' W
Admiralty chart 3315
Harbour Master: 23222
Harbour dries

There is a special charm about this small town which has an old fashioned reputation for the making of ropes and twines. Dangerous entrance during fresh onshore winds. Stand of around 1½ at HW.

LYME REGIS

Between Bridport and Exmouth

50° 43' N, 2° 56' W
Harbour Master: 02974 2137
Lyme Regis Sailing Club 3573
Harbour dries.

A pleasant, small holiday resort and fishing town, with steep streets and a history. (The Duke of Monmouth landed here in 1685). Berths alongside The Cobb.

EXMOUTH

Between Lyme Regis and Teighmouth

50° 37' N, 3° 25' W
Harbour Master: 0395 272009
River Exe, access to Exeter through canal.

Berths for visitors in Exmouth dock are still being reported as available by some guide books but, in fact, the walls have collapsed and the harbour is closed. Anchorage in river, moorings possible off Starcross.

TEIGNMOUTH

Between Exmouth and Torquay

Admiralty chart 26, 3315
Harbour Master: 773165
Teignmouth Yacht Club: 772734

Entry difficult. Heavy surf on bar is off-putting. Vacant mooring often found. A resort that has attracted the sea-bathing holidaymaker for a hundred years or so.

NEWTON FERRERS

Between Salcombe and Plymouth

River Yealm
Admiralty chart 30
Harbour Master: 0752 872533
Easy access but dries.

A popular place to call, but remote, which is probably the reason for its popularity. To the south is NOSS MAYO with a quay.

LOOE

Between Plymouth and Fowey

50° 21' N, 4° 27' W
Admiralty chart 147, 148
Harbour Master: 050 36 2839
Looe Sailing Club: 2559
Harbour Dries

A busy fishing port but visitor's moorings in West Looe. Ashore tourism reigns supreme but Looe is an attractive town on both banks of the Looe River. Gets uncomfortable in strong SE winds.

CARENTEC

Between Roscoff and Morlaix

48° 40' N, 03° 55' W
Admiralty chart 2745
SHOM 5827

A small town and holiday resort. If you are here on 15 August you can witness the blessing of the sea and pardon at the Ile de Callot which lies close N or Carentec, and divides the Riviere de Morlaix and La Penze Riviere. There are numerous above-water, drying and below-water rocks.

TREGASTEL

Between Perros-Guirec and Trebeurden

48° 50' N, 03° 31' W
Admiralty chart 2644, 2668
Bureau du port: Mairie de Tregastel
Telephone: 96.23.85.19
Yacht Club: Club Nautique de Tregastel
Good anchorage, exposed to northerlies

A small village without any distinguishing features, except the stone saint raising his arm to bless you.

PLOUMANAC'H

Between Tregastel and Perros-Guirec

48° 50' N, 03° 29' W
Admiralty chart 2644, 2668
SHOM 967, 974

A small harbour which dries completely, and is used by local fishing boats. A holiday resort, more so than nearby Perros-Guirec, and catering for families. Many restaurants in the square. Entry over sill. 20 visitor's moorings.

PRIMEL

Between Roscoff and Lannion

48° 43' N, 03° 49' W
Admiralty chart 2644
SHOM 5827, 5950

A small harbour with good anchorage, suitable as an overnight stop. A substantial quay, to which fishermen seem to be coming, (and going), at all times.

LANNION

Between Trebeurden and Roscoff

48° 44' N, 03° 20' W
Admiralty chart 2664
SHOM 967, 5960, 6065
Harbour Master 96.37.06.52

Up the Riviere de Lannion, (sometimes known as Le Leguer). The river is narrow and rather difficult with sharp bends. Lannion is a small town with streets of medieval housing, and an enormous beach nearby. Below the bridge there are quays, (drying), on both sides. The river dries as far as Le Yaudet, a village about a mile within the entrance.

TREBEURDEN

Between Morlaix and Perros-Guirec

Admiralty chart 2644, 2668
SHOM 5950, 6056
Capitainerie 96.23.66.93
Harbour entry at all times via a lifting sill.

A new marina is planned here to be available May 1991 against opposition to completion by local "Green" parties. Some shops are nearby but the town is a 20 minute uphill walk away. There are splendid beaches.

PORT BLANC

Between Perros-Guirec and Lezardrieux

48° 50' N, 03° 19' W
Admiralty chart 2668, 3672
SHOM 967, 974

A natural harbour exposed to N winds. Fairly busy with local fishing boats.

Ploumanac'h

LESSER HARBOURS

Old houses at Dinan – town puts on fête (carnival) October – every other year (1989 shown here)

SAINT BRIEUC-LE-LEGUE

Between Erquy and Binic

48° 32' N, 02° 43' W
Admiralty chart 2668, 2669
Bureau du port: Terre Plein des Ecluse
Telephone: 33.96.33.35.41
Yacht Club La Toupie et L'Anl
Lock in 2h-HW-1h

Le Legue is the harbour for Saint-Brieuc, an industrial town which doesn't seem to make any concessions to tourism, except in July when a Festival of Breton Music is organised.

DAHOUET

Between St. Cast and Binic

48° 35' N, 02° 34' W
Admiralty chart 2668, 2669
SHOM 833

Good shelter except when wind strong NW. The entrance to the harbour is marked by the Petit-Muette Light Tower. A small port with a new marina offering good facilities and welcome.

Dahouet

ERQUY

Between Saint Cast-le-Guildo and Saint Brieuc-le-Legue

48° 39' N, 02° 37' W
Admiralty chart 2668, 2669
Capitainerie Telephone 96.72.19.32
Yacht Club Cercle de la Voile d'Erquy
Harbour dries.

A fishing harbour usually full of fishing boats. There are huge beaches around this pleasant small town.

SAINT CAST-LE-GUILDO

Between Dinard and Erquy

48° 38' N, 02° 15' W
Admiralty chart 2669, 3659
Bureau du port
Telephone: 33.96.41.84.34
Yacht Club de Saint Cast
Good anchorage

The town is quite a long walk from the harbour but it is a pleasant town, a typical family type holiday resort.

DINAN

Up the River Rance from Saint Malo

Admiralty chart 2669, 2700
Bureau du port: 8 Aristide-Briand
Telephone: 96.39.56.44
Alongside moorings

It is a steep climb up to the city with its 600-year-old ramparts, but it is well worthwhile. As I remark in my book, "Through The French Canals," "masts down from here if continuing south."

CANCALE

Between Granville and Saint Malo

48° 40' N, 1° 51W
Admiralty chart 3659
Clubhouse de Port-Mer, Cercle Nautique
Telephone 33.99.89.90.22
Harbour dries, subject to this, berths available

If you are fond of oysters you must make the effort to come to this charming little port and town. Cancale oysters are known all over the world, the whole town is given over to the business of the oyster, the museum documents their history. Splendid restaurants specialise in seafood.

PORTBAIL

Between Barneville-Carteret and Granville

49° 19' N, 01° 43' W
Admiralty chart 2669
Bureau du port: La Calliourie
Telephone: 33.04.83.48
Yacht Club Cercle Nautique de Portbail
Harbour dries. Access 2½h-HW-2½

A pleasant little resort and fishing harbour.

Portbail

CARTERET

Between Cherbourg and Portbail

49° 22' N, 01° 47' W
Admiralty chart 2669
Bureau du port: Rue de Paris
Telephone: 33.04.70.84
Yacht Club Cercle Nautique de Barneville-Carteret
Harbour dries. Access 2h-HW-2h.

Visitors welcome. A marina is planned. Situated amidst some of the finest beaches in Normandy.

Carteret

BARFLEUR

Between Cherbourg and Saint Vaast-le-Hougue

Admiralty chart 1106, 1349, 2073
SHOM 847, 5609, 5618
Harbour Master 33.54.02.68
Entry difficult. Access 3h-HW-3h.
Harbour dries.

Lie along NW wall in this charming harbour which, long ago, was the biggest port in Normandy. An attractive little town.

CHANNEL ISLANDS

ALDERNEY ☆☆☆

Standard Port
ST. HELIER

Harbour Entry
Leading marks Alderney LH N.E. St. Annes Church Spire

HM Braye Harbour 2620

Lat: 49° 43' 9 N **Long:** 2° 11' W

Admiralty charts 60/233/2669/2845/3653

Approach visual navigation aids:
Ldg Lts Elbow on Front Q W 17m metal post on W base
215° old pier Rear 1so W 10s 18m metal post on W col

R/T: Alderney Radio VHF Ch 16 74 & 12 (0800-2200 hrs)

Yachting facilities: All available

Visitors moorings available: Pick up yellow mooring buoy

Distances: Jersey 28, Poole 68, Cherbourg 24, Dartmouth 64, Guernsey 22

DESCRIPTION: Alderney is the nearest of the Channel Islands to England. An "away from it all" island which is well worth a visit to experience the serenity and the uncomplicated life style. About 5½ square miles in area Alderney has a population of 2,000 and, apparently, more pubs per square mile than anywhere in the world. Braye Harbour is on the north coast of Alderney. On arrival, visiting yachts can either pick up a yellow mooring buoy – up to four craft can use each buoy – or anchor as convenient. Landing on the breakwater is not allowed. There is an uncomfortable swell in winds from the north.

Mooring charges:
£6 per boat per period

Available:
Water Electric Showers
Petrol Diesel 2772 Chandler 2772

Repairs:
Yacht 2531/2772 Engine 2531/2772
Electrical 2531/2772 Sail 2772

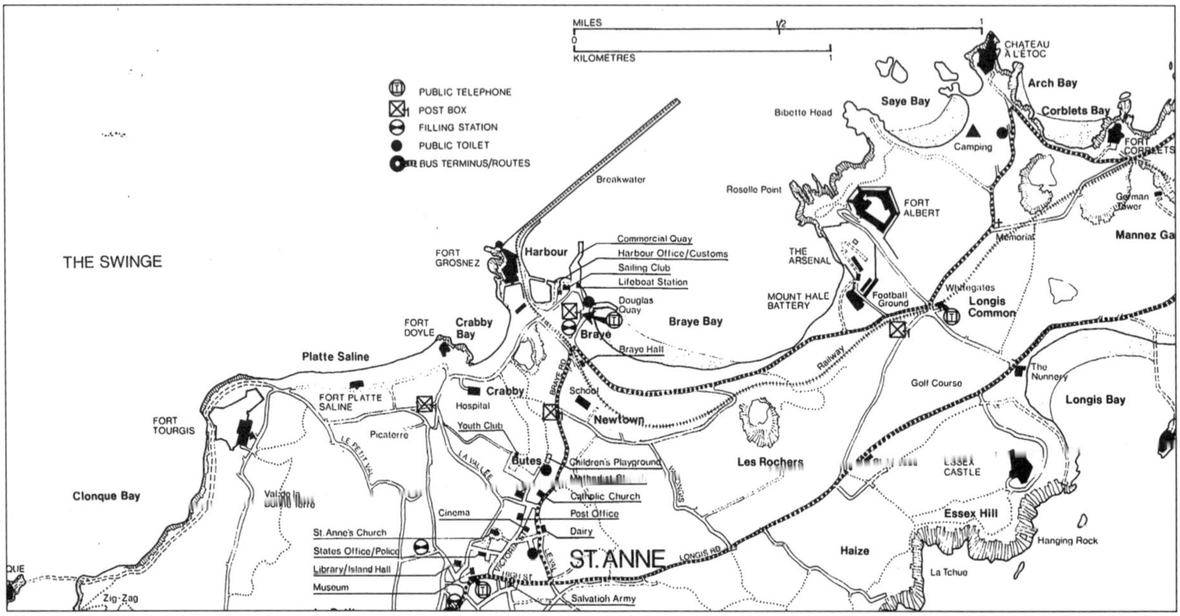

☆☆☆ ALDERNEY

Telephone Code	0481-82
Customs	Enquire 2994
Weather	Harbour Office
Tourist Office	St. Anne 2994
Taxi	☎ 3535/2611
Hire Cars	☎ 2727/2848/2919/ 2611
Doctor	☎ 2494/2077
Dentist	☎ 2456/3131/3326
Hospital	☎ 2822
Chemist	☎ 2126
Post Office	St. Anne
Bank	Lloyds, NatWest, Midland
Yacht Clubs	Alderney Sailing Club
Police	☎ 999
Laundrette	☎ 2012

Shops/supermarkets
Jeans Stores, Riduna Stores

Pubs/restaurants
Le Courier; Chez Andre; Nellie Grays, Victoria Street 3333; Divers; Seaview, Braye Harbour 2738; Harbour Lights; Belle Vue; Georgina; Moorings Hotel, Braye Beach 2421; First and Last, Braye Street 3162

Tourist attractions:
Peace, birds, wild flowers, dramatic cliff scenery, pottery, museum, fortifications, tourist railway

Aerial view of Alderney

GUERNSEY ☆☆☆☆☆ VICTORIA MARINA (Albert Marina is for local boats)

Standard Port
ST. HELIER

Harbour Entry
Subject to depth guage at sill on entry, waiting pontoons and buoys in the harbour

HM 20229

Lat: 49° 27' N **Long:** 02° 3'2 W

Admiralty charts 3140/220

Approach visual navigation aids: Little Russel and Great Russel both well marked and lit

R/T: (Port Control) VHF Ch 12

Yachting facilities: See below

Visitors moorings available: Victoria Marina up to 250 berths and 'pool' moorings 150. Moorings also available at Beaucette Marina

Distances: St. Malo 55, Lezardrieux 48, Treguier 52, Perros 54, Morlaix 78, L'Aber-Wrac'h 100, Alderney 22

DESCRIPTION: A most attractive harbour and town, a lively place to be during the summer season. The shopping area is no further away than you could throw a bottle of duty-free Pussers Rum, not that you would despite the agreeable price. There are pleasant pubs and restaurants all around. If you have never cruised to Guernsey you should make the effort to do so.
St. Peter Port is the only town on the island and it is the principal harbour. The other yacht harbour, Beaucette Marina, is on the north east of the island. A three year re-building project has been taking place here. A ferry port, busy in July and August. Entry to marina is limited by sill – waiting pontoons and buoys in the harbour.

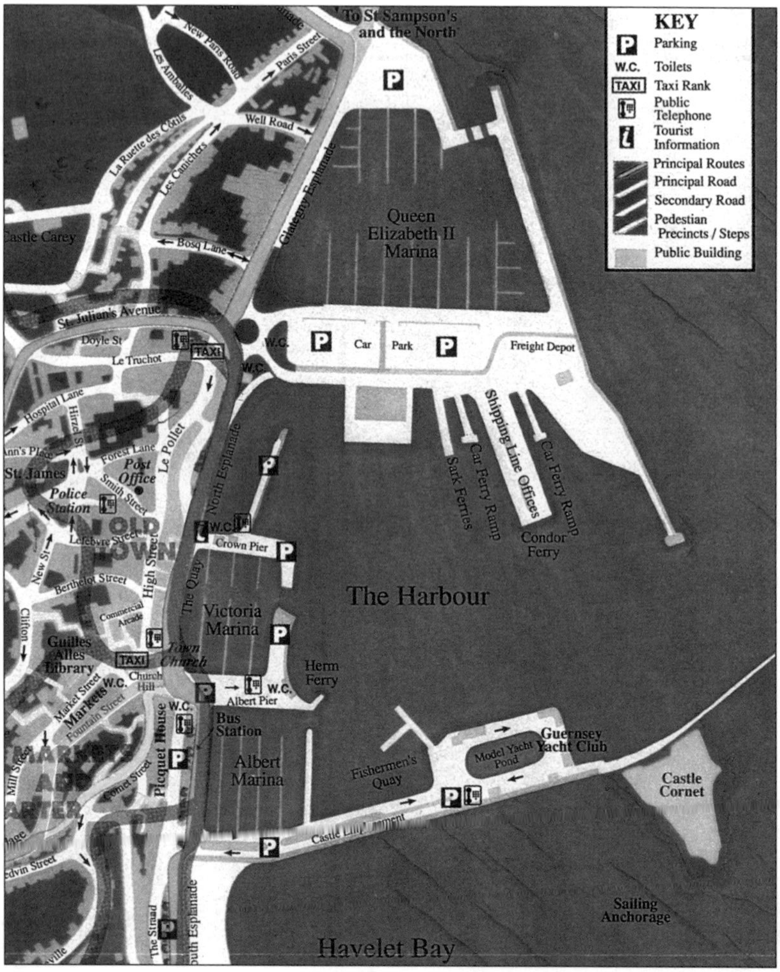

Vieux Bassin Available:
Water✓ Electric✓ Showers
Laundrette Petrol Diesel
Chandler

Repairs:
Yacht 31.89.13.71
Engine 31.89.38.54
Electrical Sail

Beaucette Marina (45000)
Mooring charges
£1.25 per day
£8.75 per week

Telephone Code	0481
Customs	☎ 26911
Weather	Jersey Radio (VHF 25) 64033
Tourist Office	☎ 23552
Taxi	☎ 23047
Hire Cars	From Marina
Doctor	Contact Harbour Office
Dentist	Contact Harbour Office
Hospital	☎ 25241
Chemist	Boots
Post Office	Smith Street
Bank	High Street
Yacht Clubs	Royal Channel Islands
Police	☎ 725111
Laundrette	Victoria Road

Shops/supermarkets
Adjacent to Victoria marina

Pubs/restaurants
Ship & Crown; Dagmar; De la Rue; Moores; Charlie's Bar; Coal Hole; Long Bar; Wellington Boot; Le Nautique; Moorings; Steak & Stilton

Tourist attractions:
Duty free shopping, La Valette Underground Military Museum, Guernsey Museum & Art Gallery, Victor Hugo's House

Victoria Marina, St. Peter Port

JERSEY ☆☆☆☆☆

Standard Port
ST. HELIER

Harbour Entry
Via automatic sill gate

HM 34451

Lat: 49° 10' N **Long:** 2° 06' W

Admiralty charts 3655/1137/1136/3278/1138

Approach visual navigation aids:
Ldg Lts Front F G W col
078° Rear F G W col

R/T: (Port Control) VHF Ch 14

Yachting facilities: See below

Visitors moorings available: In St. Helier Marina (200 berths) 79549.
La Colette 74434 (temporary)

Distances: Granville 30, St. Malo 41, Lezardrieux 46, Portsmouth 140, Binic 45, St. Peter Port 26

DESCRIPTION: A welcoming island with clearer air and a cleaner sea than you might be accustomed to. Well known for splendid beaches and a holiday atmosphere, Jersey also has a special welcome for visiting yachtsmen. Shops, pubs and restaurants are all near at hand. The main marina at the northern end of the harbour, is entered over a sill. La Colette is used while waiting for a marina berth. The marina tends to get very crowded during July and August with both French and British boats. Jersey is the biggest and most southerly of the Channel Islands. St. Helier is on the south coast of the island. On the east coast is Gorey Harbour, a good drying anchorage.

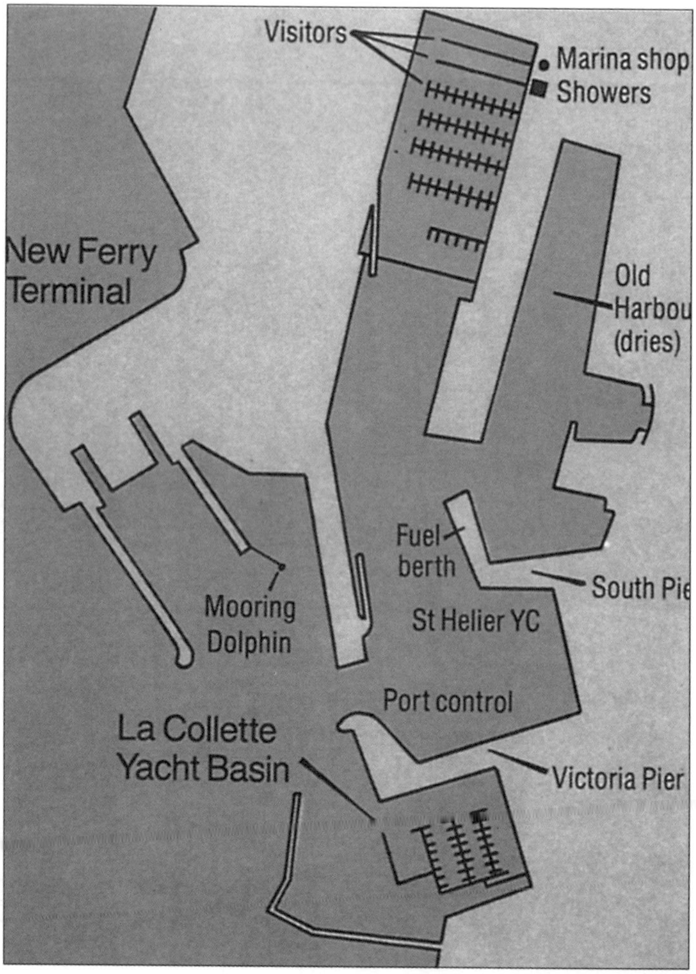

Available:
Water✓ Electric✓ Showers✓
Laundrette Petrol✓ Diesel✓
Chandler✓

Repairs:
Yacht✓ Engine✓
Electrical✓ Sail✓

Telephone Code	0534
Customs	Harbour Office
Weather	Harbour Office
Tourist Office	☎ 247749
Taxi	Rank nearby
Hire Cars	☎ 36557-23928-41363
Doctor / **Dentist** / **Hospital**	Morning medical clinic at General Hospital
Chemist	Nearby
Post Office	Broad Street
Bank	Nearby
Yacht Clubs	St. Helier
Shops/supermarkets	All nearby

Pubs/restaurants
Pomme D'Or Harbour Room, Weighbridge; Exchange Seafood Restaurant, 13 Grenville Street; Nelson's Eye, Havre des Pas

Tourist attractions:
Jersey Zoo, Jersey Museum, German Military Underground Hospital, Island Fortess Occupation, many gardens and nurseries, central market,

The Marina, St. Helier

Bibliography

GENERAL YACHTING GUIDES AND PILOT BOOKS for cruising THE ENGLISH CHANNEL

Admiralty Publications

CHANNEL PILOT NP27 BOGNOR REGIS TO ISLES OF SCILLY AND CORRESPONDING SOUTH COAST OF FRANCE
1984 with supplement to February 1988. £26.40

DOVER STRAIT PILOT NP28 THE EAST END OF THE CHANNEL TO BOGNOR REGIS AND THE CORRESPONDING COAST OF FRANCE
1985 with supplement to February 1988. £26.40

ADMIRALTY TIDE TABLES FOR YACHTSMEN NP190/91
Isles of Scilly to Portland. 1991 £2.40

ADMIRALTY TIDE TABLES FOR YACHTSMEN NP190/91
Swanage to Chichester. 1991 £2.40

I am most grateful to Alan Obin of Warsash Nautical Bookshop, 31 Newton Road, Warsash, Southampton SO6 9FY (Tel: 0489 572384 and FAX 0489 885756) who has kindly supplied the information and comments above and below. All these books are in stock with a vast number of other yachting titles. Whatever your nautical needs, *including charts,* Alan Obin can supply them. Advice too. In fact Alan Obin has compiled **THE BIBLIOGRAPHY OF NAUTICAL BOOKS** containing - would you believe it? - eight *thousand* titles of English language nautical books in print in the U.K. The price of the 1991 edition is £45.00.

CHANNEL CROSSINGS AROUND BRITAIN FOR POWER AND SAIL
Peter Cumberlidge 1990 £16.65

Specific information for making crossings in the English Channel and also the Bay of Biscay and Irish Sea.

CHANNEL ISLANDS PILOT
Malcolm Robson 1990 Spiral bound £25.00

A detailed pilot book with numerous sketches.

CREEKS AND HARBOURS OF THE SOLENT
K. Adlard Coles, revised by David Sylvester-Bradley 1987 £18.95

For many years the standard work for cruising the Solent. With sketches and photographs.

CRUISING ASSOCIATION HANDBOOK
1990 £39.75

With pilotage information and coloured plans covering the whole of the British Isles and the near part of Europe from Denmark to Gibraltar.

FRENCH PILOT Vol 1 ORMONVILLE to TREGUIER
Malcolm Robson 1989 £16.95

This pilot has sketches. The French Pilots are rather old in the tooth now but suit some people who prefer sketches to photographs.

FRENCH PILOT Vol 2 PORT BLANC to ILE DE SEIN
Details as in French Pilot No. 1.

INSHORE ALONG THE DORSET COAST
Peter Bruce 1989 £9.95

Information about the Dorset coast from Christchurch to Portland Bill.

NORMANDY AND CHANNEL ISLANDS PILOT
Mark Brackenbury 1988 revised 1990 £25.00

Calais to St. Malo including Channel Islands. Detailed pilot with photographs and charts.

NORTH BRITTANY PILOT
RCC Pilotage Foundation 1984 revised 1989 £29.95

St. Malo to Ushant. Detailed pilot with photographs and charts.

PILOT PACK NO. 1. GREAT YARMOUTH TO LITTLEHAMPTON – IJMUIDEN TO CARENTAN
Brian Goulder 1989 Spiral bound £35.00

Pilotage notes with detailed plans

PILOT PACK NO. 2. CHICHESTER TO PORTLAND – CHANNEL ISLANDS AND ST. VAAST TO ERQUY
Details as No. 1.

PILOT PACK NO. 3. BRIDPORT TO THE SCILLY ISLES – LE LEGUE TO USHANT
Details as No. 1.

SHELL PILOT TO THE ENGLISH CHANNEL Vol. 1. RAMSGATE TO THE SCILLIES
John Coote 1989 £17.50

SHELL PILOT TO THE ENGLISH CHANNEL Vol. 2. NORTHERN FRANCE AND THE CHANNEL ISLANDS
John Coote 1987 £17.50

SOLENT HAZARDS
Peter Bruce 1987 £5.95

Knowledge of the Solent shoreline and currents to help avoid hazards.

THE SOLENT
Derek Bowskill 1990 £9.95

Cruising guide from Selsey Bill to the Needles with coloured photographs and plans.

SOUTH COAST FROM THE AIR
Andrew Bray and Patrick Roach 1989 £12.95

Coloured aerial photographs of the coastline from Anvil Point to Beachy Head.

SOUTH ENGLAND PILOT Vol. 3.
Robin Brandon 1983 £17.50

Unfortunately this is the last of this excellent pilot series to be available and is rather out of date but it has an amendment sheet dated 1986.

WIGHT HAZARDS
Peter Bruce 1989 £5.95

Detailed information about the coastline of the south of the Isle of Wight to help yachtsmen.

WEST COUNTRY CRUISING
Mark Fishwick 1989 £13.95

Yachtsman's pilot and guide to ports from the Exe to Land's End. Charts and coloured photographs.

List of Agents for SHOM Charts

DUNKERQUE

F.M.C.,
Quai Freycinet III, Hangar MI-1,
59375 DUNKERQUE

BLEU MARINE,
Terre-Plein Guillain,
59140 DUNKERQUE

BOULOGNE

Librairie DUMINY,
48 rue Faidherbe,
62200 BOULOGNE-SUR-MER

LE HAVRE

NAUTIC SERVICE,
ZAC de Rogerville-Oudalle,
76700 HARFLEUR

GUERNSEY

NAVIGATION AND MARINE SUPPLIES,
North Plantation,
St Peter Port,
GUERNSEY

CHERBOURG

NICOLLET,
40 rue du Commerce,
50100 CHERBOURG

GRANVILLE

LA MARINE,
2 rue Saint-Sauveur,
50400 GRANVILLE

SAINT MALO

LIBRAIRIE MARITIME,
5 rue Broussais,
35402 SAINT MALO

VOILERIE RICHARD
3 rue de Glorioux,
35400 SAINT MALO

LIBRAIRIE NAUTIQUE DES BAS-SABLONS,
26 rue des Bas-Sablons,
35400 SAINT MALO

L'ANCRE DE MARINE,
4 rue Porcon,
35400 SAINT MALO

NAVILOC,
Port de Plaisance des Bas-Sablons,
35400 SAINT MALO

OUISTREHAM

ACCASTILLAGE DIFFUSION,
Port de Plaisance,
14150 OUISTREHAM

PAIMPOL

Librairie du Goelo,
Rue Pellier,
22500 PAIMPOL

BINIC

JEAN BART MARINE,
Quai Jean Bart, BP 15
22520 BINIC

PLERIN

L'HABITAT ET LA MER,
28 rue de la Tour,
22190 PLERIN

LANNION

ESPACE LOISIRS LEISBLEIZ S.A.,
Kersoles,
22300 LANNION

TREDARZEC (Treguier)

FOURNITURES POUR LA MARINE,
Pont-Canada,
22220 TREDARZEC

PERROS-GUIREC

SHIP MARINE,
Residence du Levant,
91 rue Ernest-Renan,
22700 PERROS-GUIREC

MORLAIX

JEGOU RITZ,
10 place des Otages, BP 186
29204 MORLAIX

BREST

ITALIQUE, S.A. JOUANNEAU,
75 rue de Siam,
2900 BREST

BELMAR,
Quai Commandant Malbert,
29200 BREST

SOCIETE 2 K,
4 rue Admiral Troude,
29200 BREST

USHIP LE COUTEUR,
Port de Plaisance, BP 31
29281 BREST CEDEX

Index to Harbours and Marinas